The Wilson Circle

The Wilson Circle

President Woodrow Wilson and His Advisers

CHARLES E. NEU

Johns Hopkins University Press

Baltimore

© 2022 Johns Hopkins University Press
All rights reserved. Published 2022
Printed in the United States of America on acid-free paper

2   4   6   8   9   7   5   3   1

Johns Hopkins University Press
2715 North Charles Street
Baltimore, Maryland 21218-4363
www.press.jhu.edu

Library of Congress Cataloging-in-Publication Data
Names: Neu, Charles E., author.
Title: The Wilson circle : President Woodrow Wilson and his advisers /
Charles E. Neu.
Description: Baltimore : Johns Hopkins University Press, 2022. |
Includes bibliographical references and index.
Identifiers: LCCN 2021018525 | ISBN 9781421442983 (hardcover) |
ISBN 9781421442990 (ebook)
Subjects: LCSH: Wilson, Woodrow, 1856–1924. | Wilson, Woodrow, 1856–1924—
Friends and associates. | Presidents—United States—Biography. | Cabinet officers—
United States—Biography. | Presidents' spouses—United States—Biography. |
United States—Politics and government—1913–1921.
Classification: LCC E767 .N48 2022 | DDC 973.91/3092—dc23
LC record available at https://lccn.loc.gov/2021018525

A catalog record for this book is available from the British Library.

*Special discounts are available for bulk purchases of this book. For more information,
please contact Special Sales at specialsales@jh.edu.*

For Hilary

CONTENTS

Helping the President

Woodrow Wilson remains a controversial figure. Nearly one hundred years after his death, historians continue to divide sharply over his presidency and his political leadership. The collapse of Wilson's health in 1919 and his failure to win Senate approval of the Versailles Treaty have tainted his legacy, as have the racism of his administration and its disregard for civil liberties after American entry into World War I. One recent critic claims that "historical memory has not been kind to Woodrow Wilson. No other president who has accomplished so much has so few latter-day admirers." Even sympathetic biographers have found it difficult to deal with these aspects of Wilson's presidency. John Milton Cooper Jr. regrets that civil rights and racial injustice did not "engage his [Wilson's] mind and spirit," and laments the fact that he never reached "his full stature as a moral leader." In May 1921, Ray Stannard Baker anticipated these divisions, concluding that "[m]en may hate him bitterly, as many do, or admire him, or try to explain him—but they cannot get around him. There he is! And he will always be discussed, fought over, hated, admired, speculated about."[1]

It is not my intention to attempt to resolve all of the many issues surrounding the leadership of his remarkable man. Rather than undertake such an impossible task, I have focused on a group of ten advisers who became a part of the new president's inner circle. I have ignored those, such as William Jennings Bryan and Albert Burleson, who served the president but never became confidants. Early in his presidency Wilson told a reporter that "a President can have no intimates, because, no matter how unselfish those intimates may be at the beginning, inevitably they will seek to take advantage of that intimacy before the end." Wilson understood that, given the scramble for power and preferment of those close to him, he was unlikely to develop deep, lasting friendships during his presidential years. Nevertheless, he also realized that, given his limited energy, he had to rely on advisers to help him maintain his physical and emotional equilibrium and to achieve his far-reaching political goals. As he later explained to Edith Galt, his presidency, if it was to be successful, required "a great diversity of talents . . . and the greatest possible variety of breeding."[2]

In 1913, Wilson brought together a diverse, impressive group of associates—especially considering the fact that he was a newcomer to national politics. His wife Ellen, the great love of Woodrow's life, understood her husband better than anyone else; Joe Tumulty, a New Jersey lawyer and politician, became his personal secretary; William Gibbs McAdoo, a bold New York entrepreneur, became his secretary of the treasury; Josephus Daniels, a North Carolina newspaper editor, became his secretary of the navy; Cary Grayson, a naval officer, became his White House physician; and Colonel Edward M. House, a Texas political operator, became his counselor. All of these advisers became, to one extent or another, friends of the president. All were struck by his magnetism, his oratorical gifts, and the power and precision of his mind. All believed that they had met a man of destiny and, looking back, realized that their relationship with Woodrow Wilson had transformed their lives.

This initial group of advisers—with the exception of Tumulty—all grew up in the South, and all, again with the exception of Tumulty, shared the president's paternalistic attitude toward African Americans. Wilson grew up around Blacks but admitted that "I have very little ease with coloured people or they with me," and he allowed Secretary of the Treasury McAdoo and Postmaster General Burleson—who were in charge of departments with the most Black employees—to begin to segregate their workers and to remove Black political appointees in the South. Rather than reach out to African Americans, Wilson defended racial segregation in federal buildings as "distinctly to the advantage of the colored people themselves." A bold reformer in so many areas, he was not willing to take on the issue of race.[3]

As the years passed, some of these advisers—House, McAdoo, Tumulty— had, to one extent or another, failed the president, and, as the challenges facing Wilson mounted, he drew new people into his inner circle. In 1916, Newton Baker, a Cleveland, Ohio, lawyer and reform mayor, became secretary of war; Bernard Baruch, a Wall Street speculator, became, after American entry into World War I, a key figure in the mobilization of the American economy; and Ray Stannard Baker, a famous muckraker jour- nalist, became the press officer of the American Peace Commission and eventually Wilson's defender before the bar of history. Finally, not long after Ellen's death in August 1914, Woodrow met Edith Galt, an attractive Washington businesswoman, and married her in December 1915. All of these advisers—even those who fell by the wayside—believed that, what- ever Wilson's flaws as a leader, they had served a great man whose legacy would endure.

Over the years, as I wrote my biography of Colonel House, I became fascinated with the men and women Wilson drew into his inner circle. This book has given me the opportunity to get to know them better, to explore a side of Woodrow Wilson that historians have often obscured, and to introduce this group of people to a new generation of readers. These advisers, and the president they served, all had their failures and short- comings, but their virtues seem evident, especially when compared to the nation's political leadership in our own dark time.

ACKNOWLEDGMENTS

As I wrote my biography of Colonel House, I got to know those advisers who became members of Woodrow Wilson's inner circle. But given the need to keep the narrative moving and to finish the book, I could not study their lives as much as I wanted to. Focusing on these ten talented people in more depth gave me the opportunity to deepen my understanding of them and their life histories and to better understand the connection they formed to the president. And after so many years of thinking about Wilson and his presidency, writing this book served as a kind of transition, as a way to leave the subject behind. Robert K. Massie, after finishing his great biography of Catherine the Great, wrote about the sadness of ending this project: "You were with the subject every day. Now this companion has departed and left you behind. He or she has concluded the time shared with you. That part of your life is over."[4]

Ray Stannard Baker remarked in *American Chronicle* that "a man must somehow learn how to live as well as how to work."[5] I am fortunate that over the years friends have helped me follow this maxim. David Hall introduced me to the glories of Pemaquid Point, Maine; Eleanor Adams always welcomed me for a visit to her magical Edgehill farm near Waterford, Virginia; David Mayers arranged for a visit to Clare Hall, University of Cambridge; and Larry McMurtry guided me to the Arizona Inn in Tucson. Two stays at the Woodrow Wilson International Center for Scholars gave me the opportunity to think more deeply about Wilson and his presidency, while John A. Thompson gave me an exceptionally thoughtful reading of the manuscript. I am also grateful to colleagues in the History

Department at the University of Miami—especially Hermann Beck, Stephen Halsey, Dominique Reill, and Donald Spivey—for their encouragement; to the late Peter Reill for his friendship; and to all those who gave my biography of Colonel House such a warm reception. At Johns Hopkins University Press, Laura Davulis and Esther Rodriguez moved the manuscript through the publication process with efficiency, and Melissa Flamson resolved permission questions with exceptional skill. Beth Gianfagna gave the manuscript a careful and thoughtful reading. It was a pleasure to work with all these talented people. My thanks, too, to Louis Galambos for continuing a conversation that began many years ago. Finally, my wife, Sabina, once again provided all kinds of critical support, while my daughter, Hilary, to whom this book is dedicated, has brightened my life in so many ways.

Quotations from the letters of Newton D. Baker, Ray Stannard Baker, Cary T. Grayson, and Joseph Patrick Tumulty are used with permission of the authors' families. I would also like to thank the rights holders for the remaining primary sources for permission to quote from that material.

— Newton D. Baker to Woodrow Wilson, Nov. 15, 1912, Newton Diehl Baker Papers, 1896–1962, Library of Congress, Manuscript Division. In Arthur S. Link, ed., *The Papers of Woodrow Wilson*, 69 vols. (Princeton, NJ, 1966–93), 25:549. Newton D. Baker to Woodrow Wilson, Nov. 11, 1918, WWP22595, World War I Letters, Woodrow Wilson Presidential Library and Museum, Staunton, Virginia. Library of Congress, Manuscript Division, Woodrow Wilson Papers. In Link, *The Papers of Woodrow Wilson*, 53:46.

— Newton D. Baker to Woodrow Wilson, Nov. 30, 1918, WWP25567, World War I Letters, Woodrow Wilson Presidential Library and Museum, Staunton, Virginia. Library of Congress, Manuscript Division, Woodrow Wilson Papers. In Arthur S. Link, ed., *The Papers of Woodrow Wilson*, 69 vols. (Princeton, NJ, 1966–93), 53:252–53. Newton D. Baker to Woodrow Wilson, July 18, 1919. In Link, *The Papers of Woodrow Wilson*, 61:53. Newton D. Baker to Woodrow Wilson, Dec. 24, 1920. In Link, *The Papers of Woodrow Wilson*, 67:3–4. Ray Stannard Baker, excerpts from *American Chronicle: The Autobiography of Ray Stannard Baker* (New York, 1945). Lord Robert Cecil, excerpt from *Diary of Lord Robert Cecil,*

British Museum, London. Reproduced with permission of the Marquess of Salisbury, Hatfield House.

— E. David Cronon, ed., excerpts from *The Cabinet Diaries of Josephus Daniels, 1913–1921* (Lincoln, NE, 1963), 33, 40–46, 117–18, 350, 474.

— Cary T. Grayson, excerpts from diary entries and letters, in Arthur S. Link, ed., *The Papers of Woodrow Wilson*, 69 vols. (Princeton, NJ, 1966–93). Edward Mandell House, previously published excerpts from House Diary, in Link, *The Papers of Woodrow Wilson*. Reproduced with permission.

— Edward Mandell House, Feb. 27, 1918, House Diary, in George Frost Kennan, *Russia Leaves the War* (Princeton, NJ, 1956), 29. Reproduced with permission.

— Joseph Patrick Tumulty, excerpts from letters in Arthur S. Link, ed., *The Papers of Woodrow Wilson*, 69 vols. (Princeton, NJ, 1966–93). Edith Wilson to Altrude G. Grayson, Feb. 11, 1916, Woodrow Wilson Presidential Library. Used with permission from the Woodrow Wilson Presidential Library and Museum, Staunton, Virginia.

— Edith Wilson, excerpts from letters in Arthur S. Link, ed., *The Papers of Woodrow Wilson*, vols. 32–34, 62, 65, copyright © 1980, 1981, 1990, 1992. Republished with permission of Princeton University Press, permission conveyed through Copyright Clearance Center, Inc.

— Edith Wilson, excerpts from *My Memoir* (Indianapolis, IN, 1939). Used with permission from the Woodrow Wilson Presidential Library and Museum, Staunton, Virginia.

— Ellen Wilson, excerpts from letters in Arthur S. Link, ed., *The Papers of Woodrow Wilson*, vols. 4–5, 11–12, 28, copyright © 1968, 1969, 1972, 1979. Republished with permission of Princeton University Press, permission conveyed through Copyright Clearance Center, Inc.

— Woodrow Wilson, excerpts from letters in Arthur S. Link, ed., *The Papers of Woodrow Wilson*, vols. 2, 6, 24–25, 27, 29–31, 33–34, 53, 68, copyright © 1967, 1969, 1978, 1979, 1980, 1981, 1986, 1993. Republished with permission of Princeton University Press, permission conveyed through Copyright Clearance Center, Inc.

The Wilson Circle

Woodrow and Ellen, seated on a lawn at Cornish, New Hampshire, ca. 1912, with their three daughters. *Left to right*: Margaret, Eleanor, and Jessie. Wilson thrived on the feminine atmosphere of his family. Library of Congress, Prints and Photographs Division, LC-USZ62-88078. Photo by Pach Brothers.

CHAPTER ONE

Woodrow Wilson

"I have a passion for interpreting great thoughts to the world"

In early April 1883, Woodrow Wilson, a twenty-six-year-old lawyer from Atlanta, traveled to Rome, Georgia, to conduct legal work for this mother. He was "absolutely *hungry for a sweetheart*," and soon after his arrival, while in church, he noticed Ellen Louise Axson, the daughter of the local Presbyterian minister. Woodrow was drawn to the delicate young woman with the intense brown eyes and chestnut-colored hair; he remembered thinking "what a bright, pretty face; what splendid, mischievous, laughing eyes! I'll lay a wager that this demure little lady has lots of life and fun in her." At the end of May, after a second visit to Rome and more walks and carriage rides with Ellen, he concluded that he was in love and would ask her to marry him. Many letters followed, and in September 1883, when Woodrow accidentally ran across Ellen in Asheville, North Carolina, he proposed. Ellen said yes, convinced, as she told her brother Stockton, that she was going to marry "the greatest man in the world." But the marriage would have to wait because Woodrow, disillusioned with the law, would enter the Johns Hopkins University in the fall in pursuit of a PhD, while Ellen, who looked after her depressed father and two younger brothers, could not in the near future leave her family responsibilities. Woodrow and Ellen would not marry until June 24, 1885. Their marriage would become a close emotional and intellectual union; shortly before his death, Wilson told his daughter Eleanor that "I owe everything to your mother—you know that, don't you?"[1]

* * *

Wilson was born on December 28, 1856, in Staunton, Virginia, the third child of the Reverend Joseph Ruggles Wilson and Janet Wilson. His father was a witty, handsome, dynamic figure, while his mother was shy, retiring, and overprotective. For a time Joseph Wilson thrived in the Southern Presbyterian church, in December 1857 moving to a bigger and more prosperous congregation in Augusta, Georgia, and thirteen years later accepting a professorship at the Columbia Theological Seminary in Columbia, South Carolina. While he was a popular teacher and a master of Calvinist theology, he encountered political difficulties at Columbia, and less than four years later moved on to a lesser church in Wilmington, North Carolina. As his own career declined, Joseph Wilson focused on the worldly success of his son. Both Woodrow's father and mother believed he was destined for great things, and Joseph Wilson showered him with affection and taught him how to use words correctly. He was, Wilson remembered, "one of the most inspiring fathers that ever a lad was blessed with." Wilson also revered his mother, telling his daughter Eleanor that "I seem to feel still the touch of her hand, and the sweet steadying influence of her wonderful character. I thank God for such a mother."[2]

Woodrow came of age in a rich cultural and intellectual environment. He enjoyed music; had an elaborate fantasy life, imagining triumphs at sea; and became fascinated with politics, placing a portrait of British Prime Minister William Gladstone in his room and declaring that "when he was a man he intended to be a statesman such as this hero of his." He developed a deep religious faith—although he had no interest in theological speculation—and considered himself a southerner, although he had no accent and the Civil War seemed to have made little impact on him. Later in life he noted that "the only place in the country, the only place in the world, where nothing has to be explained to me is the South." Woodrow grew up around Blacks—his parents had African American servants—but, as one historian remarks, they "remained invisible" to him; he never really questioned the paternalistic racial attitudes of his youth.[3]

In the fall of 1873—when he was only sixteen—Woodrow left home to attend Davidson College, a small Presbyterian school in North Carolina.

He seemed to do well at Davidson but, perhaps feeling homesick and in poor health, left after one year and returned to Wilmington, North Carolina, to live with his family. In the fall of 1875, he left home once again to attend the College of New Jersey, which everyone called Princeton for the small town where it was located. At Princeton, Woodrow thrived. He made friends easily, became a fervent fan of the football and baseball teams, and, while he found the formal instruction uninspiring, developed strong intellectual interests outside of the classroom, writing to Joseph Ruggles Wilson: "Father, I have made a discovery; I have found that I have a mind." Woodrow was fascinated with politics and the machinery of government, and particularly admired British institutions and practices and the English political commentator Walter Bagehot. As his political ambitions emerged, he would often tell his friends, "When I meet you in the Senate, I'll argue that out with you."[4]

For years Woodrow and his father had assumed that he would become a lawyer, and after his graduation from Princeton, in the fall of 1879 he entered the law school at the University of Virginia. Woodrow never considered the ministry as a career and had no interest in business, but he soon found that he was bored by the law. Once again he pursued his own intellectual agenda, reading, debating, and preparing himself for what he now thought might be a literary career. He began to sense that he was a man of destiny, writing to a Princeton friend that "those indistinct plans of which we used to talk grow on me daily, until a sort of calm confidence of great things to be accomplished has come over me which I am puzzled to analyze the nature of." In December 1880, midway in his second year, Woodrow's health broke down, and he returned to his parents' home in Wilmington. For the next year and a half he lived at home, writing essays, practicing oratory in his father's church, and preparing for the bar examination. In May 1882, Woodrow finally left Wilmington and traveled to Atlanta, Georgia, a boomtown of the New South, to join a Princeton classmate in his law practice. He soon regretted the move. He had little interest in developing his practice and had little work, complaining about "the dreadful drudgery which attends the initiation into our profession." In the spring of 1883, Wilson decided to abandon the law. He yearned for an intellectual life and had decided to become a college professor. He bought a typewriter, which, he hoped, would help him become "a speaker and writer of the highest authority on political subjects."[5]

In September 1883, Wilson moved to Baltimore, Maryland, where he entered the PhD program at the Johns Hopkins University. The emphasis at Hopkins—a new institution modeled after German universities—was on scientific research and the gradual accumulation of knowledge. While Wilson thrived in the seminary in history and political science, he had "no patience," he wrote, "for the tedious toil of what is known as 'research'; I have a passion for interpreting great thoughts to the world." He wrote ardent love letters to Ellen (one of which was nineteen pages long), pursued his political studies outside of the classroom, and in January 1885—midway through his second year at Hopkins—published his first book, *Congressional Government*. In this tome, which most critics praised, Wilson argued for more centralization of power in Washington and for responsible party government. At the age of twenty-eight he had published an original and provocative study of the American system of government.[6]

The publication of *Congressional Government* capped a brilliant stay at Hopkins, and by the spring of 1885, Wilson was eager to begin his career. He and Ellen were married in Savannah, Georgia, and in September they moved to Bryn Mawr College, which opened that fall with a faculty of seven and thirty-six undergraduates. Woodrow was a dashing young man, with a pince-nez, a long, drooping mustache, and thick sideburns. But the young instructor had a small income and heavy teaching load, and soon discovered that he disliked teaching women. And he felt ambivalent about academic life, complaining about "the disadvantages of the *closet*. I want to keep close to the *practical* and the *practicable* in politics." By his third year at Bryn Mawr he was discontent, noting "thirty-one years old and nothing done."[7]

In June 1888, Wilson received an offer from Wesleyan University, and that summer he, Ellen, and their daughters moved to Middletown, Connecticut. Woodrow prospered at Wesleyan. He quickly established himself as a compelling teacher and popular member of the faculty, and his growing reputation as a scholar and as a lecturer led, in February 1890, to an offer from Princeton University. He now experienced "a distinct *feeling of maturity*."[8]

Wilson's twelve years on the Princeton faculty marked a remarkably productive period in his life. An inspirational teacher, he was also a prolific scholar who, during these years, published nine volumes and thirty-five articles. And he was a much-sought-after lecturer who often pursued a punishing schedule (between October 10, 1895, and mid-January 1896, he made eighteen out-of-town trips). His growing reputation as one of the leading historians and political scientists of his time led to a number of offers—including university presidencies—from other institutions.[9]

Wilson did not, however, seem a driven man. He had an unusual ability to concentrate on the task at hand, while Ellen managed the household and served as adviser and confidant on every aspect of his career. During these Princeton years he had a happy home life and a wide circle of friends. The Wilson household included several servants, along with various family members who came to stay for long periods of time. Woodrow was a devoted father, often playing with his three daughters, and a gifted mimic with an endless series of dialect stories. It was a family devoted to books, one that spent many evenings reading aloud, and it was also a family that said grace at meals, read the Bible, and gave nightly prayers.[10]

These twelve years were also an intensely social period of Wilson's life; he had a wide range of friendships with both men and women. Like his father, Wilson liked to talk, delighting in good conversation and seeking out women who were "cultivated and conversable." Ellen encouraged these friendships, noting that "since he has married a wife who is not gay, I must provide him friends who are." She especially encouraged his friendship with John Grier Hibben, a professor of philosophy, four years younger than Wilson, who joined the Princeton faculty in 1891. Wilson saw Hibben nearly every day, often for tea, when the two friends would talk about literature and university affairs. Or as he put it, "I have talked with Jack Hibben and I am refreshed."[11]

Wilson paid a physical price for his extraordinary success. While he had always suffered from digestive troubles, in May 1896 he experienced severe pain and numbness in his right hand. It may, in fact, have been a small stroke, an indication of the hypertension and arteriosclerosis that would complicate his career. Alarmed, Wilson took a two-month holiday in Great Britain and returned to Princeton in apparently good health. But he now felt more restless and impatient. More than ever, his brother-in-law Stockton Axson remembered, he was "torn between the desire to live a studious and scholarly life . . . and a life of action."[12]

In October 1896, Wilson gave, in a celebration of Princeton's 150th anniversary, a speech titled "Princeton in the Nation's Service," an oratorical triumph that confirmed him as the leader of the young faculty. Wilson and many of his colleagues were disturbed by the lethargic leadership of President Francis L. Patton, and in June 1902 the university's trustees unanimously selected the young professor, who was only forty-five, as Patton's successor. He confided to Ellen that "I feel like a new prime minister getting ready to address his constituents."[13]

Granted sweeping powers by the trustees, Wilson proved to be a bold leader with a "passionate longing" to transform Princeton into one of the nation's leading universities. During his first three years he upgraded the faculty, reformed the curriculum, and worked with the prominent architect Ralph Adams Cram to redesign the campus in a Gothic Revival style. Inspired by his visits to Cambridge and Oxford, he wanted Princeton to become an American version of these great English universities, with their Gothic quadrangles and intense interaction between students and faculty. In February 1905, he proposed a tutorial system, what became known as the "Preceptorial System," one in which faculty would meet with students in small groups and hopefully inspire them to greater intellectual effort. Wilson took the initiative in recruiting the first group of preceptors, and the system became a great success. His reforms at Princeton achieved much national attention; by the end of 1905, he had become the best-known university president in the nation.[14]

During his first three years as president, Wilson's leadership style emerged. He was an impatient, visionary leader, one who could be inspiring and charming and who seemed to possess an endless supply of amusing anecdotes. But he could also be imperious and high-handed, accustomed to getting his own way and impatient and sarcastic with those who opposed him. One critic claimed that "[h]e had a cold, repellent nature."[15]

Since Princeton's president had no office staff, Wilson relied on several faculty colleagues to help, especially on "Jack" Hibben, who became his alter ego. Hibben, who had a pious and conciliatory disposition, lifted many burdens from Wilson's shoulders and knew how to soothe the high-strung president. Wilson shared all of his thoughts and ambitions with his devoted friend. It was the most intense male friendship that he would ever have.[16]

On May 28, 1906, Wilson awoke to discover that he was blind in his left eye (which would later recover partial vision). The specialist he consulted in Philadelphia concluded that he had suffered an ocular hemorrhage that was caused by high blood pressure and recommended a regimen of rest. Ellen was deeply upset, concluding that her husband had "lived too tensely" and she was more eager than ever to protect him from anxiety and worry. Determined to escape the pressures of the Princeton presidency, Wilson named Hibben as acting president and spent the summer of 1906 in England, mostly in the Lake District. Ellen and their three daughters joined him for the first part of his vacation, but after her departure he hiked by himself, sometimes as much as fourteen miles a day.[17]

In early October, Wilson returned to Princeton, refreshed by his long absence but now, as one biographer remarks, "even more focused, purposeful, and driven." He still had major reforms to enact if the transformation of Princeton into a modern university was to be completed. The first was the so-called Quadrangle Plan, or Quad Plan; the second was the creation of a Graduate College at the center of the campus. Wilson had long been upset by the thirteen eating clubs for upperclassmen on Prospect Avenue, which he believed encouraged frivolous and anti-intellectual behavior among Princeton's undergraduates. In late 1906, he proposed to the trustees the creation of residential colleges where students would live and eat and that would presumably become the center of their intellectual life. In June 1907, the trustees approved the Quad Plan, but Wilson's victory was short-lived. He had not consulted the faculty, or sought alumni support, or conferred with the dean, Andrew Fleming West, who believed the establishment of the Graduate College should be the next priority. Worse still, Wilson failed to understand that most students and alums were devoted to their eating clubs. As Dean West remarked, "The spirit of Princeton is to be killed." And during the summer of 1907, while vacationing in the Adirondacks, he discovered that Hibben, his cherished friend, opposed the Quad Plan. In October 1907, the trustees withdrew their earlier approval, and now the president, instead of seeking a compromise—as Hibben urged—became more impatient and combative.[18]

Wilson had, in fact, misunderstood Hibben, never realizing that his tactful and diplomatic friend would not support such a controversial and divisive proposal. There was no confrontation between the two men, but Woodrow concluded that Hibben was "hopelessly weak," too eager to please his wealthy alumni friends. He abruptly ended the friendship and would never reconcile with Hibben. But neither would he escape the pain that the end of the friendship brought. "Why," he asked himself years later, "will that wound not heal over in my stubborn heart?"[19]

In late November 1907, when Wilson suffered more weakness and numbness in his right arm, he decided, with Ellen's encouragement, to spend the last half of January and most of February 1908 in Bermuda. A year earlier, when he had first traveled to that "lotus land," he had met Mary Allen Hulbert Peck, a vivacious forty-five-year-old woman—estranged from her husband in Pittsfield, Massachusetts—who presided over a sophisticated salon. Now Wilson spent much more time with Mary Peck, overwhelmed by the warmth and beauty of the island and by her relaxed, fun-loving nature. In her company, he wrote, "I lost all of the abominable self-consciousness that has been my bane all my life, and felt perfectly at ease, happily myself." Mary Peck took long walks with Wilson, impressed with the "rare clear quality of his voice," and perhaps amused by his "stilted and puritanical" behavior. She discovered that her new friend did not swim, skate, dance, or smoke Or as Wilson explained, "Alas, no. My dear mother was so fearful of all those things that they were denied me." After his departure from Bermuda he began writing letters to "My precious one, my beloved Mary," pouring out his feelings and ambitions. Wilson would never again see Mary Peck in Bermuda, but he visited her in New York

City after her move there, and for several years continued to write her impassioned letters. He would remember Shoreby, her house in Bermuda, as "the home of the friend whom I had found when those I had deemed my friends were falling away from me, and all the world looked gray and bleak."[20] More than most men of his era, Wilson enjoyed the companionship of women and over the years would engage in an intense correspondence with several female friends.

In 1908, the controversy over the Quad Plan merged with the controversy over the location and control of the Graduate College. For the next two years Princeton was engulfed in what one biographer, John Milton Cooper Jr., describes as an "academic civil war." Wilson wanted the Graduate College located in the center of the campus so that graduate students could be integrated into the life of the university. Dean West, an academic dilettante with strong ties to powerful and wealthy trustees, wanted an off-campus site and a Graduate College full of medieval pomp and ceremony, a place for gentlemen rather for serious scholars. In May 1910, a large gift to Princeton for West's version of the Graduate College convinced Wilson that, as he put it," We've beaten the living, but we can't fight the dead—the game is up." His battles at Princeton had brought him national fame and had coincided with his shift from a conservative to a progressive political persuasion. The university that he had boldly transformed, however, was now so bitterly divided that Wilson faced what he termed an "all but intolerable situation." It was time to move on.[21]

By the spring of 1910, the name of the Princeton president was widely mentioned for the governorship of New Jersey. The prospect of the "rough and tumble of the political arena" appealed to Wilson. Or, as he wrote Ellen, "It would be rather jolly, after all, to start out on life anew together, to make a new career, would it not? "In mid-July he met with Democratic Party bosses, and on September 15 was nominated at the Democratic convention in Trenton. Wilson embarked on a whirlwind campaign, running on a progressive platform, and quickly became a "pungent, hard-hitting stump speaker." On November 10, he won by a wide margin. Once in office, the new governor repudiated the bosses who had given him the nomination, assumed the leadership of the Democratic Party, and pushed through a series of reform measures. His remarkable political ascent in New Jersey had won him even more nationwide attention, and in May 1911, he took a tour of the West to advance what had become his presidential ambitions. In July, a Woodrow Wilson Headquarters opened in New York City, and by September, Wilson's drive for the presidency was well under way.[22]

During the first half of 1912, Wilson's presidential campaign waxed and waned, but at the Democratic convention in Baltimore in late June he finally won the nomination on the forty-sixth ballot. With Theodore Roosevelt's bolt from the Republican Party and his leadership of the new Progressive Party, Wilson was sure to win the presidency if he could hold on to the traditional Democratic vote. On November 5, Wilson did, in fact, triumph, and he became the first Democratic president in sixteen years. On March 4, 1913, less than two and a half years after his resignation from the presidency of Princeton, Wilson was inaugurated as president of the United States.

Long before his presidential campaign Wilson had become one of the most prominent public speakers in the nation. As a youth he had practiced oratory in his father's empty church, and over the years he had trained his voice and perfected his technique. Using few if any gestures, Wilson spoke without any notes in perfect sentences. To his listeners he appeared a dignified and powerful orator, a new leader of vision and courage. Wilson relished these performances, revealing to Ellen that "I have a sense of power in dealing with men collectively which I do not feel always in dealing with them singly." More and more over the years he aspired to become what one historian describes as a "heroic oratorical statesman," convinced that "the true orator was a person of deep learning, penetrating genius, and almost magical powers of persuasion."[23]

The new president was fifty-six years old, a trim, vigorous man, with a "strong, long-jawed, animated face" and a "magnificent, resonant voice." Raymond Fosdick (who had been a student of Wilson's at Princeton) thought he was "a prophet touched by fire," a brilliant, intense man, a

The president seated at his desk. House observed that, while Wilson worked limited hours, he accomplished far more than McAdoo because he focused so intently on the task at hand. World History Archive / Alamy Stock Photo.

spellbinding orator whose ambition and sense of destiny had carried him far. His moral and political vision had inspired many Americans, and many of those who encountered Wilson over the years were convinced that they had met an extraordinary man. Stockton Axson recalled that "one knew he was in the presence of a great man as soon as he heard him utter one sentence," while Edmund W. Starling, one of the secret service agents assigned to the White House, remembered the president's voice, "so rich, so well-modulated, so vibrant with repressed energy that I was enchanted." Looking back on the Wilson years, William Gibbs McAdoo, secretary of the treasury and Wilson's son-in-law, concluded that the president was "many-sided," a "great man in the true sense." He possessed, McAdoo argued, "vision and creative power. . . . He looked over the heads of other men, above the confusion of contemporary events, to distant horizons."[24]

Wilson was an unusually solitary figure for an American political leader, one who had little taste for day-to-day contacts with politicians and reporters and with the constant intrusions of politics into his private life. Even before his election, he confided to Mary Peck that "*I* am now in a cage . . . made of triple steel and brass,—a man without individual freedom or privacy. . . . Often I find myself beating my very head against the walls in a sort of despair. I love my freedom. It is the breath of life to me. . . . You must not let me suffer the sort of blindness and atrophy public men so often suffer." Wilson was, in fact, an emotionally fragile man, one who had suffered over the years from loneliness and depression. A few months before their marriage, he had written Ellen that "my only disease is loneliness," and he soon discovered that his relationship with her gave him emotional stability and a base from which he could venture out into the world. Or as Ellen wrote, "He is almost terribly dependent on me to keep up his spirits and to 'rest' him as he says. So I dare not have the 'blues.' If I am just a little sky-blue, he immediately becomes blue-black!"[25]

Once in the White House, Wilson faced political pressures far more intense than any he had experienced before, and also found himself more isolated in a personal sense than ever before as well. He had, after all, spent most of his adult life in the academy and had not formed a wide-ranging network of political associates on whom he could rely. During the campaign Wilson worried that "politics and friendship seem mutually exclusive" and asked if it were possible to find "real, tested friendship,—friendship with insight and comprehending sympathy, that understands before the case is stated and sees as much as your own heart does? It is *that* that makes life noble and beautiful and good to live." He was in need of advisers who could serve as buffers and companions, and who could carry out many tasks he found unpalatable. But finding the right kind of people would not be easy, since the new president was a needy, passionate man, one who romanticized friendships and who expected to dominate those who drew close to him.[26]

Over the winter of 1912–13, the president's circle of advisers began to fill out. Joe Tumulty, who had served as the governor's secretary in New Jersey, now became the secretary to the president. Tumulty had a warm relationship with Wilson and his family, tracked public opinion, helped draft speeches, and supervised relations with the press and Congress. In November 1911, Colonel Edward M. House, a wealthy Texas political operator, had met Wilson, and after his election House, who had no official position, advised on a wide range of political matters. House recalled that "a few weeks after we met and after we had exchanged confidences which men usually do not exchange except after years of friendship, I asked him if he realized that we had only known one another for so short a time. He replied 'My dear friend, we have known one another always.' And I think this is true." The third new adviser was William Gibbs McAdoo, the builder of the first railway tunnels under the Hudson River. An early supporter of Wilson's presidential bid and eventually the driving force in his campaign, he was appointed secretary of the treasury. And McAdoo's marriage in May 1914 to the president's youngest daughter, Eleanor, drew him deeper into Wilson's inner circle. The fourth new adviser was Josephus Daniels, a shrewd Democratic Party operator and editor of the Raleigh, North Carolina, *News and Observer*. Daniels would serve the new president eight years as secretary of the navy and become one of his most effective and trusted advisers. Finally, during the inauguration ceremonies Wilson met Cary Grayson, the White House physician. On William Howard Taft's recommendation, he decided to keep Grayson on his staff, and the handsome, affable naval officer (he was only thirty-four) became one of the president's favorite companions. Grayson monitored Wilson's health closely, putting him on a diet and a regimen of daily exercise. The president seemed physically fit, with a round and firm neck and a quick gate, but in fact he suffered from frequent colds, headaches, and digestive problems and from cerebral vascular disease, which may have appeared as early as 1896. In April 1913, Wilson suffered a recurrence of pains in his right arm. Grayson worried about a possible circulatory problem but was careful not to alarm the president and his family.[27]

By his first summer as president, Wilson's routines had crystallized; he organized his presidency, one biographer remarks, "to preserve a central calm and to create a White House that was more of a sanctuary than a sounding board." Wilson rose at 8:00, ate breakfast at 8:30, and then went to his office, where he opened his mail and dictated replies. From 10:00 to 11:00 he received callers, who had made an appointment through Tumulty, and who were given only ten or fifteen minutes of the president's time. After lunch with members of his family, at 2:00 or 2:30, he returned to his office for more work but left by 4:00 to play golf with Grayson or take an automobile ride. Dinner was at 7:00 with family and sometimes a few friends, and then the president often went to the theater (especially vaudeville), or sang and read aloud with his family from familiar books, or, if affairs of state pressed, worked in his study. Evenings at the White House were similar to evenings at Princeton. While Ellen and Woodrow engaged in official entertaining, they made no attempt at cultural or intellectual patronage; they lived in the White House like a middle-class, intellectually and artistically inclined family that cherished its privacy and a small group of relatives and friends. Rather than mingle with a wide range of people, the president spent many hours alone reading and thinking. The journalist John Reed, who interviewed Wilson in June 1914, wrote that he "gave such an impression of quietness inside. Deep within him is a principle or a religion, or something, upon which his whole life rests."[28]

On April 8, 1913, Wilson, breaking precedent, went to Capitol Hill to address a special session of Congress on tariff reform. Throughout the rest of the year, working with Democratic leaders in the House and Senate, he pushed key reform measures through the Congress—first the Underwood Tariff Act, then the Federal Reserve Act, and later, in 1914, the Clayton Antitrust Act and Federal Trade Commission Act. During the summer of 1913, the president stayed in Washington, while Ellen and his three daughters—Margaret, Jessie, and Eleanor—moved to Cornish, New Hampshire, where they lingered until mid-October to escape the heat of the capital. Wilson pursued a solitary life, writing to a friend, "Here I am, marooned in the White House, alone in my majesty and discontent." To give the president some company, Grayson and Tumulty moved in, and the three men shared their meals, automobile rides, and games of golf.[29]

During 1913 and the early months of 1914, Wilson seemed to be thriving in the presidency. His reform agenda was nearing completion, while his health had been remarkably good throughout his first year in office. In February and March 1914, however, Ellen's energy began to decline. She suffered from Bright's disease, an infection of the kidney, and throughout the summer of 1914 her health worsened. On July 23, as she faded, Grayson moved into the room next to her bedroom while the president sat by her side until the early hours of the morning. On August 3, Grayson told Wilson to summon his daughters; two days later his beloved wife, who was only fifty-four, died at 5 o'clock in the afternoon. "God has stricken me," Wilson wrote to a friend, "almost beyond what I can bear." With the great love of his life dead, his private universe crumbled, and for several weeks he was nearly paralyzed with grief.[30]

The fall of 1914 proved to be a difficult time for the president. The outbreak of the Great War in early August disrupted the American economy and raised complicated questions about the nature of American neutrality. Moreover, Republican gains in the November congressional elections suggested that the reform impulse had ebbed and that Democrats would face a reunited Republican Party in the 1916 presidential election. Wilson was depressed, writing to Mary Hulbert (she had divorced in 1912) that "[e]very night finds me exhausted,—dead in heart and body (so far as everything concerning myself is concerned,)" and in early November telling Colonel House that "he was broken in spirit by Mrs. Wilson's death, and was not fit to be President because he did not think straight any longer, and had no heart in the things that he was doing." Wilson's family and friends tried to distract him from his grief, and in January 1915 his spirits seemed to be improving. One evening Wilson, House, McAdoo, and Eleanor examined a new presidential portrait. Instead of standing in front of the painting, as Eleanor wished, her father (House recorded) "made all sorts of contortions, sticking his tongue in his cheek, twisting his mouth into different positions, rolling his eyes, dropping his jaw, and doing everything a clown would do at a circus. She tried composing his features with her hand, and when she lifted it, he would raise his eyes to heaven."[31]

As Wilson's mood improved, he spoke of running for reelection in 1916 and displayed a renewed interest in political combat. He continued to write letters of emotional intensity to Mary Hulbert and then, around March 20, 1915, met Edith Bolling Galt, a tall, shapely widow with soft hazel eyes and dark brown hair. Vivacious and stylish, her full figure and warm, romantic temperament appealed to Wilson, and within a few weeks of their first meeting they were taking long drives and eating dinner together at the White House. Although Edith was forty-two, sixteen years younger than the president, Woodrow pressed his courtship, and on May 4, less than two months after they had met, he declared his love and proposed. While she gently rebuffed him, he continued what one biographer describes as "the most ardent chase" of his life, sending flowers every day to her house near Dupont Circle and writing a torrent of letters, some as long as twenty pages. "Here stands your friend," he wrote on May 5, "a longing man, in the midst of a world's affairs—a world that knows nothing of the heart he has shown to you and which would as lief break it as not. . . . Will you come to him some time, without reserve and make his strength complete?"[32]

While Woodrow pursued Edith, he faced growing tension with the German government. The German U-boat decree of early February 1915 had established a war zone in the waters surrounding Great Britain and Ireland and had led Wilson to warn the German government that it would be held to a "strict accountability" for the loss of American ships and American lives. On May 7, the torpedoing of the RMS *Lusitania*, one of the great North Atlantic passenger liners, threatened to bring the United States into the war and set off a long crisis in German-American relations.

During June and July 1915, as Woodrow and Edith spent weeks together at Cornish, New Hampshire, their love deepened. "You are my ideal companion," Wilson declared, "the close and delightful *chum of my mind.* You are my perfect *playmate*," while Edith wrote to her "Sweetheart" that "there are no locked doors . . . but instead all the gates are flung wide, and a perfect flood of longing rushes to you." She was eager to be "taken into partnership" with him, and Woodrow quickly obliged, writing that "I am so glad to share public matters with you—so anxious to share them with you." During the summer of 1915, when separated, Edith began receiving a "big envelope" nearly every day full of official documents, with notes of explanation written by the president. When together at their summer home Harlakenden, they would sit on the terrace overlooking the Connecticut River Valley, while, Edith wrote, "you put one dear hand on mine, while with the other you turn the pages of history."[33]

Despite her limited education, Edith was becoming one of the president's most important advisers. And she was not inclined to share her love for him with his close associates. Tumulty's "commonness" troubled her, while she dismissed House as "not a very *strong* character." Wilson defended Tumulty and House, pointing out that he needed a diversity of talent among his advisers if he was to manage all the currents of national affairs. But Edith's appearance in the inner circle around the president was bound to have important long-term consequences.[34]

In September, when Wilson was back in Washington, he was eager to clear the path to his remarriage. Tumulty and McAdoo feared the political repercussions of a White House wedding in late 1915, but Grayson and House, worried about Wilson's health and longevity, believed, as the Colonel wrote in his diary, that if the president "does not marry, and marry quickly, I believe he will go into a decline." On September 22, when House traveled to Washington to confer with his friend in the White House, the two men agreed that the announcement should be issued in the middle of October and that a wedding should follow before the end of the year.[35]

On December 18, 1915, Edith and Woodrow were married in a ceremony at her Dupont Circle home. After having supper with their guests— mostly family members—the newlyweds took a private railway car to Hot Springs, Virginia, where they began a three-week honeymoon at the Homestead Hotel. The vacation left Wilson in good spirits and prepared for the challenges of 1916.

* * *

In early 1916, Wilson's political prospects seemed doubtful. He had won in 1912 with slightly under 42 percent of the vote because of the split in the Republican Party. It seemed unlikely, however, that the GOP would remain so bitterly divided four years later. On January 28, Wilson nominated Louis D. Brandeis, known as "the people's lawyer" for a vacancy on the Supreme Court, a clear signal of the leftward shift of his administration. Wilson and congressional Democrats now planned to enact further progressive reforms and to complete the New Freedom agenda in the spring and summer of 1916. The president was reasserting his leadership.[36]

On the morning of March 6, after a long diplomatic mission to Berlin, London, and Paris, House arrived in Washington to report on his European trip. During an automobile ride of over two hours, the president's counselor had to summarize his activities in Europe while squeezed in between Woodrow and Edith in the White House limousine. The president's new wife, he now realized, was privy to all important state papers and had a lively interest in foreign affairs. In the early months of 1916, while House had traveled in Europe, Woodrow and Edith had settled into a routine that was, in important ways, different from the one he had maintained with Ellen. Edith was involved in all aspects of Wilson's life, sitting with him in his office as he dictated letters, accompanying him on the golf course or in an automobile, and staying with him after dinner when he often did his most serious work. She had few interests aside from her husband's, serving both as his constant companion and as an assistant president. The energy that Wilson had once devoted to his friendships with Grayson, House, Tumulty, and his three daughters was now focused on his new wife. As one of Edith's biographers writes, "their intimacy was foreclosing all others."[37]

While Edith criticized many of her husband's advisers, she remained close to Grayson, who on May 24 married her friend Alice Gertrude Gordon, and she also seemed, at times, to approve of House, informing Wilson's cousin Helen Bones that Grayson and House "were the only two friends the President had who were serving him without selfish ambition." Edith's love had given Woodrow a new energy and a new sense of purpose.

On May 12, the journalist Ray Stannard Baker talked with him for two hours in the White House. He found a national leader "stepping quickly and lightly," "natty" in dress, with a lively face and a quick, incisive mind, a far cry from his stern public image.[38]

Wilson spent the hot and tense summer of 1916 in Washington, pushing an ambitious legislative agenda through Congress and seeking to position his party for the fall campaign. In some cases the president took the initiative; in other cases it came from congressional Democrats. Whatever the source, over the summer the New Freedom plan was expanded, and on September 2, Wilson signed the final reform measure, the Adamson Act, which decreed an eight-hour day for railway workers. The president had once again made shrewd political adjustments and revealed his gift for political leadership. A Democratic campaign official noted that "anyone who believes that the President is not a practical man or an astute politician is making a profound mistake."[39]

Over the course of the summer Wilson suffered from digestive troubles, severe headaches, and extreme fatigue. Grayson warned him that he must "slow up" and rest or that he would not be able to keep going. On September 1, he finally left Washington for Shadow Lawn—his summer home on the New Jersey shore. There, despite the constant press of visitors and campaign events, Wilson devised ways to escape the pressure. Surrounded by family and friends, he avoided political talk over lunch and dinner and found that Edith's presence eased his burden. She accompanied him everywhere and even blotted his signature of routine government documents. "When you are here," he remarked, "work seems like play."[40]

In early October, Wilson traveled to Omaha, Nebraska, where he received an enthusiastic reception. As he defended American neutrality and spoke of the need for an association of nations, the power of the peace appeal in the Midwest and Far West became apparent. Democratic campaign managers picked up the theme, claiming that the president had kept the nation out of war and suggesting, as one Democratic Party advertisement put it, that the voters faced a choice of "Wilson and Peace with Honor? or Hughes with Roosevelt and War?" On November 2, after addressing a large gathering at Madison Square Garden in New York, Wilson returned to Shadow Lawn to await the results. Not until the evening of November 9 did his victory become almost certain. He had achieved a stunning personal triumph; his message of peace, prosperity, and progressivism had resonated throughout the nation.[41]

By the early weeks of January 1917, it seemed as if the president's efforts to end the war might finally succeed. On January 22, he stood before the Senate and gave his "Peace without Victory" speech, insisting that "there must be, not a balance of power, but a community of power; no organized rivalries, but an organized common peace." But at the end of January, news came from Berlin that Germany would begin unrestricted U-boat warfare on February 1. As America moved toward war, Wilson pondered what the next step should be. On March 7, he went to bed with a cold and sore throat and stayed in his private quarters for nearly two weeks. Every day the pressure for a decision grew more intense, and finally, on April 2, in a brief but memorable address, Wilson asked the Congress for a declaration of war.[42]

In April and May 1917, the president moved swiftly to mobilize the nation. He became absorbed in complex legislative battles, insisted on an all-out commitment to prosecute the war, and began to draw into his administration a group of powerful war managers to whom he delegated sweeping authority. The progressive journalist George Creel became head of the Committee on Public Information; the dynamic director of Belgium relief, Herbert Hoover, became head of the Food Administration; and the convivial Wall Street speculator, Bernard Baruch, took the lead in mobilizing the American economy for war. The president enjoyed Baruch's style and wit, appreciated his intellectual boldness, and liked to have him nearby. He became a key member of Wilson's war cabinet, always sitting on the president's left at its weekly meetings.[43]

The war imposed heavy new burdens on the president, who stayed in Washington throughout the exceptionally hot and humid summer of 1917. Sometimes he and Edith would escape from "the people and their intolerable excitements and demands" for a few days on the presidential yacht

Mayflower, although Woodrow brought his papers and a stenographer with him. America's entrance into the war had accelerated the rush of people and events; Wilson now had to work late into the evening on official documents. Edith continued to guard her husband's health. She and Woodrow took frequent breaks for golf, automobile rides, and vaudeville at Keith's Theater, and in September they spent a week cruising off the New England coast. Even so, the uncertainties of the war weighed heavily on the president. "There would come days," Edith remembered, "when he was incapacitated by blinding headaches that no medicine could relieve. He would have to give up everything, and the only cure seemed to be sleep. . . . He would then awaken refreshed and able at once to take up work and go on with renewed energy."[44]

On January 8, 1918, Wilson delivered his Fourteen Points address, a remarkable document that sought to rally various groups both at home and in the Allied nations behind a liberal peace settlement. In the United States the address received warm approval across the political spectrum, but it did not quiet growing discontent in both parties with what some claimed was the leisurely pace of the American war effort. Wilson moved quickly to respond to the administration's critics, and by the middle of March much of the confusion and anxiety over the nation's mobilization for war had passed. The president's leadership seemed more secure than ever.[45]

The massive German assault on the Western Front, launched on March 21, surprised and shocked Wilson, who had hoped for peace, not an intensification of the war. German forces, however, could not sustain their offensive, and by early June the Allies counterattacked with American, British, and French divisions; the tide of the war had finally begun to turn.

In mid-August 1918, Woodrow and Edith visited Colonel House at his summer cottage on Boston's North Shore. On the fourth day of the visit, House, who hoped that his friend would run for a third term, had a long talk with Grayson about the president's health. The White House physician claimed that his patient "might go on for another ten years if nothing untoward happened." And it seemed that Wilson, despite occasional complaints that "his mind was becoming 'leaky,'" was in good spirits and good health during the spring and summer of 1918, maintaining his careful regimen of work and relaxation. But House's protégé William Wiseman, who observed Wilson during his visit, noted that "[h]is attitude lately has tended to become more arbitrary, and aloof, and there are times when he seems to treat foreign governments hardly seriously." The president had, in fact, become less resilient than in earlier years, consulting fewer people and, in the case of the covenant of the proposed League of Nations, refusing to discuss his ideas with either congressional or foreign leaders. As one biographer notes, he was no longer "at the peak of his powers."[46]

In October 1918, as the German army neared collapse, Wilson drew German leaders into negotiations that led to an armistice on November 11. House, who led the American delegation in the armistice negotiations, boasted that, if he were head of the American peace commission that was to follow, with McAdoo and Hoover as his associates, he could "guarantee" the results. But the president had no intention of staying in Washington while his counselor and Allied leaders concluded a peace treaty. The peace conference—which opened on January 12, 1919—represented the culmination of Wilson's career, an opportunity for him to convince Allied leaders to conclude a peace of justice and moderation that would embody his vision of a new international order.[47] But he arrived in Paris in a weakened political position, because in the November 1918 congressional elections Republicans had won control of both the House and Senate.

During the first phase of the peace conference, which ended when Wilson left Paris on February 15, the president, so it seemed, had been dominant. He had insisted on the priority of the League of Nations and gained the conference's approval of a draft covenant that created a stronger League than many members of the Anglo-American political elite desired. But in concentrating on the covenant, he had allowed the peace conference, which was, on the day of his departure, over a month old, to put off a series of critical issues—the fate of Germany, reparations, and the problem of French security.

On March 13, an exhausted president returned to Paris. From the start, the peace conference had imposed extraordinary demands on Wilson, forcing him to work for long hours (several workdays lasted fifteen hours) and depriving him of the carefully modulated routine that he had pursued for so many years. On April 3, his health finally broke. Late in the afternoon Wilson became, as Grayson put it, "violently sick . . . seized with violent paroxysms of coughing, which were so severe and frequent that it interfered with his breathing." He had a temperature of 103 degrees, "profuse diarrhea," and intense pain in his back, stomach, and head. Over the next four and a half days he was confined to his bed, and House took his place on the Council of Four.[48]

On April 8, Wilson returned to the deliberations with a new sense of urgency. Shaken by the severity of his illness and by the stalemate of the negotiations, he made a series of concessions that broke the impasse. By early May the peace treaty was completed, and on May 7 German delegates were summoned to Versailles to receive the terms of the settlement.

After Germany received peace terms, the pace of the negotiations slowed and Wilson's health improved. He now took morning walks and automobile rides with Edith and Grayson, and family visits also helped the president relax. But Ray Stannard Baker, the press secretary of the American peace commission, noticed that Wilson seemed tired and that he had developed a facial tic and often had memory lapses. But Baker still believed that Wilson, whatever his failings, was "the great serious man of the conference—gray, grim, lonely there on the hill—fights a losing battle against heavy odds. He can escape no responsibility & must go to his punishment not only for his own mistakes & weaknesses of temperament but for the greed & selfishness of the world. I do not love him—but beyond any other man I admire & respect him. *He is real*. He is the only great man here."[49]

The peace conference had brought changes within the president's inner circle of advisers. After resigning his cabinet position in November 1918, McAdoo had opened a law office in New York, while Tumulty had remained in Washington to look after a multitude of domestic tasks. House had been, next to Wilson, the most important member of the American peace commission, but his conviction, which had emerged over the years, that his diplomatic skills were superior to those of the president had led to growing tension between the two men. When Wilson returned to Paris, he quickly realized that House had made unauthorized concessions to the French. Edith remembered him smiling bitterly and saying, "House has given away everything that I had won before we left Paris." While there was no open break between the two men, Wilson no longer confided in his counselor; after he left Paris on June 28, he would never see him again.[50]

As House's influence declined, Edith and Grayson acquired more responsibility, advising the president on a wide range of personal and political matters. Grayson in particular found that his duties had expanded; he became virtually a member of the Wilson family, eating frequently with Edith and Woodrow, listening carefully to Wilson's descriptions of each day's deliberations, and undertaking a variety of political chores for the president.

During the peace conference two new men joined the small circle of presidential intimates—Ray Stannard Baker and Bernard Baruch. Both became important figures in the president's life and would remain so until his death in 1924. Baker, a forty-nine-year-old midwesterner, was a famous journalist and a passionate reformer. Wilson liked the quiet, soft-spoken reporter and asked him to direct the American delegation's press bureau. In this position Baker had daily contact with the president and the opportunity to view the peacemaking process through his eyes. He believed in Wilson's greatness and would, in the 1920s, become his authorized biographer.

Baruch served as a loyal supporter, economic adviser, and bon vivant. As the conference progressed, Baruch and Grayson, who were close friends, spent more and more time together, especially enjoying outings at the racetrack. Edith and Grayson, aware of Woodrow's need for relaxation and male companionship, encouraged the deepening of his friendship with Baruch. Especially after Wilson's return from America and the loss of his confidence in House, the president spent more time with his economic adviser. Sometimes on Sundays Woodrow and Edith drove to St. Cloud, where they would enjoy lunch in the garden of Baruch's villa and talk in a relaxed way. Baruch, Grayson noted, "is making a great hit over here with the President, Miss E & everyone except Colonel House."[51]

* * *

On July 8, two days after reaching New York, Wilson presented the peace treaty to the Senate. He was not, however, at his best, stumbling several times and speaking in generalities instead of addressing specific criticisms of the treaty. But the president, no longer the vibrant leader of earlier years, was exhausted and in declining health. He focused his waning energies on the fight over the League of Nations, but he failed—despite the urgings of Tumulty and McAdoo—to devise his own modifications to the treaty. Instead, he allowed Senator Henry Cabot Lodge (R-MA) to unite Senate Republicans behind a series of resolutions that would severely restrict American membership in the League.

Frustrated over the stalemate in Washington, the president announced in late August that he would make a "swing around the circle," taking the League issue to the people. Edith and Grayson feared that his fragile health would not withstand the rigors of such a trip, but Wilson had always enjoyed campaigning and drawing strength from his contact with the people. He had long believed that a statesman must, at critical moments in history, rally the people behind a sacred cause. And he surely calculated that a successful tour would strengthen his hand when he returned to Washington to negotiate with opponents of the League.[52]

On the evening of September 3, the special presidential train left Union Station for a twenty-one-day trip that would carry Woodrow, Edith, Grayson, Tumulty, a small staff, and a large group of reporters all the way to the West Coast. In forty speeches—he had never spoken so often— the president made the case for the League, defending the covenant and predicting that if this experiment failed, the next war "would be the destruction of mankind." His extraordinary effort marked, as one biographer notes, the "closing lines of one of the greatest speaking careers in American History—a final burst of eloquence from a dying star."[53]

The tour gained momentum as it progressed, but Edith and Grayson worried about the endless speeches, receptions, and parades, and especially the heat. As Grayson noted, "the steel cars of the special train held the heat like ovens." They knew that Wilson was plagued by severe headaches, asthmatic attacks, double vision, and extreme fatigue. Finally, on the afternoon of September 25, twenty miles outside of Pueblo, Colorado, the special train stopped; the president was in such extreme discomfort that Grayson decided that a walk in the open air might help. Early the next morning he became so sick that Grayson convinced him to cancel the remainder of the tour and head back to Washington. On September 28, the train reached Union Station; three days later the long years of hypertension and arteriosclerosis finally took their toll. Wilson suffered a stroke that paralyzed the left side of his body and, for several days in mid-October, he was near death because of an infection in his prostate gland. Edith, once she realized the severity of his condition, took charge; she dominated a triumvirate—including Grayson and Tumulty—that managed the affairs of state. At the most important moment of his public life, Wilson lay incapacitated while three members of his much-diminished inner circle struggled to keep the government functioning.[54]

By late October, the position of the president and his supporters was bleak. Wilson was gravely ill, while Grayson issued misleading reports about his "nervous condition" and the majority of Senate Democrats dithered, unwilling to take any initiative on their own. Meanwhile, Senate Republicans coalesced behind Lodge's leadership, and on October 24, the Foreign Relations Committee reported fourteen reservations to the Senate floor. The most important of these, on Article X of the covenant, restricted America's obligation to act, and, in general, these reservations embodied a negative, suspicious view of the peace treaty that contrasted with Wilson's more hopeful vision of a new international order.

On November 7 and 17, Senate Minority Leader Gilbert Hitchcock (D-NE) conferred with Wilson and found "an emaciated old man with a thin white beard which he had permitted to grow." The president, whose emotional balance and judgment had been undermined by his stroke, regarded the Lodge reservations as a virtual nullification of the treaty and the League and claimed that it was the reservation on Article X in particular "that cuts the very heart out of the Treaty." With each side holding firm, the Senate on November 19 defeated the treaty—first with, and then without the reservations. Wilson's and Lodge's rigidity had doomed any efforts at compromise and left all sides stunned by the results of the debate.

In early December, when Senator Hitchcock again saw the president, Wilson, whose health had improved, was defiant: "Let Lodge compromise, Let Lodge hold out the olive branch." On December 14, he issued a public statement declaring that rumors that he would make any effort to break the deadlock were "entirely without foundation." He had no interest in accepting the advice of House, who warned Edith that "it seems to me vital that the treaty should pass in some form. His place in history is in the balance. If the Treaty goes through with some objectionable reservations, it can later be rectified. The essential thing is to have the President's great work in Paris live." At the very time, however, when the president needed House's conciliatory advice and personal connections, Edith ignored the overtures of the man who had once been his most trusted adviser and closest friend.[55]

In late January 1920, a bipartisan conference of Democratic and Republican senators tried to resolve the stalemate, but these efforts failed, and it was clear that only an acceptance of the Lodge reservations would bring Senate consent to the peace treaty. Both Tumulty and Edith now urged the president to compromise, but he was obdurate, suffering from mood swings and depression and from another attack of influenza. Wilson was out of touch with political reality. On February 9, 1920, when the Senate once again took up the consideration of the treaty, with the Lodge reservations, Democratic defections made it likely that it would gain a two-thirds majority. But the president stood firm, and on March 19, when the roll call was taken, the treaty fell seven votes short of a two-thirds majority. Wilson seemed reconciled to the outcome, telling Grayson that "it is evident[ly] too soon for the country to accept the League—not ready for it. May have to break the heart of the world and the pocketbook of the world before the League will be accepted and appreciated."

By the spring of 1920, the president was intensely unpopular and his administration was in disarray, but he was seriously thinking of running for a third term. He believed that the delegates might turn to him and concluded that another term would vindicate his policies. McAdoo, who had been the most dynamic and visible member of the cabinet, was the obvious carrier of the Wilson legacy, but the president would not stand aside for his son-in-law. Neither Edith nor Grayson would tell him that his candidacy was a delusion.

The triumph of the Republican presidential ticket in early November—greater than most observers had expected—was a massive repudiation of Wilson's presidency. At the end of November, Edith invited Ray Stannard Baker to the White House for lunch and moving pictures. While Baker waited in the parlor, he saw the president, "a broken, ruined old man, shuffling along, his left arm inert, the fingers drawn up like a claw, the left side of his face sagging frightfully." Edith, Baker, Grayson, and a few other guests were transported into another world as they watched films of Wilson's triumphant tour of Europe. Soon the films ended and "all that glory had faded away with a click and a sputter." Woodrow "turned slowly, and shuffled out of the doorway alone, without looking aside and without speaking." He would remain in office until March 4, 1921, but his presidency was, in fact, over.[56]

For nearly three years Wilson lived in his spacious house on S Street. Grayson continued as his physician, and Edith's brother, John Randolph Bolling, became his secretary. Despite Edith's devotion and a comfortable routine—daily automobile rides in a new Rolls-Royce, weekly visits to Keith's Theater—Wilson found the move from the White House to S Street difficult. When Baker visited the sixty-four-year-old ex-president, he concluded that "he has been lost. . . . He seems lonelier, more cut-off, than ever before. His mind still works with power, but with nothing to work upon! Only memories & regrets. He feels himself bitterly misunderstood & unjustly attacked: and being broken in health, cannot rally under it." Wilson could do no serious work, given his deteriorating vision and frequent depression. In 1923, when his health temporarily improved, he suffered, as one biographer writes, from "delusions of potency," and began to speak out on public affairs and once again to contemplate another run for the presidency. McAdoo's drive for the Democratic nomination in 1924 upset Wilson, who still would not support his son-in-law's presidential ambitions. Or as he told Baker in December 1923, "You may be sure that I will keep my eye out for every opportunity to guide the Democrats, and I hope and believe that the opportunity will not now be long deferred." In January 1924, however, Wilson may have sensed that the end was near, since he finally gave Baker exclusive access to his papers to write a biography. On February 1, as he faded, Wilson told Grayson, "I am ready. I am a broken piece of machinery," and he reassured his loyal physician, "You have been good to me. You have done everything you could."[57]

Woodrow Wilson's remarkable journey in American politics, which saw his meteoric rise and his equally meteoric fall, was finally over. His close advisers were now left with the challenge of explaining how he had inspired them and the nation, how he had achieved so much success, and how he had left a potent legacy.

Ellen Axson Wilson. She was a widely read, reflective woman, who was completely devoted to her husband's career. She understood his need for a wide range of advisers and grew close to Tumulty and House. Byron Rufus Newton Papers (MS 374), Manuscript and Archives, Yale University Library. Photo by Davis & Sanford, New York.

CHAPTER TWO

Ellen Axson Wilson

"The greatest man in the world"

When Ellen Axson met Woodrow Wilson sometime in April 1883, she sensed that there was something different about this intense young man. She had rejected previous suitors, becoming known among her friends as "Ellie, the Man Hater," but Woodrow soon convinced her that he possessed the "congeniality of mind" that she was seeking; for the first time, she had met a man she found intellectually stimulating. She soon felt "a quiet little glow and thrill of admiration, tingling out to my very fingertips," and when, in September 1883, he declared his love and proposed marriage in Asheville, North Carolina, she agreed to marry him—although they hardly knew each other—and the young couple sealed their pledge with a kiss.[1]

Ellen was born on May 15, 1860, in Rome, Georgia, a small town seventy miles northwest of Atlanta. Her father, an emotionally fragile man, was pastor of the First Presbyterian Church, but he had been devastated by his wife's death in November 1881, and Ellen, too, missed her mother; she later wrote that "I think I would give half my life to be with her, to feel her sympathy, for one short hour." Ellen was an unusual young woman. She was a voracious reader with a sharp critical sense, possessed formidable powers of concentration, and displayed considerable artistic talent, sketching crayon portraits for a small fee.[2]

Her mother's death and her father's virtual incapacity, however, had left her in a precarious situation. She was, in fact, a surrogate mother for her two younger brothers, Stockton and Edward, and also a caretaker for her father. He insisted that the family move to Savannah, Georgia, and in January 1884, he was committed to the Georgia State Mental Hospital. In late May 1884, at the age of forty-six, he probably took his own life. Ironically, her father's death—because of the small estate that he left—freed Ellen, who could now pursue her artistic ambitions. In early October 1884, she arrived in New York City to study at the Art Students League. During the winter of 1884–85—while Woodrow was in his second year at Johns Hopkins—Ellen enjoyed her new life, sometimes sketching with live models, and also explored the city, attending the theater, lectures, and art openings.[3]

Throughout the two years that Woodrow studied at Johns Hopkins, he and Ellen occasionally saw one another, but they deepened their relationship primarily through a voluminous correspondence. As Woodrow poured out his need for love and sympathy and his ambition to make a mark in the world, Ellen promised that "you shall never want for wifely love and faith and sympathy, my darling, or for anything that love can give." Convinced that Woodrow's talents would carry him far, Ellen confessed that only a man of Woodrow's stature "could have so stirred my nature to it's [*sic*] utmost depths." She decided to give up her own promising art career without, apparently, any deep regret, in order to devote herself to taking care of Woodrow. It was not, as she explained to him, that she was not ambitious, "Ah! But I *am* ambitious! and the best of it is that *mine* is *gratified* ambition, for I am ambitious for *you*—and for *myself* too, dearest, I hardly dare to say how *great* is my ambition,—would be the best and truest wife that ever man had." At the end of May 1885, Ellen left New York and, after her marriage to Woodrow in Savannah and a honeymoon in North Carolina, the young couple moved to Bryn Mawr, Pennsylvania, where Woodrow would begin his academic career. Given the depth of their devotion to one another they would, as one historian remarks, evolve into a "formidable and determined team."[4]

During Woodrow and Ellen's three years at Bryn Mawr, the pattern of their relationship began to emerge. Woodrow discovered that he liked to teach but soon became restless at the small, isolated women's college and eager to move on. Ellen devoted herself to their marriage, bearing two children— Margaret and Jessie—during their Bryn Mawr years (their third daughter, Eleanor, was born in Middletown, Connecticut), and concentrated on improving her domestic skills. She also handled family finances, provided shrewd advice on Woodrow's career, and helped him with the research for his next book, *The State*, which appeared in September 1889. Before Woodrow submitted anything that he wrote to a publisher, he would read it to Ellen, who would listen without interruption until the end. Her main goal, however, was to steady him emotionally, to give him faith in himself and confidence in his "own powers." "Dearest it is my deliberate conviction,— nay, I do not *believe* it, I *know*—that the combination of qualities found in you is the rarest, finest, noblest, *grandest* of which human nature is capable."[5]

Woodrow realized the decisive role that Ellen played in his life. "It would be hard to say, sweetheart," he wrote to her in 1889, "in what part of my life and character you have *not* been a supreme and beneficent influence. You are all-powerful in my development." From 1890 to 1902, the twelve years Woodrow spent on the Princeton faculty, Ellen continued to concentrate on creating a calm home life and caring for the extended family that always seemed to be with them. While Woodrow, after his workday was over, played with his "sweet little chicks," it was Ellen who imposed discipline on their three daughters and who looked after their education. Somehow she found the time to read widely in philosophy, poetry, history, religion, and fiction. She was a small woman, only five foot three, intensely alive, with a radiant smile, one who spoke with a soft southern drawl. While she was serious about life, her brother Stockton remembered that she had a lighter side, that when she was "gleeful, her face would brighten, her eyes sparkle, her laugher ripple over a good joke."[6]

In May 1896, after Woodrow suffered what may have been a small stroke, Ellen insisted that he spend the summer in England and Scotland. For fifteen weeks Woodrow cycled through Great Britain, visiting Oxford and Cambridge and the sites where many famous British literary figures had lived. While he rested abroad, she looked after her relatives and children and, for the first time in many years, began painting again. And she may have been relieved by the fact that Woodrow, who "needed constant attention," was away for the summer.[7]

Woodrow returned to Princeton refreshed and in October gave his sesquicentennial speech, "Princeton in the Nation's Service." Ellen sat close to the platform, full of pride in the performance of her beloved husband. "*You* are all the world to *me*," she wrote, "you elevate, you stimulate, you satisfy, you delight me: every part of me enjoys you with an infinite ardour. . . . You satisfy and delight my *pride* as well as my love." But after Woodrow experienced numbness in his right hand, Ellen watched him carefully for signs of exhaustion, and in the spring of 1899 she once again persuaded Woodrow to go to England, this time with her brother Stockton Axson. Once again she stayed at home, looking after her sick girls and now finding the time for reading and painting. A year later, Woodrow, convinced that Ellen needed a change, stayed at home while she visited friends in New Orleans.[8]

In June 1902, when Princeton's trustees chose Woodrow as the next president, Joseph Wilson, who now lived with his son, shouted to his granddaughters: "Never forget what I tell you. Your Father is the greatest man I have ever known. . . . This is only the beginning of a great career." Ellen agreed, convinced that Woodrow was the obvious choice, but she was also worried that his elevation to the presidency would bring, she wrote to a friend, "heavy sacrifices to people of our temperament." "We must leave," she continued, "our dear home and the sweet, almost ideal life when he was [a] simple 'man of letters' and go and live in that great, stately troublesome 'Prospect,' and be forever giving huge receptions, state dinners, etc. etc."[9]

Despite these doubts, Ellen plunged into their new, administrative life, replacing the high Victorian decor of the twenty-room mansion with color, light, and comfort, and redesigning the gardens outside of Prospect, as the president's mansion was named. For the first few years of his presidency, Woodrow was content, absorbed in his work and pleased to be freed finally from "a merely talking profession."[10] In the summer of 1903, Woodrow and Ellen traveled to England, France, and Italy on a "second honey moon," and the next year Ellen, Jessie, and two friends landed in Naples and embarked on a tour of the artistic treasures of Italy. She was delighted to be "rioting in [the] sensuous beauty" of Italian art and to be freed from the demands of the Princeton presidency and from the tension between her ambitions for Woodrow and her concern for his fragile health.[11]

In the fall of 1904, after Ellen returned from Italy, Stockton Axson, who was prone to depression, suffered another "nervous breakdown" and had to be put in a mental hospital until the summer. A few months later, Woodrow had a hernia operation, developed phlebitis in one leg, and had to recuperate for four weeks in Palm Beach, Florida. Worse still, in late April 1905, Ellen's young brother Eddie, along with his wife and son, died in a river accident in Georgia. Ellen was overwhelmed with grief, and the family, at Woodrow's suggestion, decided to summer in Lyme, Connecticut, where she immersed herself in the artist's colony there and began, for the first time, to paint landscapes in oil. These various family tragedies led her to doubt, in a way that Woodrow never would, her religious faith.[12]

In late May 1906, Ellen's fears about Woodrow's health were confirmed when he lost sight in his left eye. Worried that his career might be over, Woodrow and Ellen, along with their three daughters, retreated to the Lake District of England. There Woodrow regained his strength and emotional equilibrium through long walks and the development of a new friendship with the artist Frederic Yates and his wife. But Ellen now insisted that Woodrow must have a winter as well as a summer vacation, and in January 1907 he spent a month in Bermuda while she remained in Princeton to look after her daughter Eleanor, who was recuperating from surgery.[13]

As Woodrow's plans for the reform of Princeton began to meet resistance, Ellen decided that the family should spend the summer of 1907 in the Adirondacks. Woodrow, she wrote to her daughter Jessie, had been "so wretchedly ill and so depressed" that she could "hardly leave his side for a moment." But before the family left for its summer vacation, Ellen, who was deeply involved in the Quad fight, warned Jack Hibben that, despite his doubts about the plan, her husband would fight to the finish to realize his vision of reform.[14]

In mid-January 1908, Woodrow returned to Bermuda for a month-long vacation. There he became infatuated with Mary Allen Hulbert Peck. Ellen, who realized the depth of Woodrow's attachment, must, on his return, have confronted him on what she termed "emotional love." It was the only time, she later told White House physician Cary Grayson, that he had ever disappointed her. In the summer of 1908, Ellen returned to Old Lyme, where she thrived in her immersion in the art world, writing that she "felt like a girl again knocking about the countryside with a lot of young . . . girls and young men in the chummiest sort of way." Woodrow went by himself to England's Lake District, and his letters to Ellen that summer had a penitent quality, as he tried to reassure her that she was "utterly indispensable" to him and promised that "I am coming back to you, my Eileen [his nickname for Ellen], singularly well, and I hope that, being more normal, I shall be less trying."[15]

Despite his assurances to Ellen, however, Mary Peck remained an important part of his life. Woodrow never saw her again in Bermuda, but in November 1909 she moved to an apartment in New York, where he visited her often. He claimed that "I must keep in constant touch with you, if my spirits are to be steady and my tasks well done." Ellen had finally met Woodrow's vivacious friend in October 1908, when she and Woodrow visited the Pecks in Pittsfield, Massachusetts. Whatever her resentments over her husband's behavior, she tolerated Woodrow's obsession, treating Mary Peck as just another family friend and allowing her to visit the Wilson family both at Prospect and later at the White House.[16]

Woodrow's dependence on Mary Peck coincided with the growing acrimony at Princeton over his plans to reform the institution and his break with John Grier Hibben. Ellen supported her husband, urging him to stand firm and refuse to compromise with his opponents. Ellen's sister remembered that she felt that "anyone who attacked Woodrow was *wicked*," and she wrote to one friend that "if we win, we save the college, and if we lose we save our own souls, so why feel troubled?" Like Woodrow, however, she was oppressed by the "thickening clouds at Princeton," and agreed with him that he could best serve his country by leaving the university and becoming governor of New Jersey. Ellen was elated by his victory in November 1910, now dismissing Stockton's fears that a political career would "kill him quickly." She believed that he was "greatly fitted for political leadership" and, since this was what he now wanted, his family should stand behind him.[17]

As the family left Prospect, however, Ellen had doubts about its new political life. "This is all very glorious," she confessed, "but somehow I feel that it is the end of our happy home days." After Woodrow's election, the family moved to the Princeton Inn (since New Jersey did not have a governor's mansion), and Ellen (with few social obligations), plunged into state politics. She spent hours reading newspapers and every day went over with Woodrow the material that she had collected. She was curious about his new political associates and quickly drew close to his young personal secretary, Joseph P. Tumulty. Tumulty brought most political issues to Ellen's attention, and he told Woodrow, "She's a better politician than you are, Governor." Their daughter Eleanor remembered that her mother "understood people better than Woodrow, for she was more detached, and less emotional than he." As during Woodrow's academic career, however, his well-being was her chief concern. It is "very important," she wrote, "that I should 'stand by' ready to help when he needs me. He says nobody else can 'rest him.'" And she confided to a friend that her anxiety about his health, "though concealed from him, is constant and intense."[18]

In 1911, as Woodrow's presidential campaign progressed, Ellen was convinced that he was "a man of destiny," that nothing should interfere with his amazing political career. During the campaign she gave shrewd advice at critical moments and adjusted to the relentless publicity about her and her daughters. But the strain took its toll. One afternoon in Princeton— where the Wilsons rented a house—Eleanor noticed "a little figure walking slowly ahead of me. I was shocked when I realized that it was mother, whose movements had always been so eager and quick." By Election Day, Ellen was tired and tense but also excited by the prospect of Woodrow becoming president. At 10 p.m. on November 5, with the news that he was elected, she placed her hands on his shoulders, kissed him, and said: "My dear, I want to be the first to congratulate you." He was then embraced by his daughters.[19]

Ellen did not relish becoming a public figure: "life in the White House," she wrote, "has no attraction for me." Just at a time when she was receiving recognition as a landscape painter (she had a one-woman show in Philadelphia in early 1913), she would be drawn into her new job as First Lady, with little time to read, paint, or relax with friends. Even so, she was well-informed about the political issues of the day and aware of the magnitude of her husband's achievement. On March 4, when Woodrow spoke at his inaugural, she was unable to see his face from her assigned seat and then, Eleanor remembered, moved over until "she stood directly beneath him. There utterly oblivious of the thousands watching her, she gazed up at him . . . a look of rapture on her face."[20]

Ellen was an active, and in some ways innovative, First Lady. She redecorated the family quarters of the White House, dutifully hosted what seemed an endless series of official receptions (there were forty-one events between March 5 and June 11), invited many friends and relatives to visit, and found time to be alone with Woodrow during their late afternoon automobile rides in the Virginia countryside. She remained his editor and political adviser, always willing to interrupt her schedule if he needed her.[21] Aside from her keen insight into his emotional makeup, she had a wise tolerance of his political associates, recognizing that he must have a variety of advisers if he was to maintain his health and achieve his political goals. She remained close to Tumulty, who now became the president's personal secretary, welcomed Colonel Edward M. House into her family, seeking his advice on both personal and political matters (she thanked him for "being too good to us all"), and developed close ties with White House physician Cary Grayson, Secretary of the Navy Josephus Daniels, and Secretary of the Treasury William Gibbs McAdoo (who would become her son-in-law after he married Eleanor in May 1914). McAdoo remembered her "rare and beautiful spirit" and claimed that she was "*the soundest and most influential of*" his advisers.[22]

Years before she became First Lady, Ellen wrote to a friend, "I wonder how anyone who reaches middle age can bear it if she cannot feel, on looking back, that whatever mistakes she has made, she has on the whole lived for others and not for herself." Once in the White House, she soon became involved in humanitarian causes. She toured the so-called alleys, African American slums only a few blocks from the Capitol, and became a leader in the effort to reform them. She also inspected the Post Office and the Government Printing Office, where she found working conditions for women substandard. On several pressing issues of the day, however, she remained silent. Despite two of her daughters' enthusiasm for women's suffrage, she did not challenge Woodrow's reluctance to support a constitutional amendment giving women the right to vote. And in the summer of 1913, as Postmaster General Albert S. Burleson and Secretary of the Treasury McAdoo segregated their departments, she did not register any disapproval. Ellen had grown up around Blacks in the South and believed that she had an obligation to "work for the good of the Negroes." As a young woman she had attended the Art Students League in New York, which had no sexual or racial barriers. But her daughter Jessie remembered that her mother "felt much more strongly about the color line" than her father, and that she had "far more of the old southern feeling, with its curious paradox of a warm personal liking for Negroes, combined with an instinctive hostility to certain assumptions of equality."[23]

Ellen, Margaret, Jessie, and Eleanor spent the summer of 1913 in Cornish, New Hampshire. While Woodrow was "desperately lonely" in Washington, guiding reform legislation through Congress, she was reveling in the seclusion and beauty of their summer home, Harlakenden, and in the luxury of being able to paint every morning. She quickly became part of a congenial group of artists and enjoyed watching the romance of Jessie and Francis Sayre, which reminded her of her courtship with Woodrow. But she missed her husband, marooned in the heat and humidity of Washington, and followed closely his legislative battles. The nearly one hundred letters exchanged between Ellen and Woodrow that summer revealed, once again, the intensity of their love for one another. After his tariff victory in early October, Ellen could no longer contain herself, writing that now "at last, everybody in the civilized world knows that you are a great man and a great leader of men. . . . How profoundly I thank God for giving you the chance to win such victories,—to help the world so greatly;—for letting you work for him on such a *large* stage. . . . It has been the most remarkable life history I have ever *read* about,—and to think that I have lived it with you."[24]

In mid-October, Ellen left Cornish for Washington and resumed her role as First Lady. Throughout the winter she worried about Woodrow's health, writing that "the pressure *has* been very great in a score of different ways. . . . He wants me almost constantly beside him when he is ill and everything else *must* give way." As she struggled through another White House social season, her energy seemed to ebb, and on March 1, 1914, she slipped on the floor of her bedroom and took an "ugly fall." She spent the following week in bed.[25]

In the spring of 1914, as Ellen's health declined, she suffered from the heat and from nights that were filled with pain. But she helped Cary Grayson maintain the pretense that she was getting better, and for a time Woodrow believed that she was, in fact, gaining in strength. Ellen continued to worry about Woodrow, writing to a relative about her "constant anxiety about Woodrow, his health, the success of his legislative plans, etc. etc." On July 23, Grayson moved into the White House, certain that her kidney disease was now in its final stage. Shortly before she died on August 6, Ellen spoke her last words to Grayson: "Doctor, if I go away, promise me that you will take good care of my husband." Woodrow was holding her hand when she died "with a divine smile playing over her face." He looked at Grayson and said, "Is it all over?" and then got up, went to the window, and cried. "Oh my God," he asked, "what am I to do?"[26] Ellen was only fifty-four years old.

On August 10, a brief funeral service took place in the East Room of the White House, and then Woodrow and his three daughters boarded a special train to Rome, Georgia. On August 11, there was a ceremony in the First Presbyterian Church where Woodrow had first seen Ellen thirty-one years before, and then family and friends went to Myrtle Hill Cemetery, where Ellen was buried next to her father and mother. Woodrow had chosen for an inscription on her tombstone lines from a poem, "She Was a Phantom of Delight," by one of her favorite poets, William Wordsworth:

A traveller between life and death:
The reason firm, the temperate will,
Endurance, foresight, strength, and skill;
A perfect Woman, nobly plann'd
To warm, to comfort, and command;
And yet a Spirit still, and bright
With something of an angel light.[27]

Secretary of the Navy Josephus Daniels strolling near the White House in 1914. Initially many people underestimated Daniels, with his string ties, pleated linen shirts, and old-fashioned frock coats. Library of Congress, Prints and Photographs Division, LC-DIG-hec-03880. Photo by Harris & Ewing.

CHAPTER THREE

Josephus Daniels

"One of the greatest minds of his age"

On the evening of January 18, 1909, Josephus Daniels, the editor of the Raleigh, North Carolina, *News and Observer*, was sitting at his desk when he heard a voice asking, "May I invade your Sanctum?" Daniels looked up and saw that Woodrow Wilson was standing at the door. Although this was their first meeting, Daniels knew a lot about the Princeton president. He had read some of his books and had some knowledge of the battles he was fighting at his university. Daniels invited his guest to walk with him to his home, where he introduced Wilson to his wife, Addie, and asked him about the controversies raging at Princeton. Wilson proceeded, for more than an hour, to explain the issues at stake. The next day, his speech at the University of North Carolina made a profound impression on Daniels, and at the dinner after his talk Wilson charmed everyone, telling stories and anecdotes. It was the beginning of a friendship that would carry the North Carolina editor to Washington in 1913, where he would serve the new president as secretary of the navy for eight years and where he would become one of Wilson's most effective and trusted advisers. Years later, when Daniels wrote his memoirs, he remembered that "all the while I have felt that I was looking back to glory."[1]

Josephus Daniels was born on May 18, 1862, in Washington, North Carolina, the son of a shipbuilder. He had no memory of his father, who worked in a Confederate naval yard during the Civil War and died before he was three. But Josephus remembered the vivid stories of his mother, Mary Cleaves, about the destruction inflicted on Washington during the Civil War, when Union and Confederate forces fought over the town. In the summer of 1865, his mother, a woman of great vitality, moved her three young sons to Wilson, a village of fewer than one thousand people in eastern North Carolina, which Daniels remembered as the "loveliest village of the plain." It was an area with a "wide sweep of flat land, lush with vegetation," one in which cotton dominated the local economy and in which 40 percent of the population was Black. Mary Cleaves soon became postmistress, and for the next sixteen years she kept the post office in the front room of her home. Since there was no residential postal service, leading men of the town would gather there to collect their mail and to discuss local affairs. Young Josephus lingered quietly in the post office, listening and learning.[2]

Josephus was close to his mother. "If I could worship at the shrine of any mortal," he recalled, "my devotions would be at an altar erected to my mother." She raised her sons in a devout Methodist household. Each morning began, and every day ended, with family prayers and reading a chapter from the Bible. Mary Cleaves expected her sons to meet a stern code of personal behavior, avoiding ostentation, alcohol, and tobacco, and to be thrifty and hard-working. Josephus would remain a devout Methodist for the rest of his life.[3]

Josephus was an optimistic, outgoing young man, one who was generous and warm-hearted. He had a passion for baseball, liked to be around "charming" ladies and strong-willed women, and enjoyed the give-and-take of animated conversation. As a top student in the local private school (there were no public schools in Wilson), he read widely and formed a strong bond with many of his teachers.[4]

He was also industrious. He worked on local farms growing row crops and cotton, served as the business agent for two Raleigh newspapers (the state capital, sixty miles west of Wilson), and in 1880, at the age of eighteen, became the editor of the weekly local paper the *Advance*. Somehow the young man had developed a vision of becoming a newspaper entrepreneur, convinced that "a paper can do the Lord's own work in the broadening and betterment of mankind."[5]

Daniels proved to be a skilled newspaper manager, gaining the local government printing contracts and making a variety of improvements in the quality and profitability of his newspaper. He was, however, restless and ambitious; rather than stay in Wilson and manage the *Advance*, in the spring of 1885, when he was only twenty-three, he decided to leave Wilson and his mother's home and attend law school at the University of North Carolina. Later in the year, he passed the bar but never practiced law. He was intent on finding a way to enter the newspaper business in Raleigh, a city of around ten thousand people. With the help of a wealthy mentor, he gained the editorship, and then the ownership, of a weekly newspaper, the *State Chronicle*, and soon found ways to improve it and compete with the leading paper in Raleigh, the daily *News and Observer*. Daniels also fell in love. Women were attracted to this soft-spoken, kindly young man, and in September 1887, he began to court Adelaide "Addie" Bagley, who came from one of Raleigh's most distinguished old families. He "liked her fine and easy bearing, her manner and face." Josephus and Addie were married on May 2, 1888, in a large wedding that was one of Raleigh's major social events. Although both were independent and sometimes stubborn, they formed a strong bond that lasted for more than fifty years. Addie managed the couple's home and the raising of their three sons, while Josephus immersed himself in the newspaper business.[6]

Daniels quickly transformed the *State Chronicle* into a daily paper and discovered that producing a newspaper six days a week was extremely demanding. He worked late into the night, displaying the extraordinary physical and mental stamina that would last all of his long life. Aside from his family, church, and baseball, his only interests were his newspaper and politics. He dismissed physical discomfort, avoided exercise, and ate a diet of meat and potatoes. But he was rarely ill.[7]

Under Daniels's leadership the *State Chronicle* represented the younger, more progressive wing of the North Carolina Democratic Party, while the *News and Observer* spoke for the dominant Bourbon faction, for the planters and businessmen who controlled the state's government after the end of Reconstruction in 1868. In the late 1880s, the *State Chronicle* and the *News and Observer* engaged in bitter quarrels over politics and especially over winning government printing contracts that were essential for either paper's financial success. In 1901, Daniels and the owner of the *News and Observer*, Samuel D. Ashe, had a physical clash in downtown Raleigh that left both in a bad mood. The next day Daniels confronted Ashe once again in the state capitol, where the two antagonists exchanged blows and fell to the floor amid the legislators' desks before they were finally separated.[8]

By the early 1890s, the *State Chronicle* was the most widely read newspaper in the state, and Daniels had become the progressive voice of the Democratic Party. He worried, however, that a deal between Populists and Republicans could defeat the Democratic Party's candidate for governor in 1892, and "put the Negro back into office." Daniels assembled a group of young Democrats that helped his party win the governorship. At the age of thirty, he had become an influential broker within the state's Democratic Party.[9]

In the 1892 presidential election, Daniels had supported Grover Cleveland, claiming that "he is the uncrowned king of the world." With Cleveland's election, Daniels, whose newspaper was losing money, won an appointment in the Interior Department, a sprawling agency that controlled federal pensions. Daniels soon became the second in command of the department, and discovered that, in contrast to the new president, he supported lower tariffs, antitrust legislation, civil service reform, and free silver. In 1894, he resigned his position and returned to Raleigh, where he had acquired the *News and Observer*. One of his biographers notes that "in just over a decade he had risen from hustling subscriptions and advertising for his weekly papers in the coastal plain to become an owner of the state's best-known newspaper."[10]

Daniels reorganized the *News and Observer*, expanding subscriptions and advertising and no longer accepting state printing contracts. He shrewdly realized that an independent paper—one no longer dependent on government funds—could become a platform for the advancement of his political agenda. Politicians, he realized, would now have to come to him for support.[11]

The political situation in North Carolina alarmed Daniels. The Democrats' success in the elections of 1892 had only been temporary, and by 1894 that state's more radical Populists and Republicans had united into a new Fusionist Party. Daniels hoped to drive a wedge between poor whites and Blacks and eventually, in what he described as a "war to the knife," deprive African Americans of the ability to vote and bring white Populists back into the Democratic Party. But in 1894, the Fusionists won control of both houses of the state legislature, and two years later they won the governorship as well.[12]

In 1896, Daniels was more focused on national rather than state issues. He and William Jennings Bryan, who he had met three years earlier, agreed on every major issue and formed a close friendship that would last for many years. In May 1896, the *News and Observer* declared its support for Bryan's nomination, and at the Chicago convention Daniels heard the Great Commoner deliver his famous "Cross of Gold" speech. "His voice," Daniels remembered, "was made for great gatherings. As he stood there on the platform, waiting for the enthusiasm to spend itself so that he could be heard, he was every inch an Apollo, young, lithe, with flashing eyes and a great jaw that gave him power which seemed not quite in keeping with his sweetness. . . . Bryan had not been speaking for five minutes before he held the convention rapt. I had never dreamed that a mortal man could so grip and fill with enthusiasm thousands of men." He thrilled at hearing "young David with his sling who had come to slay the giants that oppressed the people." During the campaign Daniels traveled with Bryan through the East and, for a time, believed that he would win the election. After William McKinley prevailed, and war erupted between the United States and Spain, Daniels denounced the Spanish-American War and the peace treaty that brought the United States a new empire. "Whenever a greedy strong nation," he protested, "wishes to annex or exploit a weak nation, it calls its avidity 'Manifest Destiny.'"[13]

In 1898, Daniels's focus shifted back to the state level, where he led a

"White Supremacy Campaign" designed to destroy the Fusionist coalition. Through the columns of the *News and Observer* he reported the alleged "horrors of Negro domination" and challenged white men to protect the homes of their women and of the "great Anglo-Saxon race." In Wilmington, which was two-thirds Black, an armed group of white men removed the Fusionist government. The riots that accompanied the election, however, did not upset Daniels, who was determined to take the "Negro question" out of politics. He believed that only by removing African Americans from the political system could North Carolina achieve social and economic progress.[14]

In November 1898, Democrats won a sweeping victory, and two years later a constitutional amendment was passed that imposed a poll tax and literacy requirements on the state's voters. In 1903, Daniels, in his ward in Raleigh, challenged every Black voter—"except for school teachers and preachers and those known to have education"—to read parts of the state's constitution. Understandably, most Blacks did not try to vote.[15]

After the state campaigns of 1898 and 1900, Daniels became one of the most powerful men in North Carolina. He thrived, one biographer notes, on the "rough and tumble" of political campaigns and had put together a coalition of progressive Democrats that would dominate state politics for many years. On the state level he favored white supremacy, prohibition, railway regulation, and more funding for public education; on the national level he supported lower tariffs, free silver, a graduated income tax, and antitrust legislation. He combined a "mystic faith in the people" with a fierce egalitarianism, convinced, throughout his political career, that he was engaged in a struggle with a "moneyed aristocracy" that defied the ideals of Thomas Jefferson. He disliked Theodore Roosevelt, opposed what he regarded as his bellicose foreign policy, and, after Bryan's defeat in 1908, realized that Democrats must find a new leader if they were to win the presidency. In January 1909, after Daniels met Woodrow Wilson, he came to understand that the Princeton president might be the man to watch.[16]

In the winter of 1910–11, after Wilson won the New Jersey governorship, broke with the Democratic machine, and pushed his reform measures through the legislature, Daniels and the *News and Observer* now fully supported the governor's presidential campaign. In early 1912, he was instrumental in reconciling Wilson and Bryan, and he also advised his old friend to give up his hopes for the nomination. At the Democratic convention in Baltimore, Daniels played a key role in Wilson's nomination. After the convention deadlocked, William F. McCombs, the chairman of the Wilson campaign, advised the candidate to give up and release his delegates. Daniels canvassed the convention floor, concluded that Wilson had broader support than any other contender, and told him that "it may take several days, but you are sure to be nominated."[17]

Soon after his nomination, Wilson named Daniels the chair of his publicity effort, and in July and August 1912 the two men conferred often at Sea Girt (the summer home of the New Jersey governor)as they put together the campaign textbook. They agreed that Wilson's platform should be strongly progressive, emphasizing a lower tariff, antitrust legislation, support for labor, and the creation of a central bank. Wilson liked the amiable North Carolina editor and, after his election, was determined to bring him into his cabinet. In early December 1912, responding to a letter urging Daniels's appointment, the president-elect wrote that "you may be sure that what you say about Josephus Daniels appeals to my heart and as well as to my head. I have known him long enough to love him." On February 23, 1913, brushing aside the objections of several advisers, he offered Daniels the secretaryship of the navy, explaining that "I know of no one I trust more entirely or affectionately. . . . I cannot spare you from my council table." Daniels quickly accepted, writing that "it makes me happy to have come into close relationship with you—a relationship that has sweetened my life."[18]

Wilson realized, as one biographer writes, that Daniels's "cherubic face radiated an affection for humanity and concealed considerable shrewdness and intelligence." The president, a newcomer to national politics, found in his secretary of the navy an experienced Democratic Party operator who could perform many valuable tasks for his administration. He remained close to Bryan, the new secretary of state; was on good terms with Democratic leaders in the Senate; and, most important, was the kind of adviser Wilson liked to open his mind to. Daniels gave his friendship on Wilson's terms, supporting him without question. In return, Wilson responded to Daniels's love and trust with affection. Answering a warm note from Daniels in December 1914, the president wrote, "It [your note] helped not a little to keep the cloud from descending on me which threatened me all day.... You are both [Addie Daniels] of the sort that make life and friendship worth while. It is fine to have a colleague whom one can absolutely trust; how much finer to have one whom one can love! that is a real underpinning for the soul!"[19]

Daniels moved easily into Wilson's inner circle of advisers. He was a warm and sentimental man, one who idealized women and who was comfortable revealing his emotions. During the summer of 1912, as he had conferred with Wilson, he had come to know the candidate and his family. He admired Ellen Wilson, appreciated her passion for beauty, and remembered that "I came to lean upon her wisdom as much as did Wilson." After her death in August 1914, Daniels realized that the president had a powerful "need for love and companionship" and had no objection to his relationship with Edith Galt. In the early fall of 1915—when the president's remarriage was a hotly debated subject among his advisers—Postmaster General Albert Burleson appeared in Daniels's office. After conferring with prominent Democrats, Burleson explained, they had agreed that Wilson's remarriage would bring defeat in November 1916 and had also agreed that Daniels must convince the president to delay his wedding until after the election. Daniels had no intention of approaching his friend in the White House on such a quixotic mission. Or as he explained in his memoirs: "It is not necessary to quote the words I employed in declining the preferred [sic] distinction of being Minister Plenipotentiary and Ambassador Extraordinary to the President of the United States."[20]

During the 1912 campaign, Daniels had formed a friendship with Joseph Tumulty, and, early in the new administration, he came to admire Secretary of the Treasury William Gibbs McAdoo's energy and decisiveness and eventually supported him as Wilson's successor. His relationship, however, with Colonel Edward M. House, the Texas political operator who was Wilson's favorite adviser and friend, was more problematic. Daniels first met House during the 1912 campaign when, one afternoon, they had a "confidential talk" that left him with the impression that they had developed a "fast friendship." In fact, House had a low opinion of Daniels's abilities and tried to keep him out of Wilson's cabinet. After the outbreak of World War I, House became concerned about the nation's lack of military preparedness and even more dissatisfied with Daniels's leadership of the navy. In April 1916, he and Edith Wilson agreed that "the most helpful things that could be done for the President at this time, would be the elimination of good Josephus Daniels and Joseph Tumulty. She undertakes to eliminate Tumulty if I can manage the Daniels change." But House could never convince the president to remove the secretary of the navy, and in September 1917, when the *Boston Transcript* ran an article claiming that House had attempted to do so, he denied the charge in a letter to Daniels. Only years later did Daniels realize that House had never been his friend. As Daniels's son Jonathan put it, "House was an intimate man even when he was cutting a throat."[21]

Next to Secretary of State Bryan, Daniels became the most controversial member of Wilson's cabinet. As secretary of the navy he was determined to apply his progressive values to a large organization that seemed, from his perspective, badly in need of reform. He introduced programs to offer education and technical training for enlisted men, banned the use of alcoholic beverages aboard naval ships or in navy yards or stations, imposed competitive bidding on the manufacturers of armor plate and other steel products, created a new office of chief of naval operations, and insisted on civilian control of the navy. These decisions upset many senior naval officers, who regarded Daniels as a shallow political hack, and throughout his eight years in office he engaged in constant quarrels with many of his advisers. Moreover, Daniels's critics within the navy were joined by prominent Republicans, who wanted a more rapid expansion of the American fleet. As early as December 1913, former president William Howard Taft observed, "I think Daniels is proving to be more kinds of an ass than any other member of the Cabinet."[22]

But Daniels, a tenacious political infighter, persisted in his reforms; the more Daniels's critics raged, the more the president seemed to support his secretary of the navy. In January 1915, Wilson's old Boston friend, Nancy Saunders Toy, during a visit to the White House, repeated an anti-Daniels remark. Mrs. Toy recorded the president's reaction: "I have never seem the President angry before. I never want to see him angry again. His fist came down on the table: 'Daniels did *not* give the order that Tipperary should not be sung in the Navy. He is surrounded by a network of conspiracy and lies. His enemies are determined to ruin him. I can't be sure who they are yet, but when I do get them—God help them.'"[23]

Daniels picked as his assistant secretary—there was only one—Franklin D. Roosevelt. He did not know FDR well when he offered him the position during Wilson's inauguration. He knew that the young man was brash, glib, and ambitious, but he was also a shrewd judge of character and recalled that he saw in FDR the potential for future leadership in the Democratic Party. Roosevelt turned out to be a valuable assistant, although initially he viewed Daniels with condescension, ridiculing his clothes and North Carolina drawl. "When I first knew him," FDR recalled, "he was the funniest looking hillbilly I had ever seen." FDR was not always loyal to Daniels, sometimes disagreeing with his policies behind his back, and it was only later that he realized how much he had learned from his chief and how much forbearance Daniels had shown in tolerating his behavior.[24]

Initially many people underestimated Daniels, who seemed a dated figure, with his North Carolina accent, string ties, pleated linen shirts, and old-fashioned frock coats. In fact, he was a skilled manager and politician who, during his eight years in office, carried out many complicated tasks with aplomb. As secretary of the navy, as he had done all his life, he rose early and worked late, never taking a day off for illness. In contrast to the president, he had a remarkable constitution, blessed with ample physical energy and the ability to concentrate for extended periods of time.[25]

In 1913, as the various members of the cabinet settled in, Postmaster General Burleson and Secretary of the Treasury McAdoo moved to segregate their respective departments. Burleson explained to the cabinet that "he had the highest regard for the negro and wished to help him in every way possible, but that he believed segregation was best for the negro and best for the Service." Daniels, who had no objection to these efforts to separate white and Black employees, two years later became involved in the controversy over *The Birth of a Nation*. The film, a landmark in cinematography, was also a racist movie that attacked Reconstruction and defended Ku Klux Klan violence. It was based on a novel written by Thomas Dixon, a native of North Carolina, a friend of Daniels, and a Hopkins classmate of Wilson. The secretary of the navy, who loved movies, agreed to help Dixon market the film and arranged for a showing in the central post office in Washington. Since the president missed this showing, Daniels arranged for Wilson and his family to see the film in the White House. Wilson never recorded his reaction to *The Birth of a Nation*, and there is no evidence that Daniels ever regretted his role in helping to make it an extraordinary success.[26]

Initially Daniels, like the president, expected the administration to concentrate on its domestic agenda. But the secretary of the navy, who was a near-pacifist, soon found himself drawn into crises with Japan and Mexico. In May 1913, during a brief war scare with Japan, Daniels rejected the advice of senior naval advisers and of Secretary of War Lindley M. Garrison to begin naval preparations for war. And he was also cautious in dealing with the turmoil created by the Mexican revolution. Early on he realized that "what to do with Mexico is the great problem." Later, in April 1914, he authorized the landing of American troops at Veracruz to prevent German arms from reaching the government of General Victoriano Huerta. But he rejected the advice of war hawks in the administration to march on Mexico City. He could only hope that, with the passage of time, a stable government would emerge in that troubled country.[27]

Daniels was also involved in the administration's gunboat diplomacy in the Caribbean and Central America. When he took office, the Marines, who were under his command, were supporting governments in Cuba and Nicaragua. Two years later, Daniels, determined to restore political stability and to protect the Monroe Doctrine, dispatched Marines to Haiti, and in 1916 also sent them to the Dominican Republic. Despite his anti-imperialist convictions, he was the person who had to carry out the administration's interventionist policies. Years later Daniels confided to FDR that "the things we were forced to do in Haiti were a bitter pill to me for I have always hated any foreign policy that even hinted at imperialistic control."[28]

The outbreak of World War I surprised and upset Daniels. FDR noted that Daniels was "feeling chiefly very sad that his faith in human nature and civilization and similar idealistic nonsense was receiving such a rude shock." Daniels blamed Germany for the coming of war and expected a long and painful conflict; both he and Bryan believed that America must remain aloof from the conflict and pursue a policy of strict neutrality. By early 1915, however, the British blockade, along with Germany's U-boat decree establishing a war zone in the waters surrounding Great Britain and Ireland, complicated America's position and left Daniels fearful about where the president's protests might lead. By the spring of 1915, Daniels was torn between the views of his two heroes, Wilson and Bryan.[29]

The sinking of the *Lusitania* on May 7, 1915, sharpened conflicts within the administration. Some of the president's advisers, such as Secretary of the Treasury McAdoo, urged the severing of diplomatic relations with Germany—a step that almost certainly would lead to war—while others, such as Secretary of State Bryan, urged Wilson to prohibit American citizens from traveling on belligerent ships. Daniels sympathized with Bryan's position, but he was not willing to break with the president and imperil his chances for reelection in 1916. He tried to keep Bryan in the cabinet, but on June 7 learned from his onetime mentor that he had resigned. "It was," Daniels remembered, "like a bolt out of the blue. It struck me between the eyes."[30]

As 1915 progressed and Wilson's protests against Germany's U-boat warfare seemed successful, Daniels felt vindicated. The president's diplomacy had not led to war. More than ever, the destructiveness of the conflict appalled Daniels and convinced him that there were powerful political reasons for keeping the peace. In the fall of 1916, he campaigned hard for Wilson and concluded that his reelection was a "mandate from the people" to keep the nation out of war. He supported the president's peace note to the belligerents at the end of 1916, but the German U-boat decree in early February 1917 and the subsequent sinking of American ships brought the debate over war or peace, both within the nation and the administration, to a climax. On March 20, the cabinet met for what Daniels termed the "Day of Decision." After most of Daniels's colleagues urged the president to go before Congress and ask for a declaration of war, Wilson said, "We have not yet heard from Burleson and Daniels." Burleson then spoke in favor of war, and Wilson turned his head toward the secretary of the navy and asked, "Well, Daniels?" Daniels hesitated, and in a low, emotional voice said that "he saw no other course than to enter the war." "It was," he recorded in his diary, "a supreme moment of my life. I had hoped & prayed this cup would pass. . . . Having tried patience, there was no course open to us except to protect our rights on the seas. If Germany wins, we must be a military nation."[31]

Prior to America's entry into the war, Daniels had proposed, and Congress had approved in June 1916, a massive building program that would create a "Navy second to none." This naval expansion act had placed a heavy emphasis on the construction of big battleships, or dreadnaughts, but in the spring of 1917, it became apparent that the Allies, aside from massive financial support, needed large numbers of American troops. Daniels quickly realized that the navy's task would not be to fight a decisive, big-ship engagement, but rather to carry supplies to the Allies, transport American troops, and establish a convoy system that would defeat the U-boat menace and establish control of North Atlantic sea lanes. He now focused on the transformation of the navy, on doing what was necessary to keep Britain and France in the war and to defeat the German army on the Western Front. At the same time, however, he was eager for peace and upset at the prospect, in the late summer of 1918, of invading Germany. In the negotiations that began in early October, Wilson demanded more of Germany than Daniels believed prudent, but with the signing of the armistice on November 11, 1918, he felt "the first thrill of joy in years." Convinced "that something good must come out of all this suffering and travail," Daniels supported the president's vision of the peace and urged him to appoint a peace commission that would include a sitting senator and either Bryan or Taft.[32]

In early December 1918, when Wilson left for France, Daniels stayed in Washington to supervise the navy's efforts to ship food to Europe, to bring the troops home, and to plan for the postwar years. But the president wanted his secretary of the navy at the peace conference, and on March 15, 1919, Josephus and Addie left for Paris, where he would begin negotiations over the naval terms of the peace treaty. Daniels was not an Anglophile; he distrusted Great Britain and would not concede British naval supremacy in the postwar period. As a result, the tense negotiations with British Prime Minister David Lloyd George reached an impasse; there would be no grand naval settlement at the Paris peace conference.[33]

In mid-April 1919, Daniels left Paris and, after touring the front and visiting Belgium and Great Britain, reached New York on May 17. As he reviewed the complicated political situation, he realized that the president might have to accept some reservations to secure ratification of the peace treaty and urged him to meet with every senator, both Democrat and Republican, except for a few who were impossible to deal with. Daniels advised Wilson not to make his speaking tour in defense of the peace treaty, and on October 3, 1919, when he learned of the seriousness of the president's stroke, recorded in his diary that the news "fell like a pall on all hearts." Later, when two senators visited the president to determine the severity of his condition, Daniels told Cary Grayson that "if you would tell the people exactly what is the matter with the President, a wave of sympathy would pour into the White House whereas now there is nothing but uncertainty and criticism." Grayson agreed, but explained that Edith had "forbidden" him to speak of the president's true condition.[34]

During the winter of 1919–20, Daniels attended cabinet meetings and continued to consult with Grayson about the president's condition and with Tumulty about the prospects for the peace treaty in the Senate. He now supported Wilson's refusal to make concessions, convinced that Republican senators would reject any proposal that the president made. Secretary of State Robert Lansing, who Wilson would soon dismiss from

office (for his disloyalty), was critical of the behavior of Daniels and Secretary of War Newton Baker: "After the President has taken action," he
observed, "these two always endorse it. They seem to have no minds when
the President has made up his."[35]

Despite the paralysis of the Wilson administration, Daniels remained
active in Democratic Party politics. He attended the party's 1920 convention in San Francisco, where he joined with other Wilson advisers to block
the efforts of Secretary of State Bainbridge Colby to draft the president.
During the campaign of James M. Cox and FDR, Daniels spoke in the
Midwest in support of the ticket, but he soon realized that the tide was
running strongly against his party and warned the president—who did
not believe him—that the Democrats had no chance in November.[36]

On March 5, 1921, the secretary of the navy wrote his last official letter to
the president, thanking him for his support and friendship and reassuring him that he "will be hailed as the hope of mankind. One day it will
be realized and the world will remember you with gratitude."[37] Over two
months later, when Daniels reached Raleigh, he received a homecoming
welcome at a banquet attended by five thousand people. He resumed his
editorship of the *News and Observer* and also undertook extensive speaking tours, sometimes lecturing as often as five nights a week. In the editorial pages of his paper he opposed the rise of the Ku Klux Klan in North
Carolina—which threatened to revive "the Negro question"—and also
opposed the anti-evolution campaign of his old mentor, Bryan. Daniels
remained prominent in the Democratic Party, and at its 1924 convention
received some support for the nomination. But he knew that he had no
chance, observing that "the Democratic party is composed of Irishmen,
Southerners and Jews, none of whom can hope to be elected President."
He supported McAdoo for the nomination, convinced that he would revive the idealism of Woodrow Wilson and that his party should focus on
Republican corruption, Prohibition, and membership in the League of
Nations. The nomination of John W. Davis, a conservative lawyer, came as
a bitter disappointment, but Daniels, a hard-core Democrat, never thought
of abandoning his party's ticket.[38]

Throughout the 1920s, Daniels kept in touch with his onetime protégé, FDR, and, after his election as governor of New York in 1928, thought he might one day become president. At the Democratic convention in 1932 in Chicago, Daniels, still a force in his party, backed FDR for the nomination. He made two extended campaign tours and, in an article on "Franklin Roosevelt as I Know Him" in the *Saturday Evening Post*, claimed that "the two words that best describe Franklin Roosevelt are 'eagerness' and 'determination.'... He has always had a delightful eagerness in all things." At FDR's inauguration, tears filled Daniels's eyes as he watched the president, with the help of his son James, laboriously move toward the podium. He remembered "how young, and debonair, striding and strong he had been."[39] After his election, Daniels turned down the president's first offer, to coordinate the administration's transportation policies. But in March 1933 he quickly accepted his offer to become ambassador to Mexico and, two weeks later, at the age of seventy, he took the train to Mexico City. Because Daniels was in Mexico from 1933 to October 1941, he was on the periphery of the New Deal. Unlike many old progressives, however, he embraced its policies, convinced that FDR's reforms were an extension of the New Freedom. He believed that the growing concentration of power in industry and the increasing maldistribution of wealth had caused the Depression, and that only an unprecedented government response could restore the nation's prosperity.[40]

Despite his isolation in Mexico, Daniels followed American politics closely and returned home for each Democratic national convention (he had been at every one since 1896). In Mexico the new ambassador, who sympathized with Mexicans' nationalist aspirations, traveled throughout the country and displayed a remarkable "zest for life." One visitor described him as "a wonderful little man, now approaching 80, but as perky and vigorous as can be, and none of the signs of age." Daniels helped to resolve difficult economic issues between the two nations—a legacy of the revolution—and when, in March 1938, President Lázaro Cárdenas expropriated foreign-owned oil companies, he convinced FDR and Secretary of State Cordell Hull not to challenge Mexico's right to do so. As the world

crisis mounted, he concluded that regional security and hemispheric sol-
idarity must be given priority over the property rights of individuals.[41]

In October 1941—only two months before the United States entered World
War II, Daniels left his post in Mexico City and returned to Raleigh. In
1924 he had published a hagiographic biography of Woodrow Wilson, and
since the middle of the 1930s, he had somehow found the time to write five
lengthy volumes of recollections. The two volumes constituting *The Wilson Era* formed the heart of this effort, describing in loving detail Daniels's
association with Wilson and his times. On December 15, 1947, a month
before his death at the age of eighty-five, Daniels—the last surviving member of Wilson's cabinet—spoke at a meeting of the Woodrow Wilson Foundation. "These dark years," he reminisced, "are brightly lit for those who
understood that what Wilson left us was not merely a plan for peace, but
the imperishable pattern of the courage with the faith, the sacrifice with
the vision. . . . The troubles which we face now would not have dismayed
him. They will not dismay other living men who not only guard his faith,
but keep his spirit now." At Daniels's funeral in Raleigh his granddaughter
sat between Edith Wilson and Eleanor Roosevelt.[42]

Secretary of the Treasury McAdoo at his desk. McAdoo became the most forceful member of the president's cabinet, and in May 1914, after he married Eleanor Wilson, he also became the president's son-in-law. Many Democrats came to regard McAdoo as the "Crown Prince," as Wilson's legitimate heir, but the president had reservations about McAdoo and never supported his presidential ambitions. Library of Congress, Prints and Photographs Division, LC-USZ6-1532.

CHAPTER FOUR

William Gibbs McAdoo

"He looked over the heads of other men, above the confusion of
contemporary events, to distant horizons"

In February 1909, William Gibbs McAdoo, who was visiting his son at Princeton University, was waiting for a train at Princeton Junction. While he was standing on the platform, the university's president, Woodrow Wilson, got off the train from New York, and a "mutual acquaintance" introduced the two men. They then traveled to Princeton together. "He was," McAdoo recalled in his memoirs, "gracious and unpretentious in manner. He possessed, to an unusual degree, the indefinable quality of charm. There was an unforgettable clear vividness in his speech. . . . He had a way of lifting the most commonplace topic . . . to a height where it would catch the rays of the sun. . . . Almost anyone, meeting him as a stranger and not knowing his antecedents, would have taken him for a lawyer or a man of large affairs."[1] As 1910 unfolded, McAdoo followed Wilson's achievements as governor of New Jersey and in July 1911 joined a small group of men in New York City who were supporting Wilson for the presidency. In fact, McAdoo became the driving force in Wilson's campaign and, after his election, became secretary of the treasury, the dominant member of his cabinet, and in March 1914 his son-in-law. As the Wilson years passed, many of the president's supporters came to regard the secretary of the treasury as the "Crown Prince," Wilson's legitimate heir. McAdoo would never win the Democratic nomination for the presidency, but his association with Wilson would shape the rest of his life.

* * *

William Gibbs McAdoo was born on October 31, 1863, at Marietta, Georgia, the third of seven children. His father, of Scottish descent, was a lawyer and teacher who had fought in the war with Mexico; he was, McAdoo remembered, "quiet speaking, gracious in manner, and highly spirited," with a love of books. His mother, who came from an old Georgia family, was "resolute and gentle, with a matchless courage and a splendid mind, unostentatious, unaffected, unequalled." In 1863, his father joined the Confederate Army, and a year later, when McAdoo was about six months old, the family moved to Milledgeville, in the central part of the state. At the end of the war, the plantation that McAdoo's mother had inherited was in ruins, and the family could not escape the poverty and depression of the post–Civil War South. McAdoo, who was educated at temporary schools with harsh discipline, recalled that during his school days "personal courage was at a premium and no boy could refuse to fight without being regarded as a coward and suffering unendurable ostracism among his fellows." McAdoo took a variety of jobs to help his family survive, and sometimes "as I walked alone through the night my thoughts had wings and soared over the world."[2]

In 1877, when McAdoo was nearly fourteen, the family moved to Knoxville, where his father took a teaching position at the University of Tennessee. McAdoo thrived in Knoxville, a more prosperous and livelier place than Milledgeville, and two years after his family's arrival, he entered the University of Tennessee. There he debated, enjoyed fraternity life, and dreamed of attending the University of Virginia's law school. His family's finances, however, were too fragile to support further study, and midway through his junior year he took a holiday job as the assistant clerk of the United States District Court; six months later he took a full-time job as the deputy clerk of the United States Circuit Court in Chattanooga. Five months short of his nineteenth birthday, McAdoo moved to Chattanooga, where he lived in a boarding house and read law in the evening. Initially his life there was a lonely one, but in January 1885, he was admitted to the Tennessee bar, and later in the year he married and opened a law office in downtown Chattanooga. McAdoo was eager to make money and soon combined his legal practice with real estate speculation. He became excited by the prospect of converting a horse-drawn streetcar line into an electric system, and in July 1889 he bought, with the help of investors, the Knoxville Street Railway Company. But McAdoo's company was undercapitalized, and he soon discovered that the new technology was expensive and unreliable. In 1892, his Knoxville company defaulted on its debt and was taken into receivership. McAdoo now faced the prospect of financial ruin, and only after four years of litigation was he able to escape from any personal liability for the failure of his company.[3]

In June 1892, McAdoo, who yearned for a larger stage, moved his family—which now included two children—to New York. "The great city," he wrote, "with its teeming crowds, its miles of streets, and its resounding activity, was an unending source of interest and wonder. The stir and bustle of the place suited me perfectly. I felt like a born New-Yorker." He opened a small law office on Wall Street, but few clients sought out the young lawyer and the economic panic that began in May 1893 was a financial disaster for McAdoo. Desperate to reduce his expenses, he gave up his law practice, became a bond salesman, and first moved his family to a fifth-floor walk-up on the Upper West Side, then to an even cheaper place in Yonkers. By 1897, he had five children, while his wife, Sarah, had developed rheumatoid arthritis, which would leave her a virtual invalid after the birth of a sixth child in 1904. McAdoo remembered the "terrible depressions" that he felt during these years, the anxiety, headaches, nervous disorders, and the fear of failure. "The poverty," he later wrote, "the struggle, and the anxiety of this period are indescribable."[4]

With the lifting of the depression in 1897, McAdoo's prospects improved. Once again he opened a law office on Wall Street and gradually began to build up his practice. By 1901, after many difficult years, he finally began to feel prosperous. He was thirty-eight, an established lawyer with connections to the Wilkes-Barre and Hazleton Railroad and to an influential group of investors. His optimism and entrepreneurial impulses now re-emerged. "I had," he recalled, "a burning desire to acquit myself with distinction and to do something that would prove of genuine benefit to humanity while I lived."[5]

McAdoo was well aware of the fact, as were most New Yorkers, that there was no rail connection between New Jersey and Manhattan. One hundred and twenty million passengers a year crossed the Hudson River on crowded and uncomfortable ferries. McAdoo learned that in 1873 and 1883 earlier efforts to tunnel under the Hudson had failed. In October 1901, he walked through the old tunnel: "Yet, from the moment I saw the tunnel I never doubted that I would get possession of it and complete it." By the late autumn of 1901, McAdoo had given up his law practice and was completely absorbed in his daring project. As he wrote, "I experienced a sense of inner compulsion, a driving desire to do the thing for its own sake. It was also a challenge to do what was supposed to be impossible." He raised enough money to buy the old tunnel from bondholders and then proceeded to use his formidable skills as a promoter to raise the large sums needed to fund his new enterprise. He became the president of the New York and Jersey Railroad Company, and in the early summer of 1902, work began. Initially McAdoo planned to build only a single tunnel, but as the digging progressed, he expanded his plan and decided to build a second tunnel that would be part of a system that, when finally completed in 1910, included four under-river tunnels, miles of underground subways, and the Hudson Terminal Building, an elaborate office building whose twin towers became the centerpiece of the project. The whole enterprise was one of the largest engineering feats of the early twentieth century, comparable to the Panama Canal.[6]

By November 1910, more than 130,000 commuters used these tunnels every day, and McAdoo, who was the president of what was now called the Hudson and Manhattan Railway Company, had achieved fame as an enlightened, progressive businessman. He denounced monopolies and trusts, presenting himself as a different type of corporate leader; the motto of his company was "the public be pleased." McAdoo ran a customer-friendly operation, accepted unions and an eight-hour day for his employees, and equal pay for women. In July 1909, the *Boston Herald* praised him as "something more than a genius"; his fame had spread outside of New York, and he had become, by the age of forty-six, a familiar public figure. He now began to speak out on issues of the day, and in January 1911, proclaimed that "what they [the people] need is a leader. . . . A man of dynamic and militant morality, who will cleave a way through greed and selfishness for the permanent benefit of the human race."[7]

As his tunnel project advanced, McAdoo became a wealthy man. Although his salary was modest for the time—only $50,000 per year—he also speculated in stocks and real estate and acquired a house in Manhattan, and a larger one in Irvington-on-Hudson that included a domestic staff and a nurse for his wife. McAdoo now led an intense, glamorous life. He loved speeding in his high-powered Mercedes, took summer holidays in Europe, and became a favorite at high-society parties. One New York newspaper wrote, "There is something suggestive of a dreamer in his deep-set eyes, something of a dynamic energy in his long, slight, sinewy body, something of a fine race horse in the impression of his whole self. . . . He speaks lucidly and with the soft accents of the South."[8]

There was, however, a dark side to his extraordinary success. His health, which had nearly broken in the 1890s, remained fragile, while the health of his wife, Sarah, continued to decline. By 1904, she was an invalid, often bedridden, confined to the couple's home at Irvington-on-Hudson. McAdoo stayed at his Manhattan townhouse, and by early 1912 his marriage was in crisis. On February 21, deeply depressed, Sarah died of what the press reported as heart failure. Before her death, McAdoo had become involved in an affair with Florence "Daisy" Harriman, the wife of a wealthy, prominent New Yorker. At the end of 1912, as McAdoo moved on to a new phase of his life, the affair came to an end.[9]

In 1884, McAdoo, who was raised a southern Democrat, had cast his first vote for Grover Cleveland. During the 1890s, he remained a Gold Democrat, rejecting the reformism of William Jennings Bryan. After the turn of the century, he was drawn to Theodore Roosevelt's colorful personality, his aggressive foreign policy, and his willingness to expand the role of the federal government. After he had supported TR in 1904, McAdoo hoped for an appointment to the Panama Canal Commission. But McAdoo, in contrast to TR, wanted to break up the trusts, not simply to regulate them, and by the time Woodrow Wilson emerged as a presidential candidate, he had begun to move back to his Democratic roots. He first met Wilson at Princeton in 1909, then invited him to speak at the Southern Society in New York in December 1910, and six months later announced his support. He was impressed with Wilson's "strength" and the depth of his convictions, writing that "I know him to be not only a great man, but a *clean* man and a *free* man. . . . I believe, furthermore, that he is the only Democrat who can be elected."[10]

In mid-1911, McAdoo joined a small group of supporters, led by William F. McCombs, a Princeton graduate and a New York lawyer, who were promoting Wilson for the presidency. McAdoo helped McCombs, raising money and reaching out to Democrats in southern states. As the campaign developed, Wilson leaned on him more and more for advice, and in mid-April 1912, McAdoo accompanied Woodrow and Ellen on a speaking trip to Georgia. In July, at the Democratic convention in Baltimore, McAdoo served as the floor manager of the Wilson forces. On the tenth ballot, when McCombs became convinced that Wilson had lost and should release his delegates, an astonished McAdoo yelled at McCombs, "You have sold him out," and urged Wilson to remain in the race. McAdoo's feud with the irascible and neurotic McCombs would continue throughout the campaign, but for two months in the fall, while McCombs remained home after his health collapsed, McAdoo ran the New York headquarters. On Election Day, he and Josephus Daniels joined a group of family and friends at Wilson's home in Princeton to hear the returns. Wilson liked this talented progressive businessman, knew that he wanted him in his cabinet, and in early February 1913 asked him to become secretary of the treasury.[11]

In March 1913, when McAdoo took up his new post in Washington, he was fifty, seven years younger than the president. McAdoo was a tall, lean man, with a hawklike nose, exuberant manner, and youthful appearance, one who radiated energy and ambition. Secretary of War Newton Baker remembered that he had "the greatest lust for power I ever saw." McAdoo was not a well-educated man, and, as he observed in his memoir, "I have long since come to the conclusion that the vast majority of books are of no value." McAdoo was uninterested in ideas that seemed to lack any practical application. Like Wilson, he was committed to progressive reform, but he had a very different background and temperament from that of the new president he was to serve.[12]

McAdoo quickly became the most dynamic member of Wilson's cabinet, eager to expand the powers of his department and to invade the jurisdictions of his colleagues. As one biographer writes, "[F]or five years the Treasury resembled a giant battleship, constantly on the move and firing an endless barrage of new ideas and projects into official Washington." Some of those who worked with him, such as Secretary of the Navy Josephus Daniels, admired McAdoo, while others resented his fierce ambition and the ruthlessness of his empire-building. The progressive lawyer Louis Brandeis, whom Wilson would elevate to the Supreme Court in 1916, believed that McAdoo was "far-seeing, courageous, inventive, effective," but Charles Hamlin, a member of the Federal Reserve Board, claimed, "As a man . . . in spite of his brilliance, he was vindictive, rather treacherous, vain conceited & wildly jealous of anyone with him receiving credit."[13]

As McAdoo settled into his new position in the spring of 1913, he was overwhelmed by the flood of patronage requests. The Democratic Party had been out of power for sixteen years, and the Treasury Department had thousands of positions to fill in Washington and across the country. McAdoo also quickly felt the pressure from powerful southern Democrats in Congress, who urged him and other cabinet members (five of whom were southerners),to reassert white supremacy in the federal government. In April 1913, Postmaster General Burleson took the lead in segregating his department, and McAdoo soon followed. When the administration was confronted with powerful protests from northern progressives, he claimed that Black and white workplaces were segregated "to remove causes of complaint and irritation where white women have been forced unnecessarily to sit at desks with colored men." While some of the segregation orders were eventually softened, post office and treasury officials, as one historian notes, "throughout the South downgraded or discharged droves of black employees."[14]

In 1913, McAdoo was deeply involved in crafting and promoting the legislative agenda of the New Freedom, especially in the passage of the Federal Reserve Act. There were sharp disagreements among Democratic leaders in Congress over the degree of centralization, the control of the currency, and the role of the federal government in the new system. As the debate progressed, McAdoo moved toward the views of Bryan and his followers, declaring that "the right measure is the one which puts the Government in the saddle." He believed that the federal government must manage the nation's money supply, and the bill that eventually passed in December 1913 increased the power of the secretary of the treasury and turned out to be the most enduring legislative achievement of Wilson's presidency.[15]

After his arrival in Washington, McAdoo buried himself so deeply in his work that the president's personal physician, Cary Grayson, worried that his health would collapse if he kept up his frantic pace. In the fall of 1913, McAdoo began to court Eleanor "Nell" Wilson, who was, one biographer notes, "the liveliest and least inhibited" of the president's three daughters. The two danced, played tennis, went on horseback rides, and, McAdoo remembered, "talked about almost everything." The secretary of the treasury was pleased by Nell's understanding of political issues and finally proposed in early 1914.[16] Woodrow and Ellen had some reservations about the relationship, since McAdoo was fifty-one, more than twice Nell's age, and had six children who ranged in age from five to twenty-six. Moreover, Woodrow was reluctant to see his youngest daughter leave his household, since, as he wrote Mary Allen Hulbert, "the dear little girl is the apple of my eye; no man is good enough for her. But McAdoo comes as near being so as any man could." In early March 1914, when the couple's engagement was announced, McAdoo was ecstatic, writing to Colonel House, who had become his close friend, that "Miss Eleanor and I are engaged! The 'Governor' has consented and I am supremely happy. Isn't it wonderful? The days of miracles are not yet over or she never would have accepted me." On May 7, 1914, "Mac," as he was now called, and Nell were married in a White House ceremony.[17]

Wilson felt that Nell "has married a noble man," but he was also saddened by her departure. "Ah!" he wrote, "how desperately my heart aches that she is gone. She was simply part of me, the only delightful part; and I feel the loneliness more than I dare admit even to myself." The marriage changed McAdoo's relationship to the president, drawing him into his intimate family circle and putting the two men in much closer contact with each other. As House noted in his diary, "He begins to see the other side of being the President's son-in-law."[18]

Inevitably tension grew between the president and secretary of the treasury, since McAdoo, absorbed in his work, did not respect the sharp line that Wilson drew between his public and his private life. In late September 1914, House learned from Grayson that the president suffered "from indigestion and he thought one cause of it was that McAdoo and Tumulty persisted in talking business to him during his meals." House agreed to urge his friend to exercise restraint. But McAdoo was restless and ambitious, and for a time in the fall of 1914 considered leaving the administration to head the Metropolitan Life Insurance Company. He eventually decided to stay at his post in Washington but could not imagine remaining as secretary of the treasury if Wilson ran for a second term in 1916. House believed that the president would do so, but also realized that McAdoo, as early as October 1914, "has the Presidential bee firmly fixed."[19]

Looking back on the relationship between Wilson and McAdoo, the president's brother-in-law, Stockton Axson, reflected on "how easy it is that the artist's mind and the business mind should come in clash. The business mind wants to keep on with business; the artist's mind wants renewal that comes from relaxation." Eventually the president's "tone takes a little edge on. Then he adopts that worst of all his defenses—silence. The silence of Woodrow Wilson is worse than the oaths of some men, more withering."[20]

Within the president's inner circle of advisers, McAdoo became a controversial figure. He quarreled with some of his cabinet colleagues and claimed that the president's private secretary, Joe Tumulty, was "too near the interests." Secretary of Commerce David F. Houston concluded that McAdoo was a "solitaire player," unwilling to work with his colleagues. But McAdoo also formed close friendships with Grayson (who was the best man at his wedding), with Secretary of the Navy Josephus Daniels, and especially with Colonel House. House thought that McAdoo "has a fine imagination, indomitable courage, and a touch of genius"; he believed that his energy, intellect, and progressive beliefs made him a man of destiny who might become, if properly advised, Wilson's successor.[21]

During the summer of 1915, as it became obvious that Wilson was in love with Edith Galt, some of his advisers worried that an early remarriage would damage his prospects for reelection in 1916. In mid-September, McAdoo made a clumsy attempt to force the president to discuss the issue. His effort failed, but he did destroy any chance he may have had for a good relationship with the woman who would become Woodrow's wife in December 1915. Edith later told House "that she disliked McAdoo; that she had always disliked him. She considered him thoroughly selfish in as much as he would let nothing stand in the way of his ambition."[22]

In early August 1914, after the outbreak of World War I, McAdoo moved swiftly to deal with the impact of the war on the American economy, addressing the disruptions in international finance, trade, and shipping. He believed that Germany was responsible for the breakdown of peace, and, from the start of the struggle, was sympathetic to the Allies. After the sinking of the *Lusitania* on May 7, 1915, McAdoo was ready for the United States to enter the conflict, arguing that "the people of this country want peace, but they are unwilling to have it, except with honor." He viewed Germany's U-boat campaign as barbaric, a threat to freedom of the seas and, after Germany announced that it would pursue unlimited submarine warfare in early February 1917, he wrote that "I am myself full of fight and energy and am glad to have the definite issue drawn at last." He told House that "his appetite for it [war] was so strong that he would like to quit the Cabinet, raise a regiment and go to the front." McAdoo's bellicosity irri-

tated the president, who agonized over the decision for war before he finally addressed a joint session of Congress on April 2, 1917.[23]

Inevitably, McAdoo was deeply involved in preparing the nation for
war. He supervised the budget, arranged for financial support for the Allies, led four Liberty Loan campaigns, and, on December 28, 1917, became
director general of the United States Railroad Administration. McAdoo
traveled around the country on speaking tours, promoting war bonds,
meeting local political leaders, and becoming, as one newspaper reported,
"Commander-in-Chief of the Liberty Loan drive."

McAdoo quarreled, however, with Secretary of War Baker over the
organization of the American war effort. Baker was content with modest changes in the War Department, while McAdoo argued for a single
agency, the War Industries Board, that would set priorities and control
purchasing for the military. The president imposed a compromise in late
July 1917, but it soon failed, and in early March 1918, Wilson finally followed McAdoo's advice and appointed the Wall Street speculator, and
McAdoo's friend, Bernard Baruch, the head of the WIB.[24]

McAdoo's direction of the nation's railroad network, a vast enterprise
of 1.5 million employees, brought him more fame. He relished his new
position, since it combined, as his biographer Douglas Craig notes, "his
love of action and penchant for self-promotion." He now rushed to reorganize the nation's largest industry, ordering equal pay for equal work, an
eight-hour day, and making sure that his name was on every paycheck that
railway employees received.

On November 14, 1918, three days after the armistice, McAdoo submitted
his resignation as secretary of the treasury and as director general of the
US Railroad Administration. He claimed that years of public service had
damaged his health and finances, but, whatever his motives, he was leaving the administration at a critical time, when the president faced the
daunting tasks of securing a peace settlement and transforming the economy from wartime to peacetime production.[25]

McAdoo's resignation may also have been motivated by his deteriorating relationship with the president. As the war progressed, McAdoo had

become critical of what he regarded as Wilson's lack of administrative abilities, and in early August 1917, he poured out his discontents in a conversation with House. His father-in-law, he complained, "would not give him sufficient authority to properly discharge his duties," and this "lack of authority was ruining his health." House thought that McAdoo, if given all the power that he desired, "would be in complete control of the Government," and in early May 1918, when his friend once again complained that Wilson was "constantly hampering his management" of the war effort, House pointed out that "there was a feeling in Washington, which the President shared, that he, McAdoo, had an insatiable desire for power." The president, as House noted, was losing patience with his ambitious son-in-law, complaining that "he had gotten so arbitrary that he presumed that, sooner or later, it would have to come to crisis between them. . . . 'Son-in-law or no son-in-law, if he wants to resign he can do so.'" House maneuvered to keep the peace between the two men and to avoid a premature resignation that, he believed, would ruin McAdoo's chances for the Democratic nomination in 1920. In fact, McAdoo's presidential ambitions further complicated his relationship with Wilson, who was not convinced that his son-in-law ought to be the heir apparent.[26]

In August 1919, Woodrow, Edith, and Stockton Axson had a long conversation about the 1920 campaign. Wilson admired Newton Baker and David Houston, but doubted that either could be elected. He had serious reservations, however, about McAdoo: "They [Baker and Houston] are both *reflective* men—and I am not sure that Mac is a reflective man. There is no man who can devise plans with more inspiration, or put them into operation with more vigor, than can Mac, but I never caught Mac reflecting."[27]

By the early months of 1920, McAdoo faced a dilemma. He had substantial support among Democrats across the country, many of whom regarded him as Wilson's logical successor. But he could not actively seek the nomination without the president's blessing. In the spring of 1920, McAdoo tried, and failed, to see his ailing father-in-law five times. "Things are taking a turn," he confided to Grayson, "which is exceedingly embarrassing to me." Moreover, some liberal Democrats doubted his fitness for the presidency. The *Nation* concluded that "his election to the White

House would be an unqualified misfortune," while the journalist Walter Lippmann dismissed McAdoo as "a statesman grafted upon a promoter . . . [who] does not hesitate or brood or procrastinate or reflect at length. . . . McAdoo is distinctly not a safe person in the ordinary sense of the word. . . . He has length and breadth if not depth."[28]

On June 18, 1920, McAdoo announced that he would not run for the presidency. At the Democratic convention in San Francisco his name was not placed in nomination, and on the forty-fourth ballot, Governor James M. Cox of Ohio finally prevailed. McAdoo campaigned for Cox and his running mate, Franklin D. Roosevelt, but he realized that the people were disillusioned with the Wilson administration and unresponsive to his calls for more liberal reform. After Cox's crushing defeat, McAdoo concluded that he had to rethink his political prospects and decided to move to California, where he could distance himself from Wilson and establish a new political base. McAdoo relished the change, but Eleanor was upset by the move, writing to her father that "I feel as if I were chopping a great big piece off of my heart when I put four days instead of five hours, between you and us. I don't see how I'm going to stand it, Father darling. . . . I wish I knew how to tell you what you and your love mean to me."[29]

On March 1, 1922, Mac and Eleanor left New York for Los Angeles. Once there, he set up a law practice and began to plan for winning the nomination in 1924. McAdoo had national prominence, impressive progressive credentials, and powerful advocates within the Democratic Party. He hoped to unite southerners and westerners behind a campaign based on a moderate tariff, the strict enforcement of Prohibition, and agricultural and railway reform. He was reluctant, however, to denounce the Ku Klux Klan and was no longer willing to give unconditional support to American membership in the League of Nations. Much to Wilson's disgust, he advocated a national plebiscite on American membership in the League, one that would presumably guide the new administration. McAdoo seemed confident of the nomination, writing that "[u]nless there is some radical change, I think that the outcome of the Convention is not at all in doubt."[30]

In February 1924, as the Teapot Dome scandal unfolded, oil magnate

Edward L. Doheny (who had bribed Secretary of the Interior Albert Fall to acquire government oil leases), revealed that he had given McAdoo a large retainer to protect his oil leases in Mexico. While McAdoo was not directly involved in Teapot Dome, his behavior as a lawyer raised questions about his character and electability. Democrats had hoped to use Republican corruption as a major theme of their 1924 campaign; now the scandal had tainted their leading candidate for the nomination. Some of McAdoo's most important backers, such as Baruch and House, urged him to withdraw, but McAdoo refused to leave the race. He relentlessly pursued the nomination, informing House that he had no intention of becoming a "quitter" and that "[i]f I go down at all, my face will be toward the enemy but I am not going down." McAdoo confronted a difficult challenge, but Wilson's death on February 3, 1924, relieved him of the burden of his father-in-law's disapproval of his presidential ambitions.[31]

In the spring Democratic primaries, McAdoo won big victories over his chief rival, Governor Alfred E. Smith of New York. When the Democratic national convention opened on June 26 in New York's Madison Square Garden, however, McAdoo lacked a two-thirds majority. The convention, which lasted for sixteen days in oppressive heat, revealed the deep divisions that split the party. More conservative eastern and midwestern Democrats, led by Governor Smith, disliked McAdoo's progressivism and his ties to the Wilson administration, and they were determined to block his nomination. Bitter disputes over the Ku Klux Klan, the League of Nations, and many economic questions disrupted the convention. It was not until the 99th ballot that McAdoo finally released his delegates and not until the 103rd ballot that they finally chose John W. Davis, a prominent Wall Street lawyer and former ambassador to Great Britain, as a compromise candidate. McAdoo was bitter over the outcome and gave Davis only tepid support; in November he suffered a resounding defeat. McAdoo, who was sixty, still nursed presidential ambitions, but Democratic insiders felt that his time had passed. In November 1925, when McAdoo visited House in New York, the latter realized how much he missed his friend "who has so much charm, so much courage, so much vigor." He regretted that he would never be president for "he would give this country a shaking up which it needs."[32]

McAdoo relished his new life in Southern California, where he became a lawyer-entrepreneur. While his income was large, half of it went to interest payments on mortgages and debts, and he had expensive tastes, maintaining houses on both coasts, high-powered automobiles, and various club memberships. Even in the 1920s he always felt pressed financially and pursued a wide variety of business ventures (often using funds that Bernard Baruch had lent him).He confided to Baruch that "like myself, you need an outlet for your abundant energy. Neither of us can afford to dry up." McAdoo liked to live on the edge, either speeding in an automobile or flying his own plane. Or as he wrote to Nell, "you take an airline through God's majestic highway and find yourself *free*. I have never before felt the glow of real freedom and it is worth a chance even of death, to find it."[33]

After his defeat at the 1924 Democratic convention, McAdoo's influence within the party faded rapidly. In September 1927, he announced that he would not seek the presidency in 1928, and he watched with alarm as Smith moved toward the nomination and in June was nominated on the first ballot at the Democrat's Houston convention. McAdoo disliked the party's platform, complaining that it "abandoned . . . every principle for which Woodrow Wilson stood," and played no part in the fall campaign. Along with many party leaders, he doubted that any Democrat could win in 1928 and was primarily concerned with preparing the way for 1932. McAdoo now searched for a new role within the party, announcing that "a flat life makes no appeal to me" and that "except for occasional lapses, I am as full of energy, determination and spirit as I ever was, and whether I last long or not, I intend to continue to 'dare dangerously' until I go." McAdoo had not, in fact, given up his presidential ambitions, and he dismissed New York Governor Franklin Roosevelt as "one of the weakest men we could nominate for the Presidency." McAdoo informed House that the party should select "some militant and progressive man who has some hold on the popular imagination, who is free from boss and machine taint and control, and who is . . . sound on prohibition." In short, he believed that Democrats, recognizing their mistake in 1924, should turn to him for leadership.[34]

McAdoo soon realized, however, that he was out of touch; none of his friends rallied behind him. As Roosevelt's campaign for the nomination gathered momentum, McAdoo renounced his own ambitions in September 1931 and settled on the role of kingmaker. He backed Texas congressman John Nance Garner for the nomination, and, after Garner won primaries in Texas and California, McAdoo reasoned that his control of these two delegations would allow him to either block FDR's nomination or play a key role in his victory. At the Democratic convention in Chicago, on the fourth ballot, however, McAdoo made a strategic shift and threw the votes of these two delegations to FDR and guaranteed his nomination. Garner was to be FDR's running mate, while McAdoo cleared the way for his own nomination in August 1932 for a Senate seat from California. His campaign flyer announced, "Builder, executive, financier and statesman, his record entitles him to be regarded as the great administrative genius of his day." Both McAdoo and FDR triumphed in November. At the age of sixty-one he had won his first elective office, and he expected to play a major role in the new Democratic administration.[35]

The 1930s turned out to be a difficult decade for McAdoo. During 1933, he spent most of his time in Washington, while Nell remained in California. At the end of the year, they formally separated and in July 1934 were divorced (in September 1935, McAdoo would marry Doris Cross, a twenty-six-year-old nurse). Moreover, the Depression devastated his finances. During the 1920s, he had always lived beyond his means, using loans from wealthy friends to sustain his investments. With the Depression, however, he was forced to economize and to slide even deeper into debt. Nor were McAdoo's hopes for the Roosevelt administration fulfilled. He had expected to be part of FDR's inner circle of advisers, but in fact the president held him at arm's length, giving McAdoo control of patronage in California but denying him a central role in the emergence of the New Deal. Publicly, McAdoo was an enthusiastic New Dealer: "To hell," he wrote, "with hoary formulas and outworn theories in times like these!" Between 1932 and 1938, he supported every significant New Deal measure, including FDR's court-packing scheme in 1937 and his decision to run for a third term in 1940. But in private, he complained about his treatment by the president, who had denied him what he felt, as the carrier of Wilson's legacy, was his due.[36]

McAdoo was uncertain whether to run for reelection in 1938, when he would be seventy-five. Although he enjoyed his life in Washington, he was frustrated by the constraints of the Senate and fantasized about returning to private life and somehow restoring his fortune. Nevertheless, in March 1938, he announced that he would run again. This time, however, he faced a primary opponent, Sheridan Downey, who favored a more generous old-age pension plan—"Ham and Eggs"—than Social Security. McAdoo campaigned vigorously, but one adviser "was disappointed and was distressed to see how Mac had slipped as a gladiator in the political arena where he had once reigned as champion." In April 1938, McAdoo lost to a man he regarded as a "cheap demagogue."[37]

McAdoo had entered the Senate, as his biographer notes, "as a lion of Wilson progressivism and as FDR's king maker," but he left it "a much diminished figure." Out of office he continued to worry about money, but FDR eased his financial burdens by appointing him chairman of the Dollar Steamship Line. He remained, however, active in politics, and in the fall of 1940 worked hard for FDR's reelection. Earlier in the 1930s he had moved toward isolationism, rejecting the League of Nations and any collective action against German and Italian expansionism. But later in the decade, his views moved closer to those of FDR. He predicted that the European war that broke out in September 1939 would be "long and bitter" and supported the various measures championed by the president—such as the destroyers-for-bases deal in early September 1940—that gradually drew the United States into the conflict.[38]

In December 1938, McAdoo had a mild stroke and for the next two years had to cut back on what had been a frantic schedule. He had always been vain about his vitality and appearance; now he was old and ill. On February 1, 1941, he suffered a heart attack and died, leaving only a small estate to his heirs. His obituaries were mixed. Many liberals regarded him as a shallow opportunist, but the *New York Times* noted that he "was a man of singular persuasion and charm," and some of his old associates during the Wilson years caught his essential qualities. Ray Stannard Baker, Wilson's biographer, wrote that he was "dynamic rather than thoughtful," while George Creel, Wilson's chief information officer, observed that "the Secretary of the Treasury shot ahead with the speed and directness of a bullet." All agreed, however, that his career had peaked during Wilson's presidency and that in the succeeding years McAdoo had failed to achieve his two great ambitions—personal wealth and political power.[39]

In 1931, McAdoo had published his autobiography, *Crowded Years*. In it he described his personal philosophy, explaining that "I like movement and change; I like to make things better, to reshape old forces and worn-out ideals into new and dynamic forms." "What," he went on to reflect, "is life worth if one spends it like an oyster fastened securely to a rock?" And he seemed to accept the setbacks he had suffered, writing that "I have no quarrel with Fate, no matter in what moods I have found her, and no matter what her decrees have been. I have had a glorious time!" The final chapter dealt with Woodrow Wilson. In it McAdoo described some of his father-in-law's qualities—his many-sided greatness, the clarity of his mind and speech, his "sensitive, vibrant, and high-strung personality," and his loyalty to his friends and political supporters. But he also avoided what must have been a painful subject—his own gradual estrangement from the president. As the Wilson years progressed, McAdoo had become more critical of his father-in-law's leadership and more obsessed with succeeding him in the presidency. Wilson, on the other hand, had become more exasperated with his son-in-law's intrusive behavior and his empire-building and more convinced that McAdoo, for all his many talents, was not fit for the presidency. It was this disappointment that the two men eventually felt for each other that was the great, unspoken tragedy of McAdoo's life.[40]

Joseph Tumulty, the president's devoted personal secretary, looks over his chief's shoulder as he signs a document. Tumulty met Wilson in 1910 and served him loyally until 1922, when a break occurred in their friendship. Library of Congress, Prints and Photographs Division, LC-DIG-npcc-00356.

CHAPTER FIVE

Joseph Patrick Tumulty

"Not until the tears are wiped from the eyes of the world can we
grasp the vision of his greatness"

On September 16, 1910, Joseph Patrick Tumulty learned that Woodrow
Wilson was on his way to Trenton, New Jersey, to address the delegates at
the Democratic state convention. Tumulty, like other progressive Democrats, was skeptical of the new gubernatorial nominee, who appeared to
be the candidate of the party bosses. In his convention speech, however,
Wilson declared his political independence and endorsed a sweeping
program of progressive reform. As he finished his speech, the delegates
cheered wildly and rushed from their seats to greet him. Years later Tumulty remembered the scene vividly:

> The personal magnetism of the man, his winning smile, so frank and so sincere,
> the light of his grey eyes, the fine poise of his well-shaped head, the beautiful
> rhythm of his vigorous sentences, held the men in the Convention breathless
> under their mystic spell. Men all about me cried in a frenzy: 'Thank God, at last,
> a leader has come!' . . . Around me is a swirling mass of men whose hearts had been
> touched by the great speech which is just at an end. Men stood about me with
> tears streaming from their eyes. Realizing that they had just stood in the pres-
> ence of greatness, it seemed as if they had been lifted out of the selfish miasma of
> politics, and, in the spirit of the Crusaders, were ready to dedicate themselves
> to the cause of liberating their state from the bondage of special interests."[1]

Tumulty soon met Wilson and became his guide through the complexities of New Jersey politics. After the candidate's triumph in November,

he became his personal secretary, and two years later followed him to the White House. He was the only adviser who remained close to Wilson throughout his political career.

Tumulty was born on May 5, 1879, in Jersey City, New Jersey, the seventh of nine surviving children. His father, Patrick, an Irish immigrant, fought in the Civil War and in 1862 was wounded in the right leg. In December of that year, after his return to civilian life, he opened a grocery store located in a plain, two-story building in Jersey City. Tumulty's mother, who was also born in Ireland, could not read or write, but she was endowed with ample common sense and urged her children to attend school. Over the years, Patrick Tumulty prospered, branching out into contracting and real estate and moving his large family into a house of its own. His real passion, however, was politics. He served in the state Assembly and became the leader of a group of Irish Democrats who met most evenings in his grocery store. His son Joseph listened intently, remembering that "no matter how far back my memory turns, I cannot recall when I did not hear politics discussed—not ward politics only, but frequently the politics of the nation and the world. In that grocery store, from the lips of the plainest folk who came there, were carried on serious discussions of the tariff, the money question [and] our foreign relations." "Politics," he later told a reporter, "had me years before I could vote." As a boy, Tumulty joined the Fifth Ward Democratic Club, helping to raise funds, distribute literature, and get out the vote. He learned about the workings of the local Democratic machine and accepted the need for party loyalty. But he was also aware of the poverty surrounding him in Jersey City and was inspired by William Jennings Bryan's 1896 presidential campaign. He became a reformer within the Irish Democratic organization and would eventually face the dilemma, as his biographer writes, "of reconciling party regularity with the fight for social improvement."[2]

Tumulty attended parochial schools in Jersey City and in 1895 enrolled in St. Peter's College, a small, local Jesuit institution. There he pursued a demanding curriculum and excelled at public speaking, winning a gold medal for elocution. After his graduation in 1899, Tumulty read law as a clerk in a Jersey City firm and three years later was admitted to the bar. He settled down quickly, marrying his childhood sweetheart, buying a house for his family (which soon included five children), and forming what became a profitable legal partnership.

Politics, however, fascinated Tumulty, and in 1906, when he was only twenty-seven, he was easily elected to the state Assembly. For fifteen years, New Jersey had been dominated by an alliance of Republican Party bosses and big corporations. It was, one historian notes, "one of the last strongholds of an industrial-feudal order." But by 1906, a group of progressives— the "New Idea group"—had emerged within the Republican Party, and reform sentiment had also begun to spread through Democratic ranks. Progressives in both parties advocated a long list of reforms, including state regulation of railroads and utilities, a civil service commission, restrictions on child labor, and the initiative and referendum. But reformers were frustrated by Republican leaders, who controlled the governorship and legislature and blocked most reforms.[3]

Tumulty proved a popular assemblyman, easily winning his campaigns for reelection and becoming a leader of progressive insurgents in the legislature. He was a skilled tactician and fiery orator, and he might have become Speaker of the Assembly had he stayed in the legislature. By 1910, however, the demands of his law practice, the needs of his growing family, and tension with Democratic bosses convinced Tumulty not to run for reelection.

In September 1910, Tumulty had gone to the Democratic convention in Trenton determined, along with a group of Democratic progressives, to fight against Wilson's nomination. After listening to his acceptance speech, however, Tumulty had been transformed, throwing his arms around a friend and telling him that " 'this is one of the happiest days of my life.' " Tumulty, who soon met the Democratic nominee, remembered that "the democratic bearing of the man, his warmth of manner, charm, and kindly bearing were the first things that attracted me to him. There was no coldness or austerity about him, nor was he what the politicians would call 'high-browish.' He impressed me as a plain, unaffected, affable gentleman."[4]

Tumulty was not, however, impressed with Wilson's first campaign speech, which he regarded as too vague, and he urged him to deal with specific issues and to make a more definite attack on the status quo. Wilson followed his young friend's advice, quickly hitting his stride as a speaker, and soon was joined by Tumulty on the campaign tour. In early November, he carried the state with the second largest plurality in its history while Democrats captured the Assembly and five of seven congressional seats.[5]

Once in office, the new governor asked Tumulty to become his personal secretary. He considered him one of the ablest of the young progressive Democrats and realized that he needed a close adviser with a knowledge of New Jersey affairs. He was, Wilson wrote, "my delightful young Secretary and political mentor." Tumulty, who was only thirty-one, quickly became the governor's chief legislative and administrative assistant and his intermediary with the press. He was efficient, gregarious, and absorbed in the details of New Jersey politics; the two men quickly established an easy working relationship. Wilson, who was twenty-three years older than his assistant, in private referred to Tumulty as "my dear boy," while Tumulty always referred to Wilson as "Governor."

During the first four months of 1911, Tumulty played a key role—especially through his use of patronage—in helping Wilson defeat the efforts of the Democratic Party boss, James Smith Jr., to win an appointment to the US Senate, and also in helping the new governor guide a series of reform laws through the legislature. By early May 1911, Wilson had fulfilled all of his campaign promises and had become a leading candidate for the Democratic presidential nomination.[6]

The governor and his secretary, who were drawn together by the force of circumstances, lived in very different worlds. Since New Jersey had no governor's mansion, Wilson continued to live in Princeton, commuting to Trenton by car, while Tumulty commuted between Trenton and Jersey City by rail. He found that, even when he was at home, most evenings were taken up by a variety of political obligations. Occasionally Tumulty traveled to Princeton to see the governor, and on these trips he became friendly with Ellen and her three daughters. They were fascinated by Woodrow's young assistant, who was so charming and energetic, and who opened a window into the workings of New Jersey politics. Tumulty had never known people like the Wilsons, with their culture and idealism and immersion in a rarefied university life. Despite the differences in age and social position, the relationship between Tumulty and Woodrow and Ellen became personal as well as political. The young secretary developed a deep loyalty to the governor and his family.[7]

As Wilson's presidential boom mounted in 1911, Tumulty stayed in Trenton and concentrated on New Jersey affairs, since he had to be certain that the governor would win the New Jersey primary. Through the skillful use of patronage—in which he had to maintain a delicate balance between reform and machine factions—Tumulty built a new Wilson organization that won the New Jersey presidential primary in late May 1912.

Tumulty also visited the Wilson for President office in New York, where he screened the candidate's mail and gave shrewd advice on how to appease William Jennings Bryan. During the Baltimore convention, Tumulty stayed at Sea Girt—the governor's summer residence on the New Jersey shore—where he rarely slept as he received telephone reports on the twists and turns of the gathering. Along with William Gibbs McAdoo, he passionately objected—when Wilson's prospects looked bleak—to the withdrawal of his name. He was convinced that in the end Wilson would prevail. During the post-convention campaign, Tumulty became increasingly preoccupied with national affairs, accumulating valuable political information and winning over the press through his charm and good nature. With Wilson's victory in 1912, it was clear that the president-elect's secretary deserved some position in the new administration.[8]

Tumulty, who hoped that he would become the new president's secretary, aggressively sought the position. In mid-December 1912, he asked Colonel House, who was becoming Wilson's closest adviser, if he "thought his being a Catholic would be a bar to his appointment as Secretary to the President." House thought not, and in general he was impressed with Tumulty, whom he found "bright and quick." Three days later, House asked the president-elect if he had considered appointing Tumulty. "Yes," Wilson replied, "but the trouble with Tumulty is that he cannot see beyond Hudson County, his vision is so narrow." House did not dispute Tumulty's limitations but pointed out that "he had the political instinct which would be an essential asset," and warned that "in making a selection it was like walking in the country—one could always imagine that something better was beyond, but upon reaching the given point the view was still in the distance like the rainbow."[9]

While Tumulty, as one historian notes, was "pathetically eager to serve," his appointment faced considerable opposition. Anti-Catholics feared placing him so close to the president; others claimed that he was a typical Irish politician who lacked breeding and social grace. Wilson, however, was fond of Tumulty, and recognized his talents, devotion, and loyalty. On January 25, 1913, he offered him the position. Tumulty telegraphed Colonel House: "God bless you."[10]

On March 5, 1913, Tumulty took the oath of office and began a new phase of his life, one that was more than ever intertwined with that of the president. Tumulty often accompanied him to football games and baseball openings, and during the summer of 1913, when Wilson stayed in Washington to advance his legislative agenda, Tumulty and White House physician Cary Grayson moved into the White House to keep the lonely president company. The three men shared meals, automobile rides, and games of golf. As the president confided to Ellen, "Doctor Grayson and Tumulty are both living with me and we are a congenial and jolly company."[11]

Tumulty was a trim man of medium height, with (Eleanor Wilson remembered) "bright blue eyes in a round pink face." He was a skilled Irish politician, gregarious, volatile, and compassionate. His years of training in Jesuit schools had given him a strong moral code and a sharp sense of the injustices in American life. And he was well-educated. In college he had studied English literature, Latin, and rhetoric, and he had read widely in American history. Given Tumulty's unique talents and total devotion to Wilson, it is hardly surprising that he acquired more and more responsibility as the years passed. He tracked public opinion, gave political advice, helped draft speeches, supervised relations with the press, and ran the small executive office of the president. Tumulty controlled access to Wilson, seeking, if at all possible, to take care of problems himself rather than burden the president.[12]

Wilson was well aware of his dependence on his young assistant. He told the journalist Ida Tarbell that "when it is especially important that I be understood, I try . . . [a speech] on Tumulty, who has a very extraordinary appreciation of how a thing will 'get over the footlights.' He is the most valuable audience I have." Tumulty spent hours reading newspapers and journals and analyzing public opinion. He pasted clippings on long sheets of yellow paper and each evening took his "Yellow Journal" home. As Wilson remarked, "Tumulty . . . reads everything."[13]

Tumulty was fond of people, understood newspapermen, and, in general, with his Irish good humor and generosity, added warmth to the atmosphere of the White House and helped to compensate for the president's aloofness. For the next eight years he would be at Wilson's side. Tumulty was also deeply involved in the distribution of patronage, trying to end feuds among leading Democrats and pursuing a middle road between reformers and professional politicians. Tumulty's willingness, however, to work with Democratic bosses in key states, such as New York and Illinois, embittered progressives within the administration. His critics claimed that he was too willing to compromise with reactionary elements and was sometimes rash and overly emotional in his approach to public issues. They also resented his attempts to control access to the president. When House returned to Boston in mid-July 1913 after a trip to Europe, he found that McAdoo and Grayson were upset by Tumulty's behavior, and by the end of the year House complained that "Tumulty talks too much. The President desired a man of refinement and discretion and of broad vision. He has instead just the opposite and almost wholly at my instance. . . . Tumulty has good sense, but it is becoming warped by his growing egotism and jealousy concerning everyone near the President." In January 1914, during a trip to Washington, House was pleased to learn from Grayson that "there seems to be enough trouble brewing for Tumulty to drown him." House, who was the most manipulative of the president's advisers, now began to plot Tumulty's downfall. But he concealed his animosity, working behind the scenes while he maintained a facade of cordial relations with the president's secretary.[14]

Throughout 1914, House's dissatisfaction with Tumulty had grown. One of his protégés reported that he heard "complaints and denunciation" of the "scrubby Irishman" and "gutter snipe" from all sides, while House found that he differed with Tumulty over patronage in New York City (Tumulty wanted to work with Tammany Hall) and also over the direction of the administration's domestic policies (Tumulty wanted the president to reassure businessmen rather than push ahead with more reform legislation). On May 11, during one of his trips to Washington, House tried to measure Wilson's devotion to his secretary and discovered that the president "seemed upset over the idea of losing Tumulty."[15]

While House schemed to remove him, Tumulty worked to prepare for the fall congressional campaign, suggesting texts for the president's speeches and emphasizing Democratic accomplishments at home and abroad. Like Wilson, he was stunned and heartbroken by Ellen's death on August 6, and he accompanied Woodrow, his three daughters, and Ellen's brother Stockton Axson on the special train that carried her body from Washington to Rome, Georgia. Tumulty had been close to Ellen, with whom, Eleanor McAdoo remembered, "he discussed everything . . . at length."[16]

The outbreak of World War I in early August 1914 presented perplexing issues both for the president and his young secretary. Tumulty wanted to keep the nation aloof from the struggle, but he also wanted to protect America's honor and prosperity and, from the start, hoped for an Allied victory. After the German U-boat decree in early February 1915, as incidents accumulated in the North Atlantic (especially with the sinking of the *Lusitania* on May 7, 1915), Tumulty realized that there was a real possibility that the nation would be drawn into the war. He believed that the American people had doubts about the president's leadership in diplomatic and military affairs, and he knew that in the 1916 presidential election Republicans would attack the administration's national defense policies. On November 19, Tumulty warned Wilson that the people believed that the administration was "lacking in *aggressive assertiveness*," and he approved of the president's decision, on January 18, 1916, to go to the country, make a plea for reasonable preparedness, and break the impasse in Congress over defense spending. From January 27 to February 4, Wilson traveled throughout the Midwest, calling for increases in the army and navy so that the United States could remain at peace and play its part in "the redemption of the affairs of mankind." Tumulty accompanied Wilson on his speaking tour, and, with the passage of legislation in August 1916 increasing the size of the army and navy, felt that the president had removed a major political liability.[17]

After Ellen's death, Tumulty failed to realize how badly the president needed to have a woman at his side. Given his conservative moral training, he was uneasy about the passionate relationship Woodrow began with Edith Galt in March 1915. He also worried about the political repercussions of an early remarriage, urging Wilson to postpone a wedding until after the November 1916 elections.

Tumulty also misjudged Edith, who was not inclined to share her love for Woodrow with another person. In the summer of 1915, Wilson had begun sending her a "big envelope" full of official documents and had tried to explain to her the roles of his different advisers. After dispatching a memorandum from Tumulty, he pointed out that it was "characteristic of the careful way in which, after reading all the papers he can get hold of and listening to everybody talk, he seeks to sum up for me his impressions. He has done me a great deal of service in that way. . . . I have *proved* Tumulty's loyalty: that will stand any test, the most acid; and where there is absolute loyalty one can dismiss fear. The only errors will be errors of judgment,—and who does not make them?" Wilson was, however, well aware of the social gap between Edith and himself and his secretary, or what Edith referred to as his "commonness." "You know," he explained, "that he [Tumulty] was not brought up as we were; you feel his lack of our breeding. . . . *But* the majority, the great majority of the people who come to the office are not of our kind. . . . Tumulty does understand them and know how to deal with them;—much better than I would, and I need the assistance of just such a man. . . . He tells me with almost unfailing accuracy what the man on the street,—the men on all streets,—are thinking." Moreover, Wilson was convinced that "a great diversity of talents is indispensable and the greatest possible variety of breeding" was essential to the success of the administration. He was certain that Edith, once she got to know Tumulty, would like him.[18]

In late September 1915, Colonel House, sensing that Wilson's impending remarriage would shift the dynamics within the president's inner circle of advisers, sought to force Tumulty's resignation. His secretary, House informed Wilson, "did not work well with other people . . . [and] that none of his [Wilson's] close friends had been able to work with Tumulty since he had held office, and it was a serious handicap to the Administration." Nor, House persisted, could the garrulous Tumulty keep information confidential. The president, however, was noncommittal about his secretary's fate, and House's efforts to force Tumulty out of the administration failed.[19]

By the early months of 1916, Tumulty was weary, worn down by battles over neutrality and preparedness and by struggles with House and his protégés over control of the Democratic National Committee. As the 1916 campaign approached, Tumulty's influence seemed to decline, and the president often looked elsewhere for advice. Moreover, House continued to scheme to replace him; in early April 1916, he and Edith agreed that they must eliminate Tumulty and Daniels from the president's inner circle of advisers. Both realized, however, that it would be impossible to remove either man until after the president's reelection.[20]

Wilson's triumph in November 1916 brought the possibility of shifts within the upper ranks of the administration. In mid-November, House traveled from New York to Washington, where he, Edith, and Woodrow discussed possible changes in the cabinet. At one point in their conversation Edith asked, "What about Tumulty?," and Woodrow, bowing to the relentless pressure of anti-Catholic spokesmen and the arguments of his wife and counselor, finally agreed to remove his longtime secretary and offer him another position. When Wilson asked for his resignation, however, Tumulty wrote him an anguished letter, claiming that "I had hoped with all my heart that I might remain in close association with you; that I might be permitted to continue as your Secretary, a position which gave me the fullest opportunity to serve you and the country. To think of leaving you at this time when the fruits of our long fight have been realized wounds me more deeply than I can tell you. . . . You cannot know what this means to me and to mine. I am grateful for having been associated so closely with so great a man; I am heart-sick that the end should be like this." When the influential journalist David Lawrence learned of the dismissal, he confronted the president, and in a forty-five-minute conversation pointed out that no one would understand why Tumulty, given all that he had accomplished, was resigning. Wilson relented and decided to let Tumulty stay, but the bond between the two men had been weakened; Wilson would never fully trust Tumulty again, and it is difficult to imagine that Tumulty ever fully recovered from the president's loss of faith in him.[21]

At the end of January 1917, the American government learned that Germany would begin unrestricted U-boat warfare on February 1. Tumulty believed that the conflict was "a struggle between democracy and feudalism," between the rights of individuals and the "'hateful Kultur'" that Germany threatened to spread throughout the world. He watched impatiently as the president edged toward war in February and March and was relieved when, on April 2, he heard Wilson ask a joint session of Congress for a declaration of war.[22]

America's entry into the conflict changed the routines of many officials in Washington. Tumulty felt the loss of old friends and worked longer hours dealing with what seemed an endless stream of callers at the White House. "I am," he told the president, "overwhelmed here every day." He disliked the administration's censorship measures, worried that the "general mass of people" were indifferent to the war, and urged the president to speak out in a way that would arouse the nation. He wanted the government to commit itself fully to the struggle, sending troops, financial aid, and whatever else was necessary "to compel Germany to sue for peace."[23]

Organizing the American war effort absorbed the energies of many of the leaders of the administration, forcing them to curtail their political activities. Tumulty now paid more attention to domestic politics than anyone else, and it fell to him to outline a platform for the party to run on in the fall of 1918. In January, he produced a long memorandum on "The Revolt of the Underdog," arguing that "the mass of the people, underfed and dissatisfied, are clamoring for a fuller recognition of their rights to life and liberty." Tumulty wanted the party to move beyond the New Freedom, but he had trouble defining—without any help from the president—how it should do so.[24]

Tumulty realized that the political situation was ominous. The Republican Party was reunited, and its leaders were attacking the administration's war record and exploiting war weariness and various sectional issues. In June 1918, Tumulty had a long conversation with Wilson in which he gave him a plan for the fall congressional campaign and urged him to write a public letter calling for the return of a Democratic Congress. Tumulty accepted all of Wilson's ideas about the peace settlement and the creation of a League of Nations, but by the fall of 1918 he shared the hatred of many Americans for Germany and worried that Wilson's efforts to end the war would lead to political defeat in November. He was pleased when the president stiffened his demands on Germany and also pleased when, on October 25, Wilson asked the American people to avoid "a repudiation of my leadership" and to return a Democratic majority to the House and Senate on November 5. The Republican triumph, however, did not discourage Tumulty, who now planned to reinvigorate the Democratic Party and have Wilson stump the country before presidential elections in 1920.[25]

Once the president decided to lead the American delegation to the Paris Peace Conference, Tumulty knew that he would have to stay in Washington. Or as he wrote to Wilson, "I am sure that I can render better service by staying on the job here in this country and keeping you in touch with affairs here." As the peace conference progressed, Tumulty worried about Wilson's poor relations with the press and his failure to explain to the American people the reasons for all of the delays and compromises. He tried to pull Wilson back from his preoccupation with diplomacy and world order, warning at the end of January 1919 that the administration needed an aggressive program of "remedial action" to deal with economic uncertainty in America. "Washington," he explained, "is now dead and down—entirely relaxed. It should be galvanized into rushing action. . . . In short, my idea is that the President ought to get on the job in these matters with both feet, as soon as possible." Tumulty failed to appreciate, however, the difficulties of the president's position in Paris or to realize that the deliberations there had strained his health to the breaking point.[26]

In early June 1919, Tumulty warned Wilson that "there is a depression in our ranks and a feeling that our prospects for 1920 are not bright." The president's absence, he realized, was a tremendous handicap, since he could not discipline Democrats in the Congress or in the administration or, with McAdoo gone, prevent the cabinet from drifting. Tumulty realized that Republicans would oppose the peace treaty and that they would make reservation to it their "final line of defense." He was confident, however, that with the president's return on July 8 the tide would turn in his favor. He argued that his chief, "is the one man in the world . . . whose leadership can unite the liberal forces of the world in favor of a great program of international and domestic reconstruction."[27]

Tumulty's loyalty, and his mastery of domestic politics, helped restore some of the influence he had lost in 1915 and 1916. By the time Wilson returned to the United States, Tumulty realized that the peace treaty would only win Senate approval if reservations were attached. He urged the president to take the initiative and to propose reservations of his own, but Wilson, no longer the vibrant leader of earlier years, delayed, and as the summer progressed the administration lost ground in the treaty fight. In early August, Tumulty explained that "there can be no approach to normal conditions in this country until the treaty of peace is out of the way."[28]

Tumulty had long advocated a speaking tour, convinced that a trip through the Midwest and West would strengthen the Democratic Party and arouse the people's enthusiasm for Wilson's leadership. He planned the tour carefully, outlining a trip that would include forty speeches in twenty-one days. Wilson, who viewed the trip as a sacred mission, rejected itineraries that provided for a week of rest in the Grand Canyon. Shortly before the president left on September 3, Tumulty "made a comparison between the man, Woodrow Wilson, who now stood before me and the man I had met many years before in New Jersey. In those days he was a vigorous, agile, slender man, active and alert, his hair but slightly streaked with grey. Now . . . he was an old man, grown grayer and grayer, but grimmer and grimmer in his determination, like an old warrior, to fight to the end."[29]

For twenty-one days Wilson and his entourage, as one historian writes, lived as "a small closely confined group, plagued by dust and cinders, finding little relief in the commercial hotels and amidst the noisy crowds at their places of call." Tumulty sought, with the help of Grayson, to lighten the mood in the presidential car, entertaining Edith and Woodrow every evening with his Irish wit. Initially the crowds seemed subdued, but as the train moved west, the tour gathered momentum and began to turn into the mass tribute to Wilson and his vision of peace that Tumulty had hoped for. And Tumulty also began to send the president memoranda for his speeches, suggestions that he relied on more and more.[30]

When Wilson's health collapsed on September 25 near Pueblo, Colorado, Grayson warned the president early the next morning that a continuation of his trip "might prove fateful." With Tumulty's help, he finally convinced him to call off the tour. "I don't seem to realize it," Wilson confided to his longtime secretary, "but I seem to have gone to pieces. The Doctor is right. I am not in condition to go on. I have never been in a condition like this, and I just feel as if I am going to pieces."[31]

On September 28, the president's train reached Washington, and three days later, on the morning of October 2, Wilson suffered a stroke that paralyzed the left side of his body. When Secretary of State Robert Lansing learned from Grayson that the president's condition was serious, he went to the White House and asked Tumulty what was wrong. Tumulty "put his right hand on his left shoulder and drew it down along his left side," implying that Wilson had suffered a stroke and was partly paralyzed. For nearly an hour Lansing, Tumulty, and Grayson conferred about what to do. Lansing raised the possibility of Vice President Thomas R. Marshall taking over, but who should certify the president's disability? In a vivid, emotional account in his memoir, Tumulty remembered telling the secretary of state, "You may rest assured that while Woodrow Wilson is lying in the White House on the broad of his back I will not be a party to ousting him. He has been too kind, too loyal, and too wonderful to me to receive such treatment at my hands." Neither Tumulty nor Grayson would acknowledge the president's disability, and after an inconclusive cabinet discussion on October 6, the issue was dropped.[32]

When Edith realized the seriousness of Woodrow's condition, she took charge. She discouraged any talk of his resigning from office, insisted on concealing the severity of his illness from the public, and assumed a major role, with the help of Tumulty and Grayson, in the workings of the government. Edith dominated the triumvirate that now managed affairs of state, controlling access to her husband and not even allowing Tumulty to see him until mid-November. For October and most of November, only Edith decided what issues would be brought to Woodrow's attention, while Tumulty and Grayson issued bulletins from the White House that were vague and optimistic. Tumulty understood the need for concessions if the peace treaty was to be approved by the Senate, but he would not challenge the president, who dominated Democratic strategy in the treaty fight. On November 19, the treaty was defeated, first with and then without the Lodge reservations. Tumulty was shocked; it was the worst defeat of his political career and shattered all of his hopes about rebuilding the Democratic Party and achieving a Wilsonian peace.[33]

By early December, the president's condition had improved, and Tumulty saw him more often. On December 28, he tried to lift his spirits, writing on his sixty-third birthday that "the clouds are going to pass and the memory of your work will stand as an everlasting monument to liberalism and the highest ideals of Christianity." But he confided to Josephus Daniels that "if he [Wilson] had [died] when [he] brought the treaty home it would have let him loom larger in history." Tumulty tried to convince Wilson to become involved in negotiations over reservations, explaining to Edith on January 15, 1920, that the "psychological moment" had been reached when the president must put forward his own interpretation of the treaty (Tumulty enclosed the draft of a letter to Senator Gilbert Hitchcock outlining acceptable terms.)But Wilson never responded to Tumulty's proposal; he was still too ill to deal with the contents of the letter, and neither the efforts of his wife or his physician could move him toward a compromise.[34]

On February 27, 1920, Tumulty wrote to the president that Democratic forces in the Senate "are rapidly disintegrating" and that "the ordinary man on the street is for ratification even with the Lodge reservations." But Wilson ignored this warning, and on March 19, the treaty with the Lodge reservations attached suffered a narrow defeat. The treaty debate was over; Tumulty's attention now turned to the forthcoming presidential campaign.[35]

Since late March, Tumulty had urged Wilson to announce that he would not seek a third term. The president, however, had no intention of doing so. He believed that if the Democratic convention deadlocked, the delegates might turn to him as "someone to lead them out of the wilderness," and he wanted the fall campaign to be a referendum on the peace treaty. Wilson had nothing to say about a wide range of pressing domestic issues. At the San Francisco convention, despite an emotional outpouring for the president, most delegates were convinced that he was not fit to run. And party insiders—including Tumulty—intervened to prevent his name from being placed in nomination. On July 6, on the forty-fourth ballot, Democratic delegates in San Francisco nominated Governor James M. Cox of Ohio. Tumulty worked hard for Cox, but the party was divided and demoralized, and Tumulty soon discovered that Cox's campaign managers were incompetent. He tried, without success, to persuade Wilson to intervene, but he would not directly answer Republican critics of his administration. On November 1, Tumulty, aware that the tide had turned against Cox, wrote to Edith to reassure her that "we are associated with the greatest force for good in the world. We know this in our very souls and no mere results of tomorrow can alter or change this in the least." As the scale of the Republican triumph became apparent, Tumulty remarked that "it wasn't a landslide. It was an earthquake."[36]

The winter of 1920–21 was a gloomy one in the White House, as Wilson and his loyal retainers absorbed the magnitude of their defeat and the collapse of their dreams. On March 3, 1921, Tumulty wrote his last letter from his West Wing office to his brother Philip, confiding that "I have lived in the presence of a great man and I have tried hard to serve him." The next day, after Wilson drove to the Capitol and participated in the inaugural ceremony, Woodrow and Edith, accompanied by Grayson, Tumulty, and a valet, drove to their new home at 2340 S Street. The Wilson era was over.[37]

In the spring of 1921, Tumulty, who was only forty-two and still had a large family to support, started a law practice in Washington. While he worked long hours, he remained fascinated with national politics and remained loyal to the Democratic Party and to Wilson's legacy. In November 1921, he published a hastily written, hagiographic memoir (one that Wilson did not like), but there was no role for Tumulty at S Street. Edith's brother, Randolph Bolling, became the retired president's secretary, and a variety of prominent Democrats stopped by for political conversations. Edith kept Tumulty at a distance, and Woodrow no longer took his longtime adviser into his confidence.[38]

No doubt his exclusion from the president's inner circle of advisers upset Tumulty, who sought to find some way to regain the confidence of the man who was still his idol. On April 5, 1922, Tumulty wrote to Wilson, asking him to provide a brief message for the Democrats' Jefferson Day banquet in New York. Wilson refused to do so, and Tumulty, before leaving for New York, visited his mentor and somehow went away with the impression that he would not object to an innocuous greeting. Days later newspapers reported on the speech given by Cox and a message from the ex-president that, in fact, Tumulty had composed. "My husband," Edith remembered, "was thunderstruck" by the newspaper articles; he now demanded an explanation from his former secretary. Tumulty's efforts to explain his behavior, as one historian remarks, only "dug a deeper hole for himself." He had, after all, fabricated Wilson's message and betrayed his trust. In the end, he could only prostrate himself, writing to Wilson that "I will never engage in a controversy with you. No slight bruise nor public rebuke from you can in any way lessen my devotion to and affection for you. . . . If you decide that this message of greeting which I delivered has embarrassed you in any way and that I must be rebuked, I shall not complain." After the incident was over, Wilson remarked that "if Tumulty had been my son and had acted as he did, I would have done the same thing." Tumulty was now banished, like Jack Hibben years before. Wilson never saw him again, although he never questioned his loyalty or forgot his service. Aware of Tumulty's political gifts, in October 1923, he encouraged Democratic leaders in New Jersey to support him for the US Senate.[39]

In early February 1924, as Wilson's death neared, Tumulty stopped at S Street, determined to have one last encounter with his old chief. Grayson agreed to let him do so, but Wilson was sleeping and soon slipped into unconsciousness and died on February 3, 1924. Edith did not invite Tumulty to the small service at S Street, but McAdoo arranged for him to attend. Tumulty left no record of the anguish he must have felt over his estrangement from Wilson, but the day after his death he issued a statement claiming that "his spirit still lives—the spirit that tried to wipe away the tears of the world, the spirit of justice, humanity, and holy peace."[40]

After Tumulty's departure from the White House, his law practice thrived, and he collected a wide range of friends, hosting a luncheon table at the Shoreham Hotel and welcoming congressmen to his office in late afternoon gatherings. During the 1920s, he sided with the conservative wing of the Democratic Party, in 1924 and 1928 supporting the presidential campaigns of New York Governor Al Smith. Even in 1932, he preferred either Smith or Texas congressman John Nance Garner for the Democratic nomination. When the Democrats chose Franklin D. Roosevelt at their Chicago convention, Tumulty observed that "the mountain moved and brought forth a mouse, and the tragedy of the whole thing is that even he will win."[41]

Despite his reservations, Tumulty supported FDR in 1932 and 1936, but, like most old Wilsonians, he never really understood the New Deal. He approved of some of FDR's social reforms but disliked the paternalistic aspects of the New Deal and felt that it had led to a dangerous expansion of the federal government. In October 1936, he observed in a speech that "personally, being an individualist, I do not like regimentation or planned economy any more than you do." Only his strong ties to the Democratic

Party and his memory of Wilson kept him from a break with the Roose-velt administration.[42]

As the years passed, many of Tumulty's recollections of the Wilson years faded, but his memories of the western tour remained vivid, and more and more he focused on Wilson the peacemaker and on "his indomitable courage." Tumulty was fortunate to live long enough to see a part of Wilson's vision, the creation of the United Nations, fulfilled before his death on April 8, 1954, at the age of seventy-four.[43]

Colonel House, his granddaughter Louise, and Wilson, relaxing at Roslyn, Long Island, June 1915. House became virtually a member of Wilson's family, staying in the White House during his many trips to Washington and becoming, until Woodrow met Edith, the most important of his advisers. Courtesy of the author.

CHAPTER SIX

Colonel Edward M. House

"No man of his time touched so deeply the conscience and
aspirations of mankind"

On November 24, 1911, Colonel Edward M. House, a Texas political operator, met with Woodrow Wilson at the Gotham Hotel in New York. House
recorded that "we talked as hard as we could for an hour and a half and he
left reluctantly and only because he had an engagement and made as early
a date to meet again as he could." House noted that Wilson was not "the
biggest man I have ever met but he is one of the pleasantest and I would
rather play with him than any prospective candidate I have seen." After
over a decade of waiting for "the man and the opportunity," House had
finally found a presidential candidate he believed he could influence and
who seemed likely to win the Democratic nomination.[1]

Five days later, the two men met again at the Gotham Hotel. House
remembered that "our second meeting was even more delightful. We
dined alone at the Gotham and talked together for hours. We talked about
everything, I believe, and this time we could go into details and analyze
our thoughts. It was remarkable. We found ourselves in agreement upon
practically every one of the issues of the day. I never met a man whose
thought ran so identically with mine." A few years later, House recorded
that "a few weeks after we met and after we had exchanged confidences
which men usually do not exchange except after years of friendship I asked
him if he realized that we had only known one another for so short a time.

He replied 'My dear friend, we have known one another always.' And I think this is true."[2]

Edward Mandell House was born on July 26, 1858, the last of eight children. His father, Thomas William, had left England for America and had arrived at the raw, small town of Houston in late 1837 or early 1838. He proved to be a resourceful entrepreneur, rapidly expanding his various businesses and becoming by the outbreak of the Civil War a leading merchant and wealthy citizen. His mother, Mary Elizabeth Shearn, died when Edward was only eleven; he did not retain any vivid memories of her. His father was the dominant parent, one who sought to mold the careers of his children and look after their education.

Edward came of age during the Civil War and Reconstruction, and remembered vividly the excitement of wartime Galveston, where his father's ships sought to outrun the Union blockade. After the war, T. W. House bought a large sugar plantation near Houston. Edward adored the time he spent there, riding through the fields filled with corn, cotton, and sugar cane, and sometimes moving beyond his family's land to the "beautiful but limitless prairies to the west of Houston." As I have written, he had a privileged youth, "full . . . of big skies, distant horizons, and a sense of the limitless possibilities of life."[3]

Edward also recalled the violent atmosphere of post–Civil War Texas. He rode and shot as early as he could remember and was fascinated with the local gunfighters and their code of honor. In 1874, his father, concerned about his unruly children, decided to send Edward to a primitive boarding school in Virginia. Two years later he moved to Hopkins Grammar School in New Haven, Connecticut. He proved to be an indifferent student, more interested in the hotly contested presidential election of 1876 than in his studies. In the fall of 1877, he entered Cornell University, where his days drifted pleasantly by, filled with casual reading, pranks on his fraternity brothers, and hunting in the surrounding countryside. In the autumn of 1879, T. W. House became seriously ill and Edward returned to Houston to help look after him. For three months he sat with his father every other night. "My affection for him was such," he remembered, "that

I wanted to care for him to the limits of my strength." But efforts to cure the great merchant failed, and on January 17, 1880, he died. His son Edward was twenty-one.[4] The death of T. W. House was a tremendous blow to Edward. He had idolized his father, who "seemed to me then [in 1880], as he seems to me now [in 1916], among the ablest men I have ever known. He was of that intrepid band that made Texas what she is today."[5]

Edward had no taste for a business career, but in the spring of 1880, his brother T. W. Jr. asked him to return to Houston and help with the management of his father's estate. Edward's task was to inspect the family's lands scattered throughout Texas, and he especially relished trips to the large family ranch near the Rio Grande. Those trips, he recalled, were "filled with a certain exhilarating joy. The reckless freedom of the life, the campfires at night, sleeping under the skies, the soft dry air, the awakening at dawn, the riding with a free rein over the vast, undulating flower strewn prairies intoxicated the senses and stimulated the imagination. In the silent watches of the night and in the quieter moments of the day, I dreamed great dreams—many of which have since come true."[6]

In early 1881, House met Loulie Hunter, the daughter of a prosperous plantation owner, a woman of charm and beauty who was a fitting partner for the youngest son of one of the leading families of Texas. On August 4, 1881, Edward and Loulie were married, and after their wedding the young couple left on a year-long grand tour of Europe, where their first child was born. In the summer of 1882, the House family returned to Houston; three years later Edward decided to move to Austin, the state capital, a city with a mild climate at the edge of the Hill Country of central Texas. He was only twenty-eight, a slight, intense man, with prominent cheekbones, a recessive chin, a thick, closely cropped mustache, and a black, already receding hairline. Edward and Loulie soon assumed a prominent place in the social life of the capital, and in 1892 they moved into a new home, designed by a New York architect, which became one of the great mansions of Austin. He also hired Frances B. Denton, called Fanny, as his personal secretary. She gradually became Edward's confidante as well as virtually a member of the family and would serve House loyally until his death in 1938.[7]

During his early years in Austin, Edward was absorbed in his family, supervising the construction of his new home, and pursuing his varied business activities. Inevitably, however, he met the leading political figures of Texas and was drawn into the political ferment of the capital city. He admired the colorful, dynamic governor, James Stephen Hogg, who had swept into office in 1890 on a wave of discontent. Hogg pushed a series of reform measures through the legislature, but in 1892, both conservative Democrats and angry Populists contested his reelection. Drawn to Hogg's vivid personality and intrigued by the challenges of the campaign, House agreed to manage the governor's reelection effort. Hogg prevailed with a plurality of the vote, but it was, House remembered, "a bitter fight and the wounds lasted many years."[8]

Hogg's reelection brought a new role for House. The governor, in recognition of House's value as a political associate, commissioned him a lieutenant colonel on his staff, and gradually the press and others began to refer to "Colonel House" rather than "Ed House." House advised on questions of patronage and served as a middleman between Hogg and various people and groups. While the two men became close, House was the junior partner in the relationship; during Hogg's second term he served his political apprenticeship, learning more about the political diversity and peculiarities of the state.

In 1894, a now united Democratic Party faced a serious Populist challenge, and House agreed to manage the campaign of Charles Allen Culberson, who had served as Hogg's attorney general. House led a desperate Democratic organization that was willing to use bribery, intimidation, and ballot-box-stuffing to retain its hold on the reins of power. Culberson's victory was a triumph for a rejuvenated Texas Democratic Party and for House, the manager of his campaign. Although only thirty-six, he was now widely recognized as the mastermind of Culberson's victory and as a powerful force in Texas politics.[9]

As Culberson settled into his new office, House seemed to be everywhere, helping with plans for the inaugural ball and dealing with the nettlesome question of patronage. "I went to his office at the Capitol," House recalled, "nearly each day, went over his mail with him and sometimes continued my work there until nightfall." He relished the power that he now possessed. Hogg had been a major force in Texas politics prior to his association with House; in contrast, House played a key role in elevating Culberson to the governorship and soon became the dominant partner in the relationship.[10]

Culberson dealt with the public side of politics, while House thrived on all the private wheeling and dealing. Both had supported Hogg's reform legislation, but neither had any vision of moving beyond it, and both were eager to avoid divisive national issues. Most of all, Culberson and House were determined to maintain their hold on the governorship.

House gradually assembled a core of close political associates, a group that he termed "our crowd." These men combined energy and intelligence with a fascination with the machinery of politics. They conferred with House often and handled most of the innumerable details of political organization and campaigning. Several moved through the shadowy world of Texas politics where the struggle for the African American and Mexican American vote took place. All looked to House for guidance and inspiration and formed lasting bonds of friendship with him.

From the start of his political career, House avoided the limelight, leaving public honors and offices to others. During the twelve years he was active in Texas politics—1892–1904—he avoided most state conventions. His refusal to run for public office gave the appearance of selflessness, of being above the petty bickering and ambitions of others, and also kept him out of the eye of the political storm and allowed him to avoid many of the demands made on public officials. "Keep yourself as much in the background as possible," he advised one protégé, "and let everybody do the talking excepting yourself. Nothing ever kills a man's influence so quickly as to be too much in evidence."[11]

Operating largely behind the scenes, House developed the gifts for intrigue and manipulation that had emerged when he was a student at Cornell. He sought to avoid direct clashes or open antagonism, concealing his own position by working through others and encouraging those he opposed or disliked to believe that he was their true friend. He understood the personal nature of Texas politics and the need to cement his political alliances with patronage. House had no illusions about the bonds of loyalty—he knew that the ability to reward the faithful was a key element of his political power.[12]

As House managed "our crowd," changes took place in the rhythms of his personal life. By the late 1880s, the House family had begun to spend a portion of each summer on the East Coast. Gradually Edward, Loulie, and their two daughters settled into a pattern of visits to New York City and long vacations on Boston's North Shore. Along a few miles of rocky coastline the elite of Boston summered, and there House gained relief from the heat of Texas and from the demands of politics, as well as the opportunity to mingle with upper-class Bostonians. Slowly the lure of the North Shore pulled House away from Texas and the demands of his political career there.[13]

House managed Culberson's reelection campaign in 1896, holding off another determined challenge of the Populist Party. Two years later—when Culberson left the governorship for the United States Senate—House and his associates backed Congressman Joseph D. Sayers for the governorship. Sayers won easily in 1898, and his reelection was never in doubt. Well before then, however, House and his associates had begun to ponder the governor's successor in 1902. Inevitably House's name came to the forefront. His continuing triumphs in gubernatorial campaigns, along with the intense loyalty of his friends, created mounting pressure on him to enter the race. One businessman indicated the depth of this support when he wrote: "I have not taken off my coat in a political contest since I was 22 years old. But if this thing comes to pass [House running for governor], coat, shirt & all goes off and I stand stripped, greased, ready and eager for the fight."[14]

Gradually House sorted through his ambitions, and by 1900 he seems to have established his priorities and resolved on a course. House decided to remain the leader of a faction, a behind-the-scenes wire-puller, although he continued to console himself with the thought that he could hold public office if only he desired to do so. But the price was too high; official responsibilities would alter the comfortable rhythms of his life and pull him back to Texas, with all its dense heat and political strife, at the very time he was enjoying society in New York and Boston. House also feared the physical and psychological toll of public service, and the poor health he experienced in 1898 and 1899 only strengthened his determination to continue his less stressful role of confidential adviser. He also knew, however, that he could not dominate Texas governors forever.[15]

In the years after the turn of the century—what House termed his "twilight years"—he established a migratory rhythm that took him away from Texas for all but four or five months of the year. He thought of transferring his political skills from the state to the national level, but knew that he could not draw close to William Jennings Bryan, who won the Democratic presidential nomination in 1896, 1900, and 1908. Bryan was too set in his ways and too emotionally self-sufficient; he had no need for an adviser such as House. Moreover, the early years of the twentieth century were an era of Republican supremacy. During the summer of 1908, House, who was traveling in Europe, watched from afar still another Democratic defeat. As a youth he had dreamed great dreams, but despite all of his achievements in Texas, the reality fell far short of his hopes. At the age of fifty, his career in Texas politics had come to an end, while a career in national politics seemed unlikely to replace it. Neither the pursuit of more wealth or European tours allowed House to escape from the disparity between what he had achieved and what he had dreamed of becoming.[16]

By 1910, Texas politics had become a sideshow for House, as he searched for a promising Democratic presidential candidate. In the spring and summer of 1911, House quietly watched Wilson's drive for the presidency gain momentum. In mid-September, House returned to New York and picked up the threads of the campaign. In October, he met the two leaders of the Wilson for President movement, William F. McCombs and William Gibbs McAdoo, and undertook a variety of political chores. After meeting Wilson on November 24, he was convinced that he finally had "both the man and the opportunity." During the fall he saw Wilson often, conferring with him in New York or talking on the phone when the candidate was in Princeton. House confided to his brother-in-law that "my relations with

him are closer than anyone knows. In writing to me he signs himself sometimes 'Gratefully yours' and other times 'Affectionately yours' and I believe that he feels it." House did not record his feelings on Election Day,
but Wilson's victory in early November was the culmination of years of
waiting and dreaming.[17]

In the fall of 1912, as the presidential campaign intensified, House had
begun to consult with his political allies and to think about the composition of a Democratic administration. On December 18, two days after
Wilson returned from a vacation in Bermuda, the two men lunched at
House's apartment in New York, where they deliberated over a variety of
key positions. Although he did not know him well, House supported Tumulty's appointment as the president's secretary. He knew McAdoo much
better, for during the campaign the two men had engaged in long talks
about the nation's social problems. House became McAdoo's promoter, in
part because he shared his ideals about social justice, in part because he
shrewdly recognized that McAdoo needed him, that House could play an
essential role in helping him to achieve his tremendous ambitions.

As the process of choosing the cabinet dragged on, McAdoo visited
House, or talked with him on the telephone, nearly every day, seeking advice and reassurance. McAdoo realized the one-sidedness of their friendship, observing to House that "I tell you everything I know and you never
tell me anything." House continued to advise patience and restraint, writing that "the more I see of McAdoo the better I like him. He is a splendid
fellow, whole-souled and generous without a tinge of envy and, with it all,
he is honest and progressive. His thoughts are in line with my own." Mc-
Adoo's ordeal lasted until early February 1913, when Wilson finally offered
him the position that he coveted: secretary of the treasury.[18]

While House promoted McAdoo and Tumulty, he also tried, unsuccessfully, to keep Josephus Daniels out of the cabinet. Most of all, however,
he sought to be of service to Wilson, controlling the flow of information
that the president-elect received about prospective cabinet appointees and
staying in close touch with him. Wilson wanted House to join his cabinet,
but his new adviser declined. He preferred to retain his autonomy, "being
a free lance . . . and to have a roving commission to serve wherever and

whenever possible." He had never been tied down by an official position and no doubt sensed that if he was to retain his influence with the president, a certain amount of distance was essential.[19]

On March 2, 1913, House left New York for Washington on what would become, over the next seven years, a familiar journey. Two days later he attended the inauguration, and on March 8, he had a "delightful talk" with the president about the cabinet. House was pleased with his effort and optimistic about his role as a confidential adviser. During the spring of 1913, he traveled to Washington six times to consult with the president, and on April 14, House recorded, Wilson "was generous and fine in his praise of my work. He declared he did not know how he could do without me and thanked me again and again for what I am trying to do." House worried that Wilson "seemed depressed" and tried to lift his spirits. The two men were at the beginning of what would become a long, complicated relationship.[20]

Wilson and House were an odd couple. The president was fifty-six, two years older than House, and was taller and heavier with a "long-jawed, animated face" and a "magnificent, resonant voice," while House (Raymond Fosdick, Wilson's Princeton student, who knew both men well, remembered), was "a small, frail, courteous, bright-eyed man with a gentle voice and winning manners." House liked the feminine atmosphere of the president's immediate family and the Wilsons' daily routine, with its emphasis on family meals and plain food. "The Wilsons," he noted approvingly after a dinner at the White House, "are living simply. We had fish, veal cutlets, rice, peas and potatoes, a simple lettuce salad with ice cream. It is a household in which there are no pretenses and where everything is in good taste." It was, in fact, a household similar to his own, although both of House's daughters were married, while all three of Wilson's daughters lived in the White House.[21]

House appeared at the right time, when the president was in need of advisers who could serve as buffers and was also in need of male companionship, since his long and close friendship with John Grier Hibben had ended in 1907. House had a combination of personal and political qualities that strongly appealed to Wilson. House's gentle, deferential manner, his lack of an assertive masculinity, put the president at ease. His own apparently fragile health elicited Wilson's sympathy and concern, and his frequent assurances of affection and esteem helped to satisfy one of Wilson's deepest needs. Moreover, House had impressive political skills that complemented those of the president. He was unusually gifted in drawing people out, estimating their abilities, and winning their confidence, without offering the same in return. His many years in Texas politics had made him a patient and crafty political infighter, experienced in dispensing patronage and in attempting to maintain harmony among the many factions within the Democratic Party. During the winter of 1912–13 House joined the circle of intimates around the president who were dedicated both to advancing his political career and to maintaining his physical health and emotional stability.

For a man of allegedly frail health, House had displayed a remarkable degree of stamina during the winter of 1912–13. He had worked long hours, beginning generally around 9:00 a.m. and often continuing late into the evening, collecting information, conferring with aspiring politicians, and advising the president. He made many trips to Washington, where his schedule was equally arduous, and missed his annual winter stay in Texas. Evenings at the theater were his only regular escape from the constant pressure of patronage and the assembling of the cabinet.

House realized, however, that the arrival of warm weather (he had developed heat phobia in his youth) would bring a change in his routine, and as early as April 23 he warned the president that "the weather will soon begin to grow warm which warns me that I am not to see much more of you until the Autumn." Breaking away for his annual trip to Europe would provide a much-needed rest and also deflate the publicity that was beginning to worry him, especially an article in *Collier's Weekly* titled "The President's Silent Partner." House did not know how much Wilson would tolerate and concluded that his growing fame was all the more reason to leave for Europe.[22]

When House left for Great Britain on May 21, he was "very tired and slept a large part of the time during the voyage. I did but little and thought not at all." His journey to London and Paris was in part a vacation, and in part an attempt to strengthen Anglo-American understanding and to lessen tension between Germany and Great Britain. The climax of his visit came on July 3, when he had a luncheon meeting with Foreign Secretary Sir Edward Grey. Five days later, House left Liverpool, and on July 16 he arrived in Boston. Fearful of the heat in New York and Boston, he traveled directly to his summer cottage at Beverly Cove, Massachusetts. He would not return to his apartment in New York until September 21 and would not see the president until he traveled to Washington in mid-October.[23]

During 1913, House, despite his long absence in Europe, followed closely the progress of the president's reform legislation. He supported tariff reduction and was especially concerned about the reform of the nation's banking system, working with Wilson to put together the Federal Reserve Act of December 1913. House had little interest, however, in the controversy that erupted in the spring of 1913 over the segregation of African Americans in federal bureaus and agencies. House had traditional southern, paternalistic attitudes toward African Americans; in *Philip Dru*, his novel of the future, he wrote that "we have placed his [the Black man's] feet upon firm ground, and are leading him with helping hands along the road of opportunity."[24]

In the unending struggle for preferment around the president, House had a unique position. He was both a close friend and a close adviser and, more than any of the others, could gain access to the president and influence his decisions. On his return from Europe, House received a warm welcome from the White House, and in early September Wilson wrote to him that "I am fairly longing to see you." The president eagerly awaited the arrival of cool weather for a reunion with his counselor. In return, House was effusive in his compliments, reassuring him that "it is a splendid future that I see before you and God grant you strength to carry all your noble undertakings to completion."[25]

When House was separated from the president, he received a steady flow of political gossip from various members of the administration. He had grown close to McAdoo, and watched with fascination McAdoo's emergence as the most forceful member of the cabinet. House and McAdoo often discussed personal and political matters, and after a mid-August visit from the secretary of the treasury, House concluded that McAdoo "has a fine imagination, indomitable courage, and a touch of genius"; he believed that McAdoo's energy, intellect, and progressive beliefs made him a man of destiny. And House appreciated his friend's emotional dependence, observing in late November, "He is as emotional as a woman. He said he would rather be with me than any man in the world, and he acts as if he meant it."[26]

Inevitably, however, House's intimacy with the president pulled him into controversies within his inner circle, particularly the growing tension between McAdoo and Tumulty. By the end of 1913, House had turned against Tumulty; he was determined, sooner or later, to remove the young secretary from his proximity to the president.[27]

As House grew closer to Wilson, he began to assess his strengths and weaknesses. He had no doubts about Wilson's intellectual gifts, but he complained (only in his diary) about his friend's reluctance to consult with his cabinet and with congressional leaders. House continued to serve as a kind of companion for the president. When he was in Washington, the two men ate meals together, went to the theater, and occasionally wandered through the White House, studying various objects. Wilson pressed House to conform to his routines, demanding that he sleep in the White House rather than at a friend's residence and lengthen his stays in Washington. House was virtually a member of the Wilson family, forming close personal ties with Ellen and with Wilson's three daughters and with members of his extended family. Wilson's cousin Helen Bones told House's wife, "When Uncle Woodrow and the Colonel are together the families feel the country is safe, and that nothing can happen."[28]

In March 1914, while House was in Washington, he learned that Ellen was ill and confined to her room. He also learned from White House physician Cary T. Grayson (who "tells me everything concerning the Presi-

dent in the most minute detail in order to get my advice" that Wilson's
medical problems were serious, that he might be suffering from "hardening of the arteries." Grayson told him that "in 1905 the President had an
almost complete breakdown at Princeton [in fact, it occurred in 1906] and
it was uncertain whether he could resume his duties." House must have
wondered how long his friend could survive the far greater stress of the
presidency.[29]

On May 16, 1914, House left for another diplomatic mission to Europe,
one that he called "the great adventure." He spoke to government leaders
in Berlin and London, and at the end of July, after his return to the United
States, he learned that Austria had declared war on Serbia at noon on July
28. As war erupted in Europe, House also learned of Ellen's death. "I never
dreamed," he wrote to his friend, "that Mrs. Wilson was so mortally ill and
her death leaves me unnerved and stunned. It only proves again how near
to us the Angel of Death hovers." Ellen's death intensified the desire of the
two men to end their long separation; in late August, House drove from
Boston's North Shore to Cornish, New Hampshire, for a reunion with his
friend. For two days the president read aloud, told "humorous stories"
about golf, and reminisced about his Princeton days. On the second afternoon, Wilson finally allowed his grief to break through the surface. As
always, House listened sympathetically, seeking to ease Wilson's sadness
and loneliness.[30]

In the fall of 1914, House could not avoid the question of whether the
president would run for a second term, a question that was complicated
by uncertainties about his health. Woodrow, still depressed by Ellen's
death, shared his doubts with his counselor, claiming that "if he knew he
would not have to stand for re-election two years from now, he would feel
a great load had been lifted from him." House, however, wanted Wilson to
head the ticket in 1916 and urged him to add to his fame through a foreign
policy that "would bring him world-wide recognition."[31]

Throughout November and December 1914, House kept in close touch
with the president, who leaned heavily on him for political advice and also
for companionship and emotional support. During these two months

House traveled to Washington five times, while Wilson visited him in New York twice. On November 4, when Edward and his wife Loulie arrived at the White House for a four-night stay, they found Wilson in a fragile emotional state. On their third evening together the two talked of "the trouble brewing between McAdoo and Tumulty," and House told the president that McAdoo thought Tumulty "too near the interests." Wilson, House recorded, "became flushed and excited and wanted to know if McAdoo had gone crazy." Visibly upset, the president went on to say that "he was broken in spirit by Mrs. Wilson's death, and was not fit to be President because he did not think straight any longer, and had no heart in the things he was doing." House tried, without success, to lift his friend's spirits before they went to bed.[32]

House wanted the president to make foreign policy the administration's highest priority and at the end of 1914 convinced him that he should undertake another mission to Europe to explore the prospects for American mediation of the conflict. On January 24, 1915, House traveled to Washington to consult one last time with the president before his departure. The next evening, as they said goodbye, House recorded the scene carefully for posterity: "The President's eyes were moist when he said his last words of farewell. He said: 'Your unselfish and intelligent friendship has meant much to me' and he expressed his gratitude again and again calling me his 'Most trusted friend.' He declared that I was the only one in all the world to whom he could open his entire mind. I asked if he remembered the first day we met, some three and a half years ago. He replied: 'Yes, but we had known one another always, and merely came in touch then, for our purposes and thoughts were as one.'"[33]

House arrived in London on February 6, and for nearly five weeks he consulted with leaders of the British government. He then traveled to Berlin and Paris for shorter stays, and in late April returned to London, where he planned to remain "indefinitely." He relished his life there, mingling with Britain's cultural, political, and social elite, and believed that a long residence in London would allow him to monitor the policies of the belligerent governments. But the sinking of the *Lusitania* on May 7 forced a change in his plans. Convinced that the diplomatic standoff between Germany and the United States could lead to American entry into the war, he informed the president that he could be of "better service" in Washington and on June 5 sailed from Liverpool.[34]

House reached Roslyn, Long Island (where his son-in-law had a summer home) on June 13. Although he had last seen the president on January 25, a few days before he left for Europe, he had no plans to travel to Washington, since he feared the heat in the capital and wanted to get in touch with "the feeling in America" before conferring with Wilson. The president, however, was eager to see his counselor, and decided to stop at Roslyn on his way to vacation with his family at Cornish. Before Wilson arrived, House learned that in late March, when House was in Berlin, Wilson had met Edith Bolling Galt, had quickly fallen in love, and less than two months after they had met asked her to marry him.

At some point during their talk at Roslyn, Wilson told House of his love for Edith and asked him if a remarriage "would lessen my influence with the American people." Fortunately, House had been forewarned of the president's romance and quickly approved his plans for remarriage. He had long been worried about Wilson's longevity and now felt "that his health demands it [remarriage].""I also feel," he recorded in his diary, "that Woodrow Wilson today is the greatest asset the world has. If he should die or become incapacitated, it is doubtful whether a right solution of the problems involved in this terrible conflict and its aftermath would be possible." House did, however, urge his friend to delay his marriage until the spring of 1916.[35]

Despite the brevity of their meeting at Roslyn, as the summer progressed Wilson and House felt that they were back in touch with one another. "But I need not explain anything to you," Wilson wrote on July 21. "You know as well as I do what my motives are, so soon as I form them." At the end of July, Cary Grayson appeared at House's summer cottage and for nearly two hours poured out intimate details of Wilson's personal life. Grayson was upset by "the President's infatuation with Mrs. Norman Galt.

It seems the President is wholly absorbed in this love affair and is neglecting practically everything else." House regretted that Wilson "had fallen in love at this time," and realized that "he will be criticized for not waiting longer after Mrs. Wilson's death." But he sympathized with the president's lack of privacy, noting in his diary that "there is someone to watch every turn and movement that he makes."[36]

Over the summer of 1915, as Woodrow and Edith spent weeks together at Cornish, their love deepened. House, who had not yet met Edith, had no way of knowing that she was neither as well-educated nor as tolerant as Ellen had been. Despite the president's efforts, Edith was not inclined to share her love for him with another person. After reading some of House's letters, she became skeptical of his value as an adviser. Or, as she wrote, "I know I am wrong but I can't help feeling he is not a very strong character. I suppose it is in comparison to you, for really every other man seems like a dwarf when I put them by you in my thoughts. I know what a comfort and staff Col. House is to you Precious One and that your judgment about him is correct, but he does look like a weak vessel and I think that he writes like one very often." Wilson responded to his "own Darling" with the fullest assessment of House that he ever composed:

> And, then, dear House. About him, again, you are no doubt partly right. You have too keen an insight and too discerning a judgment to be wholly wrong, even in a snap judgment of a man you do not know! House *has* a strong character,—if to be disinterested and unafraid and incorruptible is to be strong. He has a noble and lovely character, too, for he is capable of utter self-forgetfulness and loyalty and devotion. And he is wise. He can give prudent and far-seeing counsel. He can find out what many men, of diverse kinds, are thinking about, and how they can be made to work together for a common purpose. He wins the confidence of all sorts of men and wins it at once,—by deserving it. But you are right in thinking that intellectually he is not a great man. His mind is not of the first class. He is a counselor, not a statesman. . . . We cannot require of every man that he should be everything. You are going to love House some day,—if only because he loves me and would give, I believe, his life for me,—and because he loves the country and seeks its real benefit and glory. I'm not afraid of the ultimate impression he will make on you,—because I know you and your instinctive love and admiration for whatever is true and genuine. You must

remember, dear little critic, that sweetness and *power* do not often happen to-gether. You are apt to exact too much of others because of what you are yourself and mistakenly suppose it easy and common to be.[37]

On September 22, 1915, House arrived in the nation's capital, his first trip there since the end of January. He quickly discovered that many of the president's advisers—including McAdoo and Tumulty—were upset over his plans for an early remarriage. House was drawn into the center of the controversy, listening to Wilson as he explained his relationship with Mary Allen Hulbert and discussing with him the timing of the wedding an-nouncement. The two agreed on the middle of October for the announce-ment and for the wedding to follow before the end of the year. House be-lieved, as he wrote in his diary, that if Wilson "does not marry, and marry quickly, I believe he will go into a decline."[38]

On September 23, the president, relieved that the path of his remar-riage had finally been cleared, wrote to Edith, "I had a fine talk with House last night, which cleared things wonderfully. . . . He is really a wonderful counsellor. . . . I am sure that the first real conversation you have with him, about something definite and of the stuff of judgment, you will lose en-tirely your impression that he lacks strength. It is a quiet, serene strength, but it is great and real. I am impatient to have you know him." That same day Woodrow's new partner and his trusted adviser finally met at the White House. "She and I," House wrote in his diary, "became friends im-mediately," and they agreed to get together the next day for a private talk. On September 24, over late afternoon tea, Edith and Edward each sought to charm the other. Edith told him that Woodrow spoke of him with "af-fection" and had described their "first meeting and . . . the delight it was to find one whose mind ran parallel to his own upon public questions." House tried to captivate her with his vision of Wilson's future greatness, confiding that "if our plans carried true, the President would easily out-rank any American that had yet lived." House found Edith "delightful and full of humor" and was relieved "to think the President will have her to cheer him in his loneliness."[39]

Woodrow's romance had already begun to change the dynamics within

Woodrow, Edith, and Colonel House, October 1918. After the president's remarriage in December 1915, House discovered that Edith, who spent all of her time with Woodrow, was dismissive of most of his advisers and curious about affairs of state. Bettmann via Getty Images.

the president's inner circle of advisers. House was pleased to see that Tumulty's influence had lessened, but he was concerned about McAdoo's behavior. The secretary of the treasury's clumsy attempt to delay Wilson's remarriage had disturbed House, as did his quarrels with members of the new Federal Reserve Board. House had once been close to McAdoo, but since his marriage to Eleanor Wilson in May 1914 the two men had drifted apart. "McAdoo," House wrote, "had gotten pretty well from under my influence." In mid-December, three days before his father-in-law's wedding, House found McAdoo "depressed over his finances" and his position within the administration. McAdoo, House noted, "thinks Tumulty is working against him all the time, and the President is listening to Tumulty, which indeed is more or less true." House could only attempt to reassure his insecure friend.[40]

During the fall of 1915, against the backdrop of the war in Europe, Woodrow's courtship moved toward completion. House engaged in his own courtship of Edith, trying to win her friendship and protect his special relationship with the president. For her birthday he sent "blood red roses," and arranged to have her portrait painted as a wedding gift to the president. But he worried about rumors of Wilson's "immoral" behavior and the political impact of his remarriage. And House was surely upset when Edith told him that the president "had shown her some of my European correspondence." House felt a growing resentment over Wilson's transference of affection to Edith and over the extent to which she was changing his relationship with the president. Late in November, he complained in his diary that the president "is so engrossed with his fiancée that he is neglecting business." Realizing that Edith had now become a member of Woodrow's inner circle, on November 30 House drew her into his study after lunch and urged her to ignore the importunities of Wilson's friends and "to let [sic] the President alone to think out his problems in the future as he had done in the past." House did not record Edith's reaction to this advice but clearly he hoped that she would not disrupt his own role of confidential adviser.[41]

On December 15—three days before the president's wedding—House arrived in Washington for a final visit prior to his departure for Europe on another diplomatic mission. After lunch Woodrow showed him the diamond brooch he had gotten for Edith and other presents that had arrived for her. He and House ate dinner alone and afterward visited Edith at her home near Dupont Circle, where they "sat for half an hour in intimate personal conversation." "She expressed regret," House noted cryptically, "that we were going to Europe and also that I was not to be at the wedding. She said it did not seem right, but I made it clear that it would be an impossibility on account of the hurt feelings it would engender."[42]

In fact, House's decision not to attend the wedding is puzzling. He was not leaving for Europe until December 28; his explanation that his attendance was impossible because "of the hurt feelings it would engender" is unconvincing. The wedding was, to be sure, a small one, including only thirty-eight relatives and close friends, but House had a unique relationship with the president and had been instrumental in clearing away the obstacles to an early remarriage. His refusal to attend the wedding revealed a curious insensitivity, for he disappointed both Edith and Woodrow. It is hardly surprising that, when House left Washington on the evening of December 15, Wilson's goodbye must have been so perfunctory that he did not bother to record it.[43]

On December 28, 1915, House left for Europe to pursue—with Wilson's agreement—a bold plan to use American mediation to end the Great War. Throughout January and February, he conferred with leaders in Berlin, London, and Paris in a futile attempt to convince them to accept Wilsonian intervention. On the morning of March 6, 1916, the day after his return to New York, House arrived in Washington to report on his European journey. He soon discovered that Edith had a lively interest in foreign policy and was involved in all aspects of Wilson's life. She had become his constant companion and virtually an assistant president.[44]

As the end of May approached, House planned to escape the heat of the city by retreating to Sunapee, New Hampshire. His friend in the White House was sympathetic with his counselor's fear of heat. "Be sure," he advised, "not to linger too long in this heat. Much as I hate to see you go further away, you must take no risks." During a visit to Lake Sunapee, McAdoo complained that his father-in-law did not confide in him and that "the new Mrs. Wilson was antagonistic to him." The treasury secretary claimed that he looked forward to a return to private life, but House, who had followed his emotional ups and downs for years, was skeptical. He believed that McAdoo wanted to be president and, looking beyond Wilson's second term, wondered what kind of president he would make. House thought McAdoo was "able and has great courage," but lacked "discretion." "I am not sure," House concluded, "he would not make a great President because in addition to his other qualities he has imagination."[45]

On September 16, House finally returned to New York and quickly plunged into the presidential campaign. Both Edward and Woodrow, caught up in the demands of the campaign, missed their leisurely visits and talks. On November 2, House took a "final survey of the field" and concluded that "the fight is won." On November 12, after the result was no longer in doubt, House found the president a "a happy and contented man." House, too, was relieved, because Wilson's reelection had ended four years of anxiety over the president's political future and opened up a vista of further accomplishments on the national and international stage.[46]

On November 14, House traveled to Washington, where he and the president planned to discuss many matters the campaign had forced them to defer. House, who had always favored a pro-Allied mediation effort, now found that Wilson—who had lost his patience with the Allies—wanted an independent American effort, one that would demand that the belligerents end the war. The two men sharply disagreed, and on November 25, when House returned to Washington, they continued to argue over the best way to achieve peace. On December 17, Wilson finally completed a softened version of the original note, one that asked the warring nations to state the terms on which they would stop the fighting and work for the restoration of peace. Even so, House was upset. He concealed his feelings from the president, but complained in his diary that his friend had failed to distinguish between the Allies and the Central Powers and that he had "nearly destroyed all the work I have done in Europe."[47]

December 18, 1916, was the wedding anniversary of Woodrow and Edith. During the first year of their marriage, one biographer writes, she became accustomed to "monitoring the nation's events in person," working at her husband's side, sitting in on many of his conferences, and accumulating grudges against all of his advisers.[48]

On the surface, House's relationship with Wilson did not change, but their sharp disagreement over the president's peace note in late 1916 had furthered loosened the emotional ties between them. On his first visit to the White House in 1917, when House learned that Wilson planned to ask Ambassador Walter Hines Page in London to resign, both Edith and Woodrow suggested that he should take Page's place. House quickly convinced the two, so he claimed in his diary, that this would not be a wise move, but House seemed to miss the significance of the suggestion. For four years Wilson had pressed him to visit more often and stay longer; now with Edith at his side, he could contemplate sending him abroad on an ambassadorial assignment.[49]

Despite Edith's attempt to exile House in London, she continued to share with him her complaints about other members of her husband's inner circle. The behavior of Grayson, who was pushing for an appointment to rear admiral, disappointed House and also troubled Edith, who felt that "Grayson had been pushing his own fortunes in an indelicate and objectionable way." With Grayson's apparent fall from grace and a rumor that Tumulty might resign, House observed that "the little circle close to the President seems to have dwindled down to the two of us, Mrs. Wilson and myself."[50]

Nor did Secretary of the Treasury McAdoo escape the displeasure of the president and his wife. McAdoo's belligerence—he wants, House noted, "war to the hilt"—and his intrusions on his father-in-law's privacy, irritated the president, while Edith confided to House that she had always disliked him. House took a more balanced view of McAdoo's personality, observing that "he is an affectionate and generous friend." He also realized that McAdoo, with all of his "shortcomings . . . is the great driving force in the Cabinet." He urged his intense friend to concentrate on the Treasury Department and "to leave the president and the other departments alone."[51]

For a time in January 1917, House and Wilson believed that the war might come to an end. House helped Wilson draft his "peace without victory" address, which the president delivered to the congress on January 22. House declared that it was "a noble document and one which I think will live." But at the end of the month the American government learned that Germany would begin unrestricted U-boat warfare on February 1. Both the president and his counselor realized that their peace efforts had failed and that the United States would have to confront a new and more deadly phase of the Great War.

In February and March, House watched with growing impatience as

Wilson agonized over his decision for war. On March 26, he decided that he must go to Washington, convinced that he needed "to talk matters out with the President." Once there, however, he discovered that he and Wilson agreed on the need for a declaration of war against Germany and that he approved of the content of Wilson's war message. House was in the audience when the president addressed Congress on April 2. He believed that "history may record this the most important day in the life of our country—one of the most important, indeed, in the life of the world."[52]

In the spring of 1917, the rush to prepare the nation for war increased the pressure on House. He noted in his diary that "the days are a continual turmoil now. Telephone calls, telegrams, letters and personal interviews occupy every waking hour." The administration's early mobilization efforts pleased House, but he was uneasy over the leadership of the president, who lacked, so he claimed, "the power of large administration." House ignored the fact that Wilson was beginning to draw into his administration a group of powerful war managers to whom he granted sweeping authority. Wilson especially admired the convivial Wall Street speculator Bernard Baruch and made him the purchasing agent for the Allies. House sought to block Baruch's ascent, explaining that "I believe Baruch is able and I believe he is honest, but I do not believe the country will take kindly to having a Hebrew, Wall Street speculator given so much power. He is not the type that inspires confidence." But aware of Wilson's fondness for Baruch, he did not take his objections directly to the president.[53]

The president, unaware of his counselor's critique of his wartime leadership, continued to give House additional responsibilities. In early September, during a visit with House on the North Shore, Wilson asked him to put together a group—which would become known as "the Inquiry"—to collect data for the peace conference. On October 9, when House visited the president in Washington, Wilson decided that his counselor should serve as the American representative at the Inter-Allied Conference in Paris. "No one in America," he insisted, "or in Europe either knows my mind and I am not willing to trust them to interpret it." On October 29, the House Party, as it came to be called, left New York for Europe. Not until mid-December, after extensive consultations with Allied leaders in London and Paris, did House return to America.[54]

In early January 1918, House traveled to Washington, where he helped the president complete the draft of what would become his Fourteen Points address. Once again, Wilson's boldness as a political leader impressed House. "The more I see of him," he recorded in his diary, "the more firmly am I convinced that there is not a statesman in the world who is his equal." House remained concerned, however, about the administration's war effort, and found that the president did not seek his advice on most domestic issues. He still valued, however, House's foreign policy expertise, consulting with him about the composition of the American peace commission. And he told one of House's protégés that his counselor had "a wonderful gift for getting a detached view-point and fixing on the really important issues."[55]

In June 1918, as House settled into another summer on the North Shore, he was pleased with the position he had achieved. "Someone said recently," he carefully recorded, "'Magnolia is the first port of call for foreigners coming over, and the last port before returning home!'" House, convinced that the tide of war on the Western Front would soon turn, wanted the president to assume leadership of the League of Nations movement. He reasoned that American power might be greater in the autumn of 1918—before the war ended—than in 1919, and that the time had come for the president to engage in diplomacy, in give-and-take with Allied leaders.[56]

On October 6, 1919, a German note arrived in Washington, asking for peace negotiations based on the Fourteen Points. The president now became engaged—with help from House—in negotiations with the German government over the terms on which the war should be ended. By the middle of October, Wilson realized that he must dispatch his counselor to Europe to negotiate with the Allies. House, Wilson told one British diplomat, "knows my mind entirely; but you must ask them [British leaders] to realize how hard it is for me to spare him. On many problems he is the only person I can consult."[57]

On October 25, House and his entourage arrived in Paris, where he quickly plunged into negotiations with Allied leaders. After a series of tense meetings, House believed that he had committed the Allies to a peace based on the Fourteen Points, that he had "won a great diplomatic victory," but in fact the so-called pre-armistice agreement did not commit the Allies to all that much. On November 11, German delegates accepted the harsh terms proposed by the United States and the Allies, and the war finally came to an end.[58]

In mid-August, nearly three months before the fighting stopped, House had concluded that if Wilson attended the peace conference, it would be best if the president did not sit on the American delegation and instead continued his role as an outside observer. The armistice negotiations confirmed House's belief, if he ever had any doubts, that he possessed superior diplomatic skills. He had gone to Europe on special missions every year of the war, and by the end of the conflict had met leaders in Berlin, London, and Paris, and had become especially familiar with Britain's ruling elite. House fervently hoped that Wilson, whatever the length of his stay in Europe, would make him the head of the American peace commission.

He was, however, badly out of touch with the president's convictions. The peace conference represented the culmination of Wilson's life, an opportunity for him to convince Allied leaders to conclude a peace of justice that would embody his vision of a new international order. While Wilson regarded House as a valuable emissary, he had always viewed him as a counselor, not as a statesman, and during the armistice negotiations may have developed some doubts about House's ability as a diplomat. On November 12, he told his cabinet that he would attend the peace conference.[59]

Woodrow and Edith arrived in France on December 13, and received a tumultuous welcome, first in Brest and then in Paris. While House busied himself with preparations for the peace conference, the president traveled, first to England, then to Italy; not until January 12, 1919, nearly a month after his arrival, did he and Allied leaders have their first meeting at the Quai d'Orsay in Paris.

During the first phase of the peace conference, which lasted until February 15, when Wilson left Paris, the president sat on the Council of Ten along with the political heads of the chief Western powers and their foreign ministers. Wilson and House insisted that all major issues should be put off until an agreement was reached on the covenant of the League of Nations. In late January, a League of Nations Commission was setup, chaired by Wilson, with House as one of its members. He worked behind the scenes to gain acceptance of the president's version of the League, and on February 14, Wilson read the final draft covenant to a plenary session of the peace conference. The president explained that the covenant was "not a straightjacket, but a vehicle of life. A living thing is born." House believed that the president's address was a great triumph; after Wilson finished speaking, he slipped him a piece of paper that read: "Your speech was as great as the occasion. I am very happy."[60]

The president, who planned to be gone a for month (catching up on a large accumulation of official business in Washington), chose House as his replacement on the Council of Ten. Both men realized that crucial issues—such as Germany's frontiers, reparations, and French security—remained to be dealt with, but Wilson expected that major decisions should wait until his return. House, however, concluded that the time had come for decisive action. He now worked with British and French leaders to speed up the peace conference and, in the process of doing so, accepted a substantial part of French demands on Germany. House was proud of his decisiveness, boasting in his diary that "when the President is away I never hesitate to act and to take as much responsibility as either of the others" (as if, in fact, he too was a head of state).[61]

When the president arrived at Brest on March 13, House greeted him and, on the train ride to Paris explained what had been accomplished during his absence. While the exact exchange between the two men is lost in time, Wilson realized that during his absence things had not gone well and that House had made tentative but damaging compromises on key issues. Wilson did not reprimand his counselor, but the trust he had placed in him for so many years now disappeared. The change in their relationship, however, took place slowly. As one historian writes, "They needed each other too much—House for his own self-esteem, Wilson for a thousand practical services—to have their bond cut at one stroke."[62]

Wilson quickly sought to reestablish the American position and to speed up the deliberations. He now began to meet only with Georges Clemenceau, David Lloyd George, and Vittorio Orlando, but on April 3, Wilson became violently ill and asked House to take his place on the Council of Four. Over the next four and a half days, while the president was confined to his bed, House once again moved to the center of the negotiations. After Wilson recovered, he realized that, if the peace was to be concluded, he would have to compromise on major issues. By the middle of April, after days of intense negotiations, many of the French demands had been met, and the Council of Four invited German delegates to Paris later in the month to receive the terms of the treaty.[63]

As the peace conference stalemated, and especially after Wilson fell ill on April 3, the discontents and frustrations of the president's intimates focused on House. In early April, Ray Stannard Baker, the press secretary of the American delegation, had a long talk with House,

> who was sitting on his long lounge with a figured blanket over his chilly legs—quite serenely dictating his diary to Miss Denton. More & more he impresses me as the dilettante—the lover of the game—the eager secretary without profound responsibility. He stands in the midst of great events, to lose nothing. He gains experience to put in his diary, makes great acquaintances, plays at getting important men together for the sheer joy of making them agree. He is a matchless conciliator but with the faults of his victim for he conciliates over the border of minor disagreements into the solid flesh of principle. . . . This bright, lively little man, optimistic in the presence of tragic events.[64]

During his illness Wilson brooded about many matters, including his relationship with his counselor. It was Edith, however, who forced a confrontation. On April 21, when House appeared to discuss events at the conference, she read to him a news report—written by a journalist close to House—which praised his role at the peace conference. House quickly left the room, no doubt aware of the fact that Woodrow and Edith now realized that he was trying to overshadow the president. Edith's conversation with him was to be their last face-to-face encounter. They never spoke again.

During the second half of the peace conference Wilson and House still met often or talked on their private telephone line. But their relationship was now decidedly more formal. Finally, on May 30, House admitted in his diary what had been true for several months—that "I seldom or never have a chance to talk with him seriously and, for the moment, he is practically out from under my influence." House now moved toward a major, more critical reassessment of Wilson's leadership: "I am quite sincere in believing that the President will rank with the great orators of all time. In truth, I believe that it is as an orator that he excels rather than as a statesman. The feeling has become fairly general that the President's actions do not square with his speeches. There is a *bon mot* going the round in Paris and London, 'Wilson talks like Jesus Christ but acts like Lloyd George.' "[65]

On June 28, German officials arrived at the Hall of Mirrors in the Palace of Versailles to sign the peace treaty. House witnessed the ceremony, and in the evening went to the Gare des Invalides to see the president and his party off as they boarded the train to Brest. He had a final conversation with Wilson, one that "was not reassuring." He urged the president "to meet the Senate in a conciliatory spirit. I was certain that if he treated them with the same consideration he had used with his foreign colleagues here, all would be well." His optimism, however, left Wilson unmoved: " 'House, I have found one can never get anything in this life that is worthwhile without fighting for it.' I combated this, and reminded him that Anglo-Saxon Civilization was built on compromise. I said that a fight was the last thing to be brought about, and then only when it could not be avoided." The two men would never see each other again.[66]

House spent the summer of 1919 in London, where he helped set up the League of Nations, and in mid-September returned to Paris, where he once again took up the remaining issues of the peace conference. On October 12, he was back in New York, eager to pick up "the thread of affairs." The news from Washington was bleak, particularly after the Senate failed to approve the peace treaty on November 19. House wished that Wilson had turned the presidency over to Vice President Thomas Marshall during the period of his disability. With Marshall in command the treaty would "have gone through with such mild reservations as to leave no question of its acceptance by the other powers." He worried that Edith would not allow Woodrow to see his letters and complained that "the small entourage of the President evidently feel that he should be kept in office at all costs. In doing so they are crucifying his reputation." House lamented the influence of Baruch and Grayson and did not realize that Edith was determined to keep him away from her husband. Over the years she had tolerated House, but his behavior at the peace conference had confirmed her earlier doubts, and now she cut him off from contact with her crippled husband. At the very time when Wilson needed House's conciliatory advice and his personal connections, Edith ignored the overtures of the man who had once been his most trusted adviser and closest friend.[67]

In the early months of 1920, from his vantage point in New York, House watched the final chapter of the League debate with a sense of foreboding. All his efforts to reach his old friend the president had failed, and he remained uncertain about their relationship. House believed that if only he had "a moment with the President," he could convince him to turn the government over to Marshall and to issue a public statement explaining that "he had fallen ill before his work was finished." If Wilson left office in a dignified way, he was certain that "he would have become a world martyr. . . . The treaty would have been ratified at once and the work for which he was responsible would have lived." He blamed the coterie around Wilson for his stubbornness, failing to understand the devastating impact of Wilson's stroke on his emotional balance, or to realize that the president himself, far more than Edith or Grayson, was the instigator of his own self-destructive behavior.[68]

By May 1920, House was discouraged. The president was intensely unpopular, his administration was in disarray, but he would listen "to no one." House wondered "how I influenced him so many years and yet retained his friendship and affection." After he returned from a summer in England, he realized that the campaign of the Democratic Party's nominee, Governor James M. Cox of Ohio, had no chance of prevailing. But he was not prepared for the scale of the Republican triumph, which was a massive repudiation of Wilson's presidency.[69]

* * *

In the early 1920s, House returned to familiar routines. He enjoyed his prominence as an elder statesman, traveling to Europe every summer, following events their closely, and hoping that his friend McAdoo would receive the Democratic nomination and carry the party to victory in 1924. Late on the morning of February 3, 1924, House learned that Wilson had died. Initially he planned to travel to Washington and attend the funeral, but Tumulty called and said that he had not been invited. Rather than risk a confrontation with Edith, House attended a memorial service at Madison Square Garden, where he sat on the platform while ten thousand people crowded into the great hall. "I have never," he recorded, "attended a more impressive and touching service." Three days later he published in the *New York Times* an effusive tribute to his old friend, concluding that "no man of his time touched so deeply the conscience and aspirations of mankind."[70]

House had always been concerned about his historical reputation, and in 1921 he commissioned a young Yale historian, Charles Seymour, to edit his letters and diaries. The first two volumes, which appeared in early 1926, portrayed House as moving shrewdly and quietly through the corridors of power in both America and Europe, rarely making a misstep in either domestic affairs or international diplomacy. *The Intimate Papers of Colonel House* left the reader with no doubts about Wilson's greatness as a political leader, but the president's shortcomings were also a prominent theme that ran through the narrative. In various diary passages, House noted Wilson's alleged defects—his strong prejudices, his one-track mind, and his slowness to appreciate the importance of world affairs. The result was a reversal of the roles of the two men, one that made House the dominant partner in their extraordinary collaboration and reduced Wilson to a subordinate position. In an editorial, the *New York Times* noted that the two volumes "might give the impression that the errand-boy considered himself of more consequence than the employer."[71]

In November 1928, the third and fourth volumes of *The Intimate Papers* finally appeared, covering the period from the American entry into the war until the end of the peace conference. In these volumes Seymour would not admit that a sharp break had occurred between the two men.

Rather, he argued, the "friendship lapsed. It was not broken." At the conclusion of volume 4, Seymour quoted from a letter House had written him
on April 20, 1928:"My separation from Woodrow Wilson," House claimed,
"was and is to me a tragic mystery, a mystery that can never be dispelled,
for its explanation lies buried with him."[72]

By early 1931, House realized that Governor Franklin D. Roosevelt of New
York—assistant secretary of the navy under Wilson—was the leading Democratic contender for the presidency. For a time House hoped that a new
version of "our crowd" would take over FDR's campaign. But the New York
governor, while he courted old Wilsonians, had no intention of allowing
House and his lieutenants to replace his seasoned advisers. While House
had some reservations about FDR, he was pleased with his sweeping victory in November 1932. But at the age of seventy-four, in uncertain health,
and with a cordial but somewhat distant relationship with the new president, House felt none of the excitement that had swept over him twenty
years before, when his friend Woodrow Wilson had won the presidency.
As the new administration took shape, House realized that FDR was not
the same kind of leader as Wilson. Wilson was a solitary figure, one who
had relied on House to deal with a wide range of people. "FDR's methods"
House observed, "are different from those of Wilson. He has many advisers but no one is very close to him." House realized that "my health is not
equal to my trying to do for him [FDR] what I did for Wilson."[73]

House seemed uncertain what to make of the flood of legislation passed
during the Hundred Days. He was, however, impressed with Roosevelt's
qualities of leadership, and in the fall of 1933 he refused to join conservative Democrats in an open rebellion against the New Deal. He was, he
insisted, "a friend of the President and all the advice I had to give would
be given him privately." House would support FDR throughout the 1930s;
he had no intention of breaking openly with the party he had joined as a
young man in Texas.[74]

The 1930s proved to be a difficult decade for House. The Depression forced
him to reduce his standard of living—he could no longer afford trips to

Europe—and his declining energy left him on the political sidelines. In early January 1938, Charles Seymour visited House at his New York apartment. He found the elder statesman reconciled to the fact that his life was coming to an end. House was, however, still obsessed with his break with Wilson. Once again the old man placed much of the blame on Edith, claiming that the "rift" began right after the Armistice, when House's alleged diplomatic triumph had received "extravagant praise." Both Woodrow and Edith had been offended by Edward's advice that the president not attend the peace conference, and, once there, the two men "were separated by half of Paris and did not see each other so constantly as had been our custom." After Wilson's return in March 1919, there was a further change, since "unfriendly persons had carried to Mrs. Wilson the story . . . that during the President's absence I had yielded to unwise suggestions of compromise. . . . As the Peace Conference closed there was no coolness between us; merely a slackening of intimacy." House reviewed his relations with the president after his stroke, concluding that Wilson had no reason for "hard feelings against me. . . . But he didn't have the force to break through the ring [of House's enemies] and resume relations." And so, House concluded, "my separation from Wilson was not a break. It was caused by the illness of each of us, that drove a wedge between us. When a rift was opened it was kept open by those who did not wish us to come together. . . . My love and admiration for Woodrow Wilson have never faltered or lessened."[75] Even at the end of his life, House refused to reflect deeply on his behavior during the Wilson years or to accept any blame for what had happened. He died on March 28, 1938, still perplexed, at the age of seventy-nine, by the reasons for Wilson's withdrawal of confidence, the great failure of his life.

Dr. Grayson and the president, sharing some observations. Grayson began as the president's physician but soon became a frequent companion and the monitor of his health. Granger Historical Picture Archive.

CHAPTER SEVEN

Cary T. Grayson

"... [T]he embodiment of the loftiest spirit, the supreme mind of his generation, one of the immortals of the world's history"

On March 3, 1913, the day before the inauguration, president-elect Woodrow Wilson and his wife, Ellen, came to the White House for tea with William Howard Taft and his wife, Nellie. Before Wilson left, Taft drew him aside and introduced him to White House physician Cary T. Grayson. "Mr. Wilson," Taft said, "here is an excellent fellow that I hope you will get to know. I regret to say that he is a Democrat and a Virginian, but that's a matter that can't be helped." The next day, at a buffet luncheon at the White House after the inauguration was over, Annie Howe, Wilson's sister, slipped on a marble staircase and cut her head. Grayson was on hand to stitch the wound. After treating her, the young physician—he was only thirty-four—came into the Oval Room and chatted with the new president and his family. Eleanor McAdoo remembered him as "a charming man with a handsome aristocratic face, speaking ... in a soft attractive voice, with a chuckle that sounded like tearing silk. We were all delighted with him."[1] Nearly a week later, when Wilson fell ill, Ellen asked Grayson to come to the White House and examine him. The doctor's modesty and background appealed to Woodrow, who a few days later invited him to lunch with Secretary of the Navy Daniels. During the luncheon the president told Daniels, "'Mr. Secretary, there is one part of the Navy I must ask you to let me have. I want you to let me appropriate this part,' laying his hand upon the arm of Grayson as he said it. ... 'I wish this part of the Navy for my very own.'" Grayson quickly accepted the offer, for he was drawn to the president and his family and remembered his first impression: "The picture will always be vivid in my mind—how clear-cut Mr. Wilson's features were, how intensely determined he was—completely calm and at ease." And he remembered his first glimpse of Ellen's "cordial, beautiful smile." It was the beginning of what would become a close relationship that would last until Wilson's death in 1924.[2]

Cary Travers Grayson was born on October 11, 1878, at Salubria, his family's historic plantation house near Culpeper, Virginia. The Graysons, who were of Scottish ancestry, had been physicians for three generations, and Cary's father, John Cooke Grayson, enlisted as a surgeon in the Confederate Army at the beginning of the Civil War. His mother, Adelena, died when he was a child; his father died when he was twelve. John Cooke often urged his young son to emulate his family's distinguished forebears, while Adelena, he recalled, advised him "to deal fairly, keep his temper and observe the Golden Rule."[3]

Somehow, with the help of friends and relatives, Cary prospered, working his way through William and Mary College and graduating Phi Beta Kappa in 1898. In 1902, he received a medical degree from the University of the South and then moved on to an internship at Columbia Hospital for Women in Washington, DC. A year later he enlisted in the navy, where he received additional training at the US Naval Hospital. He was eager to see the world and was assigned to the armored cruiser USS *Maryland*, which in December 1907 left as part of the Great White Fleet's round-the-world cruise. On his return, he joined the medical staff of the White House, and on January 13, 1909, when Theodore Roosevelt decided to prove to army officers that his physical exercise order was reasonable, Grayson joined the president, Surgeon-General Presley Marion Rixey, and presidential aide Archie Butt in a 104-mile horseback ride. Using a relay of four horses, the four men left the White House at 3:40 a.m. and returned at 8:40 p.m., riding the last thirty miles in the dark, with a sleet storm blowing in their faces. Clearly the short, handsome young physician, an expert horseman, had learned how to win the confidence of powerful men.[4]

* * *

As Grayson settled in as the president's personal physician, he learned all he could about his new patient's medical history, about his headaches and gastric disorders and about the ruptured blood vessel that he had suffered in his left eye in 1906. He took away medications that upset Wilson's stomach and the stomach pump that he had used to siphon out gastric acid. It seems unlikely, however, that Grayson understood the extent of Wilson's hypertension and cerebrovascular disease or the way in which, as they progressed, they would ravage his health. Nevertheless, he warned him that "he had four hard years ahead of him and that he owed it to himself and the American people to get into as fit condition as possible and to stay there." Grayson insisted that the president must accept a new regimen, one that "included plenty of fresh air, a diet suited to his idiosyncrasies as I discovered them by close study, plenty of sleep, daily motor rides, occasional trips on the *Mayflower*, and especially regular games of golf, together with treatment for a persistent case of neuritis from which he had long suffered." Inevitably, as Wilson adopted these new routines, Grayson, as he recalled, "was quickly drawn into close, personal association with him."[5]

During the summer of 1913, Ellen and her three daughters vacationed at Cornish, New Hampshire, while Woodrow labored in the heat of Washington, pushing his legislative agenda through Congress. In order to keep the president company, Grayson and Tumulty moved into the White House. Tumulty left on weekends to join his family on the New Jersey shore, but Grayson, a bachelor, became the president's constant companion. The two men dined together, played golf most days, attended the theater twice a week, and sometimes cruised down the Potomac on the *Mayflower*. Woodrow reported to Ellen that the three were a "congenial and jolly company" and that Grayson and Tumulty "wear extremely well." Wilson was drawn to the young naval officer, who was deferential and conscientious and, when the occasion presented itself, a skilled raconteur.

Grayson soon became a close friend of both McAdoo and House. He and McAdoo were two of the most eligible bachelors in Washington, and during the winter of 1913–14 they attended many social events together.

When McAdoo married Eleanor Wilson in early May 1914, Grayson was his best man. Grayson met House at Wilson's inaugural and found him, on first impression, to be a "quiet, modest, unassuming, clearheaded man." He identified with House, sided with him in his quarrels with Tumulty, and began telling the Colonel, as House recorded, "everything concerning the President in the most minute detail in order to get my advice." House knew from the start that the president's health was fragile, and he was eager for information that would reveal how Wilson was dealing with the burdens of the presidency and whether or not he would be able to run for a second term. In late March 1914, Grayson "alarmed me [House] somewhat by saying that the Philadelphia oculist Dr. Swinehart [George E. de Schweinitz] who had the President under his care for ten years or more, told him, Grayson, that there was some indication of the hardening of the arteries. The President does not know this, neither does any member of his family. It seems in 1905 [actually, 1906] the President had an almost complete breakdown at Princeton and it was uncertain whether he could resume his duties." Both Grayson and House were clearly worried that the leader to whom they had attached themselves might suffer from a serious illness.[6]

In early March 1914, Ellen fainted and fell on her bedroom floor. Grayson became preoccupied with her health and how to tell Woodrow—who resisted hearing any bad news—that the kidney disease from which she suffered was almost certain to prove fatal. Throughout the summer of 1914, Ellen's health declined, and on July 23, as she faded, Grayson moved into the White House. On August 4, Grayson told Wilson to summon his daughters, and two days later, as Ellen sensed that her death was near, she drew Grayson close and whispered, "Please take good care of Woodrow, Doctor."[7]

On August 20, Grayson wrote to House, revealing the anxieties he had suffered during Ellen's long decline. "A few days after your departure for Europe [on May 16, 1914]," Grayson confessed, "alarming symptoms developed with Mrs. Wilson. . . . I felt it my duty to save the President from all worry, anxiety and distress as long as possible. This was an awful load to struggle under. He gradually realized the seriousness of the case and about a week before the end I told him that I thought the daughters should be here—he understood. You cannot imagine how I felt through it all and ... I longed for you many, many times. I went to our dear, and true friend, McAdoo, and told him all."[8]

At the end of August, Wilson and Grayson traveled to Cornish, where the young physician hoped the president would begin what was sure to be a long, painful recovery from Ellen's death. When House arrived for a visit, Grayson gave him "all the mischievous petty, White House gossip. It seem[s] impossible for the President to escape espionage concerning his most intimate personal affairs." On September 26, after Wilson returned to Washington and House to New York, Grayson appeared at House's apartment to give him news of tensions in the White House. House learned that the president suffered from indigestion because McAdoo and Tumulty insisted on talking business during meals. He was given the unenviable assignment of telling the secretary of the treasury that he must restrain himself. And Grayson also told House, drawing on information that only he possessed and that House longed for, that after the president's counselor left Cornish, Wilson confided to him that "I am thankful for such a friend. If there were more like him we would not need government."[9]

In December 1912, Grayson had met Alice Gertrude Gordon (her friends called her Altrude), a high-spirited young women—she was fourteen years younger than Grayson—whose father, a wealthy mining engineer, had died the previous year. He had asked a friend, Edith Galt, to look after his motherless daughter, and in 1911 the two women had spent five months traveling in Europe and had become close friends. Late in the summer of 1914, Altrude—with whom Grayson had fallen in love—asked the young doctor to treat Edith, who had fallen ill after a trip to Maine. After his successful treatment, Grayson began writing to Edith, asking for her support in his courtship of Altrude and also telling her of the president's depression. Wilson was, Grayson confided, feeling the loss of Ellen more than ever, and the day before, when the doctor went to see his patient, "tears were streaming down his face.... A sadder picture, no one could imagine. A great man with his heart torn out."[10]

In early 1915, when Wilson and Grayson were motoring through Washington, they passed Edith on the street, and the president suddenly asked, "Who is that beautiful woman?" Grayson, who was searching for ways to bring Woodrow out of his lethargy, arranged for Edith and Wilson's cousin Helen Bones to become friends. Sometime in March, when Edith and Helen returned to the White House for tea, they stumbled across Wilson and Grayson returning from a game of golf. Edith's warm, romantic temperament appealed to Wilson, and within a few weeks after their first meeting, they were taking long drives and eating dinner together at the White House. Woodrow pressed his courtship, and less than two months after they had met, he asked Edith to marry him. While she gently rebuffed him, he continued his pursuit, sending flowers every day to her house near Dupont Circle and writing a torrent of letters.[11]

Grayson understood that Woodrow's love for Edith was highly therapeutic. He urged her to see the president as often as possible, confided to Edith "his hopes and fears" in his courtship of Altrude Gordon, and told Edith "such beautiful things about you [Woodrow] that my heart expanded and glowed."[12]

In June and July 1915, Woodrow and Edith spent weeks together at Cornish. Grayson, who was with the president at his New Hampshire retreat, knew that he must remarry. But he also seemed upset by the extent to which Wilson was carried away by his new romance. On July 31, 1915, Grayson appeared at House's summer cottage in Manchester, Massachusetts, and poured out intimate details of his patient's personal life. He was, House recorded, upset by "the President's infatuation with Mrs. Norman Galt. It seems the President is wholly absorbed in this love affair and is neglecting practically everything else." Grayson also "mentioned some things which are rather disturbing but which I do not care to put in the diary."[13]

During her time with Woodrow at Harlakenden, Edith became familiar with the issues he confronted and with the advisers on whom he relied. She was opinionated in her judgments, complaining of Tumulty's "commonness," and also dismissed House as not "a very *strong* character." But she was generous in her judgments of Grayson, writing that "I have always felt you were like a son to me" and thanking him "for all you did for me. I will never forget it."[14]

Wilson was devoted to Grayson and, in the late summer of 1915, worried about what seemed, for a time, his unsuccessful courtship of Altrude Gordon. "I must confess," he wrote to Edith, "that *as a lover* Miss Gordon is inscrutable to me." He was, however, more critical of his physician than Edith: "The dear doctor you know. He has every sterling quality, and his mind thinks good, sound sense. He is full of right and generous feeling. He is a restful and most satisfactory companion and a loyal friend. He every day wins anew my warm affectionate regard. He is true gold. But he is not intellectually stimulating. He does not wake my mind up and quicken its paces." While both Grayson and Tumulty wore well, "I must admit," Wilson confessed, "that I am often bored."[15]

In the fall of 1915, Grayson, along with House, worked to smooth the path for the president's remarriage. On October 6, the White House announced the engagement of the president and Mrs. Norman Galt, and on December 15, when House arrived in Washington to confer with Wilson before his departure for Europe, he and Grayson went into a half-hour session "relating to family and household matters." "I seem to be the receptacle," he complained, "for everything and everybody when I am in Washington. It is tiresome, though in a way, gratifying." House did not linger to attend the small ceremony three days later, but Grayson was there, and on May 24, 1916, Woodrow and Edith attended Grayson's marriage to Altrude in New York City. The president was delighted with his physician's marriage, confiding to Altrude that "I have known few men whom I admired and trusted and loved as I do Grayson and his happiness means a great deal to me."[16]

Grayson was pleased with the way in which Wilson's marriage seemed to improve his health. After Woodrow and Edith returned from their honeymoon, he observed that "I never saw either of them look finer." Throughout the spring and summer of 1916, as political pressures mounted, Grayson continued to monitor the president's condition. He worried about Wilson's gastric disorders, severe headaches, and extreme fatigue. At the end of the summer, Grayson warned Wilson that he must slow up and rest or he would not be able to keep going. When Woodrow and Edith moved to Shadow Lawn (their vacation home in Long Branch, New Jersey) on September 1, Grayson and Altrude followed them, occupying a cottage near the main house. On election eve they were with Wilson, along with members of his family, as they awaited the results. When the returns from the West Coast finally tipped the election in Wilson's favor, Grayson was relieved by the president's extraordinary victory, but he also must have felt anxiety over whether his patient's health would sustain him for another four years.[17]

On July 2, 1915, Wilson had written Secretary of the Navy Daniels, raising the possibility of Grayson's promotion to rear admiral. But nothing could be done until the passage of the personnel bill of 1915, which, for the first time, gave the rank of rear admiral to officers in the Medical Corps. While the Navy Department had abolished promotion by seniority in all grades, the fact remained that Grayson, if promoted, would move ahead of 114 more senior officers. Despite his affection for Grayson, the president was sensitive to charges of favoritism, and on January 3, 1917, when House arrived in Washington, he found that Edith was also troubled over the issue. "She feels," House recorded, "as we all do, that Grayson has been pushing his own fortunes in an indelicate and objectionable way. She said the President was so disturbed over it that he lay awake nearly all night. He feels that he should refuse Grayson this advancement." Wilson, however, soon overcame his reservations and on January 18 sent Grayson's name to the Senate. Some Republican senators objected and filibustered the nomination, but on March 6, Wilson sent Grayson's name back to the Senate, and it was finally confirmed. House felt that the controversy would reduce Grayson's influence with Woodrow and Edith, but their annoyance with him soon passed, and he remained their physician and friend.[18]

In early March 1917, right after his inauguration, Wilson suffered from exhaustion and a severe cold. Grayson ordered him to bed, where he stayed for nearly two weeks. America's entry into World War I on April 6, 1917, put further pressure on the president, who now had to mobilize the government and the nation for war in Europe. He continued to pursue Grayson's regimen of daily exercise and leisure, and seemed to maintain his strength throughout the war, suffering from an occasional cold and congested nasal passages. Aside from traveling with the president and treating his various ailments, Grayson also meddled in matters far removed from his duties as White House physician. In October 1917, he accompanied his friend McAdoo on a nationwide tour to sell the second Liberty Loan and reported to House that every place the secretary of the treasury went he was "mentioned as the next President." Like House, Grayson was aware of Edith's dislike of her husband's son-in-law (she never forgave him for his opposition to their marriage in 1915) and warned House that "we have all got to be very careful about mentioning McAdoo's name around the White House for future honors—especially with the female members." He also reported that Tumulty "is an entirely changed man. . . . His attitude toward McAdoo and yourself reversed from the past three years. He is always praising you—and most enthusiastic about McAdoo." Grayson promised to do his best "in the interest of harmony and loyalty," but he was also intent on following the maneuverings within the president's inner circle of advisers and in protecting his own position.[19]

Both Grayson and House closely watched the president's health. When House visited Washington in late February 1918, he noted that Wilson "looks better than upon my last visit, [but] I can see indications of fatigue. He does not remember names as well and he does not think to do the things we decide upon." Grayson admitted to House that "while he gave the impression to everyone that the President worked day and night, he and I knew that eight hours work a day was about all he was equal to." Wilson's limited energy, however, did not concern House. "I believe the President," he recorded, "can do more in eight hours than any man I know. He wastes no time in talking or useless arguments or energy of any sort. McAdoo has more energy and staying powers, and works perhaps twice as many hours as the President, but he does not accomplish as much because he wastes so much energy in talking."[20]

In the spring of 1918, McAdoo, who was restless and ambitious, had become a problem for both House and Grayson. He had become embroiled in a dispute with Federal Fuel Administrator Harry Garfield over the price of coal for the nation's railways (which were now under federal control). McAdoo's threat to resign upset House, who used Grayson as a go-between with the disgruntled secretary of the treasury. On May 19, House instructed Grayson to see McAdoo the next morning and persuade him to stay in office. Grayson did so, but after a conversation lasting three and a half hours found his friend "in an excitable condition" and, rather than report directly to House, phoned House's trusted son-in-law, Gordon Auchincloss. Eventually McAdoo gave way and the crisis passed, but the episode indicated the extent to which Grayson and House had become collaborators (with House as the senior partner) in maintaining harmony in the inner circle around the president.[21]

In mid-August 1918, when Woodrow, Edith, and Grayson visited House on Boston's North Shore, House "sounded" Wilson on the question of a third term and concluded that he would be a candidate. Given the magnitude of the challenges that lay ahead, both Grayson and House agreed, as the latter observed, that "there is no one but the President who has the proper background and outlook. The Republican Party is devoid of suitable material; nor is there anyone in the Democratic Party who could fill the President's place in such work." Two days later, House "had a long talk with Dr. Grayson . . . as to the President's health and as to whether he thought he could stand another term." Grayson, House discovered to his relief, "thought he might go for another ten years if nothing untoward happened."[22]

On November 12, 1918, Wilson told his cabinet that he would attend the peace conference. Grayson realized that, given the president's conviction that a League of Nations must be at the center of a new world order, "[h]e must go." "Such was his faith," Grayson continued, "and he was fully aware that he himself must be the chief apostle of that faith." On December 3, 1918, when Woodrow and Edith left on the SS *George Washington* for the ten-day voyage across the Atlantic, Grayson was perhaps the most important member of their entourage. Once in Paris, he rode with the president and his wife through massive crowds to the Murat Palace, where they stayed during the first phase of the peace conference. Since the opening of the conference was delayed, Grayson traveled with Woodrow and Edith, first to Great Britain, then to Italy. Finally, on January 12, 1919, Wilson and Allied leaders began their deliberations in what became known as the Council of Ten. After listening to one of these sessions, Grayson concluded that the president "towers above the others . . . [who] are not in the same class with our great man. . . . He is a marvel and all realize it—and are afraid of him." Grayson took most of his meals with Woodrow and Edith and often sat with them after dinner while the president described the day's deliberations. He also fretted about the long days Wilson was com-pelled to endure and about his lack of rest and exercise. Grayson's inti-macy with Woodrow and Edith now deepened; he gradually assumed responsibilities—as a special emissary and press officer—that went far beyond his duties as a medical doctor.[23]

On February 14, the president left Paris for his voyage back to the United States. During the first phase of the peace conference Wilson had been remarkably healthy, and on March 4, when Grayson gave him a thor-ough examination, he found that "his blood pressure, blood examination and urinalysis were unusually good for a man of his age [sixty-two]." On the return voyage aboard the *George Washington*, Grayson confided de-tails of the president's health to Ray Stannard Baker, the press officer of the America Peace Commission. Baker claimed that "Grayson is one of the men who ought to have credit for a League of Nations, if ever it is estab-lished, for he has done a wonderful service in preserving & keeping in good order the precious life of the President." Wilson had come to the White House, Baker optimistically concluded, in poor health, but "to-day he is in practically perfect health & can stand no end of work & strain: and this is due, in no small degree, to the daily care of Grayson who watched him like a hawk."[24]

When the *George Washington* arrived at Brest on March 13, House was there to greet the president, and on the way back to Paris he had a long talk with Wilson about the situation at the peace conference. Grayson recorded a full account of their meeting in his diary: "Leaving Brest the

President and Colonel House went into conference and Colonel House told the President of the various developments, including the apparent desire on the part of the French authorities to have the League of Nations covenant side-tracked and a preliminary peace treaty signed which would include the complete disarmament of Germany, the creation of a Rhenish Republic, and would in effect do what the President had declared on a number of occasions he would not countenance—absolutely denude Germany of everything she had and allow Bolshevism to spread throughout that country." Grayson quickly sensed the coolness between the president and his counselor and realized that in the final phase of the peace conference he could no longer rely on his friendship with House.[25]

During the second half of March, while Wilson engaged in arduous negotiations, Grayson found various ways to protect the president. On March 29, Lady Northcliffe (the wife of the British press baron) came for lunch and began to ask pointed questions about the deliberations. Wilson, following his physician's advice, explained "that I [Grayson] was in a great sense his guardian and that I would not allow him to dwell too much on business matters during his meals or during such short periods of relaxation as it was possible to secure." After dinner, while Woodrow played solitaire and Edith knitted, Grayson sat and talked with the president, "making every possible effort to divert his mind from the difficult task which had confronted him during the day."[26]

On April 3, Wilson fell violently ill and had to leave a meeting of the Council of Four. Grayson thought that the president suffered from influenza, although retrospective analyses suggest that he had contracted a serious viral infection. Whatever the diagnosis, Grayson knew that his patient's condition was serious, and for several nights he sat with him at the side of his bed, sometimes long after midnight. On April 7, when Wilson was better, he asked Grayson: "Do you see any change in House; I don't mean a physical change; he does not show the same free and easy spirit; he seems to act distant with me as if he has something on his conscience." Grayson was not entirely frank in his reply, avoiding any direct criticism of House and instead blaming his son-in-law Gordon Auchincloss, who had swollen up so much that "should he remain here much longer, he will bust." Grayson had, in fact, finally broken with House, who, he concluded, had on more than one occasion undermined the president's position. House had become " 'The Great American Acquiescor,' " the "champion Yes, Yes-man with Lloyd George, and Yes, Yes, with Clemenceau."[27]

In early April, Grayson poured out his anxieties about the peace con-ference in a long letter to McAdoo. He condemned those close to the president who were attempting to compromise and whose behavior "sim-ply makes my blood boil." Grayson worried that Wilson might suffer a relapse, especially considering the fact that he was "working beyond his endurance." The day before, Grayson wrote, Wilson had received a dele-gation right after breakfast, then went to a meeting of the Council of Four that did not adjourn until lunchtime, then entertained the queen of Ro-mania for lunch, and at three o'clock attended the plenary session of the peace conference, which adjourned just before dinner. After dinner he went to a meeting of the League of Nations Commission and did not fi-nally get to bed until after 1:00 a.m. Nevertheless, Grayson concluded that "with the President's great brain and courage I am confident that every-thing ultimately is going to come out all right. But I feel that he is going through a lot of unnecessary strain by not having the proper help." Gray-son longed for McAdoo's presence at the peace conference, telling his long-time friend that "your cooperation, vision, and more than all else, your boldness and your courage and good common-sense are just what the President needs in this crisis." At the end of April, Grayson's spirits had not improved. "These are terrible days," he confided to Tumulty, "for the President physically and otherwise."[28]

Grayson tried to help, urging Wilson to get more exercise, to rest on Sundays, or to drive to Bernard Baruch's villa at St. Cloud, where he could enjoy the company of the convivial financier. He also found that Wilson relied on him more and more as an adviser, one with whom he could dis-cuss issues of the peace conference. On April 24, the two men had a long talk about the crisis over Italian territorial claims. The president showed Grayson maps and explained the Pact of London and various other issues under discussion. And once again, in the privacy of his diary, Grayson denounced House as the "King of Compromisers," who was telling the Italians that in the end he could convince Wilson to yield.[29]

In early May, Grayson was once again worried about the pressure on the president. "I have never" he confided to his diary, "seen the President more fatigued then he was at dinner time this evening. He could not have had a harder or more difficult and fatiguing day." When Ray Stannard Baker appeared for peace conference news, Wilson, rather than talk to Baker himself, told Grayson to brief him. After dinner Grayson spent an hour relaxing with Woodrow and Edith, and once again he was impressed with Edith's devotion to her ailing husband.[30]

Over the course of the peace conference Grayson had observed many of its leading personalities—David Lloyd George, Georges Clemenceau, John Pershing, Ferdinand Foch, and Arthur Balfour—and he had concluded that "the President is the best informed and the most skilled diplomatist in the European countries today. He knows the details of all countries and the philosophy of their governments as a whole." Despite the "deception and trickery" of his adversaries and the failure of some of his advisers, Grayson, as the conference drew to a close, remained convinced that Wilson was the greatest leader of his time.[31]

Grayson realized that, because of the Republican Party's "organized campaign of misrepresentation," and the lack of effective Democratic leaders in the Senate, "[i]t is very plain that the President has a Herculean task before him when he returns to the United States." On the voyage back to America, Wilson had trouble organizing his thoughts and writing the speech he planned to give before the Senate.[32] That speech, delivered on July 10, was a failure, and nine days later Wilson developed headaches, a cramped hand, and difficulty reading and speaking. Grayson insisted that Woodrow and Edith spend the weekend on the *Mayflower*, and, once back at the White House, put the president to bed. As the editors of *The Papers of Woodrow Wilson* note, the doctor "may or may not have understood the cause of Wilson's illness [which was his long-standing hypertension and cerebrovascular disease], but he did recognize that his patient was a very sick man," with diminished capacities of leadership, and that a speaking tour might lead to a major breakdown. For a time after the July 19 stroke, Grayson convinced Wilson to cancel his western trip, but the president soon returned to his obsession with the tour that he hoped would rally the American people behind the peace treaty. In late August, when Grayson went to his study to make a final appeal, the president was ready with a response: "I know what you have come for. I do not want to do anything foolhardy but the League of Nations is now in its crisis, and if it fails I hate to think what will happen to the world. You must remember that I, as Commander in Chief, was responsible for sending our soldiers to Europe. In the crucial test in the trenches they did not turn back—and I cannot turn back now. I cannot put my personal safety, my health in the balance against my duty—I must go."[33]

On September 3, Grayson, along with Woodrow, Edith, and Tumulty, headed west on the special presidential train. From the start of the trip Grayson knew that his patient was not in good health, and he did all that he could to ease the strain on him. He insisted that Wilson not add to his burdens with rear platform speeches, and in the evening, after dinner, Grayson drew out Tumulty, who sought to entertain Woodrow and Edith with his "explosive Irish wit." At every stop, however, the president was greeted by dense crowds, and from early on in the tour Wilson suffered from asthma and pounding headaches; by the time he reached Portland, Oregon, Grayson wrote that "the strain of the trip was showing on the President, and it required all of my skill to keep him fit so that he could meet the engagements before him."[34] On September 25, outside Pueblo, Colorado, Wilson's headaches became so severe that Grayson stopped the train and went for a long walk with the president. Early the next morning, as the pain became unbearable, Edith called for Grayson, who found his patient "in a highly nervous condition, the muscles of his face were twitching, and he was extremely nauseated." After Wilson fell asleep, Grayson awakened Tumulty, and they and Edith agreed that the trip must be called off. When Wilson woke up, Grayson told him that "he owed it to the country, as well as to Mrs. Wilson and his children to stop now before very serious developments should occur." The president finally relented, telling his faithful aides, "I don't seem to realize it, but I seem to have gone to pieces. The Doctor is right. I am not in condition to go on. I have never been in a condition like this, and I just feel as if I am going to pieces." As Grayson recorded, those in the president's entourage felt a "deep sorrow" as the trip was canceled and the train sped back to the nation's capital.[35]

On September 28, when the train reached Union Station, Grayson immediately imposed a strict "rest cure" on the president. Wilson, his physician decreed, "should not be bothered with any matters of official character," especially any questions of a controversial nature. He could not, in short, meet with members of his cabinet or with other officials. For a few days Wilson seemed better, but early in the morning of October 2, he awoke, found that his left hand was limp, and fell to the floor in the bathroom. Edith called Grayson and, after his arrival, together they put Woodrow to bed. Stunned by his patient's condition, Grayson exclaimed to Irwin Hoover, the chief White House usher, "My God, the President is paralyzed," and summoned Wilson's ophthalmologist and neurologist for consultation. The three physicians agreed that he had suffered a stroke, a clot in an artery of the brain; his left side was paralyzed. The next day Secretary of State Lansing, who realized that the president was very ill and might be disabled, found that Grayson, like Tumulty, would not be a party to suggesting that he was unable to carry out his duties. When the cabinet convened on October 6, Grayson told its members that Wilson's mind was "not only clear but very active." And Grayson's frequent bulletins to the press described the president's "nervous exhaustion" but obscured the nature of his illness.[36]

For nearly a month the president was so ill that he was unable to carry out any of the functions of his office. Edith made a series of critical decisions. She discouraged her husband from admitting that he was incapacitated and resigning from office, insisted on concealing the severity of his illness from the public, and assumed a major role in the workings of the government. Edith decided what issues would be brought to his attention and what visitors he would see. She led a triumvirate—including Grayson and Tumulty—that managed affairs of state. Documents and letters that flowed to the president would often be returned with her handwritten notes on them, filled with spelling and grammatical errors, prefaced with the message that "the President says." As one biographer notes, Edith, Grayson, and Tumulty decided that "what best served Woodrow Wilson best served the country," and "enshrouded the Presidency in as much secrecy as possible." Josephus Daniels, who knew that the president was partly paralyzed, urged Grayson to be honest with the American people, but he replied: "I think you are right. I wish I could do so and state that the paralysis is partial and he will probably get over it or get over it enough to return to his full duties. But I am forbidden to speak of it. The President and Mrs. Wilson have made me make a promise to that effect. You are the only person except his son-in-law that knows his condition." Grayson's emotional bond with Edith and Woodrow ran so deep that he could not imagine challenging their decisions. At a critical moment of his public life, Wilson lay incapacitated while three members of his much diminished inner circle—House and McAdoo were gone—struggled to carry out his wishes and to keep the government functioning.[37]

By the end of October, Wilson's health had improved enough so that Edith allowed carefully managed visits. She controlled access to her husband's bedroom, while Tumulty tried to handle official business and Grayson kept a close watch on his patient's health.[38] By early 1920, government business was piling up, the press was debating Wilson's physical condition, and, in late January, the president, weakened by a viral infection, talked with Grayson about resigning. Grayson urged him to do so, but Edith strongly opposed resignation, and in early February, Woodrow's physical condition dramatically improved. He now found that his doctor's two-year-old son, Gordon, was a stimulating companion, and he also became more assertive and obstructive. On March 3, he left the White House grounds for the first time in five months. He was still, however, subject to mood swings, and Edith and Grayson continued to shield him from pessimistic news. On March 15, the peace treaty failed, for a second time, to win a two-thirds majority in the Senate. That night Grayson visited the troubled president several times. "Doctor," he said, "the devil is a busy man." He then asked Grayson to read from the Bible and said, "If I were not Christian, I think I should go mad, but my faith in God holds me to the belief that He is in some way working out His own plans through human perversities and mistakes."[39]

As the spring unfolded, the president began to consider running for a third term. He believed that if the Democratic convention deadlocked, the delegates might turn to him as "someone to lead them out of the wilderness." Wilson now gave the appearance of being well and held regular cabinet meetings, but Grayson and Edith knew that he was still a very sick man, and both feared that another campaign would end in his death. Grayson worked behind the scenes to make sure that delegates at the Democratic convention in San Francisco (which met on June 28) did not rally behind the president. He told one prominent Democrat, Carter Glass, as he left for the convention, "If anything comes up, save the life and fame of this great man from the juggling of false friends," and gave another party insider, Robert Woolley, a frank account of Wilson's physical condition: "No matter what others may tell you, no matter what you may read about the President being on the road to recovery, I tell you that he is permanently ill physically, is gradually weakening mentally and can't recover. He couldn't possibly survive the campaign." At the convention, party insiders closed ranks against Wilson and nominated Governor James M. Cox of Ohio on the forty-fourth ballot.[40]

In the aftermath of the Democrats' sweeping defeat in early November, Wilson drifted. His physical health continued to improve, but his emotional swings grew more extreme. Or as Grayson put it to Ray Stannard Baker, "He takes it less easily, does not make light of it or joke as he did. He more easily loses control of himself & when he talks is likely to break down & weep." Wilson's temper flared; he shouted at nurses and even at this loyal physician. He also often called for Grayson in the middle of the night, whether he needed him or not, and engaged him in long conversations. One longtime aide, Charles Swem, complained that the president was being treated like a child, "humored, petted, and coddled and justifying all his weaknesses by the plea that he is sick."[41]

Throughout the winter of 1920–21, Wilson's bitter mood persisted. After attending Harding's inauguration on March 4—it was physically impossible for him to stay for the swearing-in ceremony—Woodrow, Edith, Grayson, Tumulty, a valet, and a Secret Service agent left for the ex-president's new home on 2340 S Street (for the purchase of which Grayson had rallied some of Wilson's closest friends). President Harding had assigned Grayson to Washington, where he could continue to serve as Wilson's personal physician. In late March 1921, Wilson had prostate trouble, and by mid-May he stayed in bed most days. Grayson thought that the ex-president was too passive and urged him "to get at some work that will engage, even to exhaustion, his self-consuming mind," but his patient was not, in fact, improving. Worse still, his good eye began to fail. In late January 1924, Grayson, badly in need of a rest, traveled to South Carolina for a shooting expedition on Baruch's estate. After a few days, Edith, worried about Woodrow's health, summoned him back to Washington. At first Grayson was not alarmed, but the next morning he realized that Wilson's condition was serious and that his body was shutting down. When Grayson told Woodrow that his death was imminent, he responded, "I am ready. I am a broken piece of machinery." Then he put his hand on Grayson's arm and said, "You have been good to me. You have done everything you could."[42]

On Sunday, February 3, Wilson died at 11:15 a.m. Grayson went to the front door of the S Street house to announce the ex-president's death to the assembled reporters. As he read a detailed account of the cause of Wilson's death, his eyes filled with tears. His long vigil had finally come to an end. As one biographer notes, he "had promised Ellen Wilson on her deathbed that he would look after her husband." He had kept that promise.[43]

After Wilson's death, Grayson led a busy and varied life. He and Altrude lived at The Highlands, a twenty-three-acre estate on Wisconsin Avenue, and in 1928 bought Blue Ridge Farm near Upperville, Virginia, where Grayson could breed thoroughbred horses. A skilled rider since his youth, he studied horses and often told his friends that "the outside of a horse is good for the inside of a man." Grayson shared his passion for horses, and for hunting, with Baruch, and over the years the two friends enjoyed the races at Saratoga Springs and hunted in Czechoslovakia and at Baruch's estate in South Carolina. Like Wilson, Baruch found Grayson to be a man of "keen intelligence, deep religious feelings, and a highly developed sense of duty," combined with a "wit and charm which endeared him to Wilson as it did to everybody." Grayson also remained close to Ray Stannard Baker, encouraging him to complete his great biography and giving him medical advice for his various ailments.[44]

Most of all, throughout the 1920s and 1930s, Grayson was fiercely determined to protect the president's legacy. In 1924, he wrote some recollections of the personal side of Wilson—which were published posthumously—and in early 1926, with the appearance of the first two volumes of Charles Seymour's *The Intimate Papers of Colonel House*, Grayson responded with a critical but perceptive essay on the House-Wilson relationship (published long after his death in *American Heritage Magazine* as "The Colonel's Folly and the President's Distress.")Grayson pointed out that House—despite Wilson's intellectual dominance of the relationship—gradually came to see himself not as a subordinate adviser but as the "great conciliator" of the Allies. Or as Grayson put it, "too many trips to Europe, too much association with the great folk of the world, too much delegated responsibility, and too many adulators, spoiled the Colonel House I had known in the early years of the Wilson administration. Europe was too far away from Texas. The stage was too big, the pageantry too impressive, the praise too seductive, and, gradually, Colonel E. M. House of Houston and Austin Texas, of the Texas governor's staff . . . got his head turned." Two years later, Grayson revealed in a biographical sketch that he was gathering material for a book that "will divest certain Warwicks of their borrowed plumage and reveal Wilson in a new light to the peoples of every race and clime." But he never completed the project.[45]

Grayson was devoted to Franklin D. Roosevelt, and in 1933, and again in 1937, chaired his inaugural committee. In 1935, he became the chairman of the American Red Cross, a position he held until his death, at the age of fifty-nine, on February 15, 1938. He died nearly a month and a half before the death of Colonel House, the man whose friendship he had once valued so highly.

Secretary of War Newton Baker, speaking at a patriotic event in 1917. Baker did not join Wilson's cabinet until March 1916, but he became one of the president's closest advisers and most fervent admirers. Like the president, he was a gifted orator. Library of Congress, Prints and Photographs Division, LC-DIG-hec-09797. Photo by Harris & Ewing.

CHAPTER EIGHT

Newton D. Baker

"You are still the captain of my soul"

Between 1889 and 1892, Newton D. Baker, an undergraduate at Johns Hopkins University, attended the lectures of a visiting professor from Princeton, Woodrow Wilson. Apparently the young student did not meet the distinguished scholar, and the paths of the two men would not cross again until April 1912, when Baker, now reform mayor of Cleveland, Ohio, became involved in the Wilson campaign. But Baker turned down the new president's offer of a place in his cabinet; he did not, in fact, join it until March 1916. As secretary of war from 1916 to 1921, he became one of Wilson's closest advisers and most fervent admirers. But he never recorded his first impressions of the man he would serve so loyally for so many years.

Baker was born in Martinsburg, West Virginia, on December 3, 1871. His mother was a fervent supporter of the Confederacy and a High Church Episcopalian; his father joined the Confederate Army in 1861, served under J.E.B. Stuart, and fought at Gettysburg. He returned home just before the peace settlement at Appomattox, and in September 1865 enrolled in medical school at the University of Maryland. Two years later, he returned to Martinsburg and set up the medical practice that he would maintain until his death in 1909. His son was a quiet, sensitive boy who accompanied his father in the horse and buggy he used for his medical rounds and who read the books he kept in his office. Father and son discussed a wide range of topics, and "Newt," as he was called, acquired from his father a romantic view of the South and of race relations there. His family had owned slaves before the Civil War, and Baker had warm memories of his black "mammy": "I still remember her as the comforter and protector of my youth, and certainly I learned from her humbly given, but profoundly potent lessons about humility and goodness."[1]

Despite his service for the Confederacy, Baker's father was a tolerant man who did not resent the victory of the North. Or as his son remembered, "My father accepted in word and spirit the results of the war and from my earliest childhood taught me to rejoice that our country was reunited."[2]

In 1889, Baker traveled to Baltimore, where he attended Johns Hopkins University. He prospered there, joining a fraternity and immersing himself in the social and intellectual life of the university. After his graduation in 1892, he stayed for an additional year so that he could read in Roman law and jurisprudence. He then moved on to law school at Washington and Lee University in Lexington, Virginia, managing to complete a two-year legal program in one year. Baker was a superb student, and during his years at Johns Hopkins and at Washington and Lee he had acquired an impressive education.

In 1894, after he graduated from law school, Baker returned to Martinsburg to set up a law practice. He lived at home, without a wife, and clients were slow to appear. He must have been relieved when in January 1896 US Postmaster General William L. Wilson, who had served in the Confederate Army with his father, asked him to become his private secretary. Baker found political life in the nation's capital stimulating and was impressed with President Grover Cleveland, who he found a "sturdy and solid character." Baker was a gold standard Democrat who supported free trade and civil service reform, and who disliked William Jennings Bryan and his allegedly radical ideas. Nor did he have much respect for the new Republican president, William McKinley. In June 1897, he left Washington, toured Europe during the summer, and then returned to Martinsburg in September, where he once again set up a law firm, this time with two other lawyers.

But Baker was restless and ambitious, and he was drawn to Cleveland, a rapidly growing industrial powerhouse whose financial and legal establishments had close ties to West Virginia. In January 1899, he joined a Cleveland law firm. Three and a half years later, he married Elizabeth Leopold. The couple raised three children and had a warm, traditional marriage that lasted thirty-four years.[3]

Baker soon became, as one biographer notes, "a rising star in Cleveland's legal community," but his legal career was cut short by the election of Tom Loftin Johnson as mayor in 1901. Johnson, a charismatic reformer, called for municipal ownership of streetcar lines and other utilities and soon drew together a talented cabinet that helped him transform the city and gain a reputation, as the progressive journalist Lincoln Steffens declared, as "the best mayor of the best-governed city in the United States."[4]

Johnson drew the young, idealistic lawyer into his orbit, making him a legal adviser and eventually, after the city charter was changed in 1903, supporting his election as city solicitor. Johnson was impressed with Baker, convinced that "he ranks with the best, highest paid, corporation lawyers in ability and has held his public office at a constant personal sacrifice." In turn, Baker was inspired by Johnson's vision and intelligence, recalling that "my association with Mr. Johnson was intensely stimulating, intellectually and morally. He was one of the few really great men I have ever known, and undoubtedly everything I have done or thought since I knew him, has been in some way affected by his splendid mind."[5]

In the early years of the twentieth century, Baker, who soon became the mayor's most trusted adviser, was at the center of the bitter, prolonged battles that Johnson fought with powerful utility companies, especially the Cleveland Electric Railway Company. Baker was involved in virtually endless litigation, arguing three cases before the Supreme Court, and, to the surprise of many observers, he emerged as a successful politician. He won election as city solicitor for five successive terms, until he became mayor in January 1912.[6]

Baker was a small man, five feet six inches tall and weighing 125 pounds, with a reserved personality and a love of books. Initially his opponents underestimated him, but they soon discovered that this bookish man was a skilled politician. In 1905, Baker's followers introduced him as "the Napoleon of Democratic eloquence, our Little Corporal, Newton D. Baker," and, as the years passed, he would gain fame as an orator. Like Woodrow Wilson, he spoke extemporaneously, in a conversational tone, using few gestures, with a candor and conviction that appealed to audiences first in Cleveland and then across the country.[7]

Baker was a more pragmatic leader than Johnson, willing to work with both reformers and business groups to carry out his program for the rapidly growing city. He achieved municipal home rule, brought about major improvements in Cleveland's infrastructure, and supported municipal utilities in cases, such as the production of electricity, where private utilities were performing poorly. He became known as the "Big Little Mayor," admired for his honesty and decency and for his devotion to the welfare of Cleveland's citizens. Baker's new age of civic reform, one biographer notes, included "more beautiful parks, cleaner streets, upright government and widespread adherence to justice as the ideal of social and economic relations." In November 1913, he was reelected to a second term as mayor. Baker's reformism, however, had its limits. He was deeply committed to stability and order and suspicious of federal authority. The economic slump of 1914 hit Cleveland's industries hard, laying off thousands of workers and bringing widespread despair in the city's industrial neighborhoods. But Mayor Baker would not engage in municipal public works or expand the city's welfare system. He insisted that private relief organizations should deal with the unemployment crisis.[8]

Baker gradually developed a reputation as a successful municipal reformer, and as his interest in national politics grew, he moved toward the progressive wing of the Democratic Party. He overcame his initial opposition and supported William Jennings Bryan in 1900 and 1908 but complained that "his thinking is certainly not of a modern type." Convinced that the Democratic Party "is essentially a radical party," Baker was looking for a new type of Democratic leader.[9]

Initially Baker was skeptical of Woodrow Wilson, concerned about the depth of his commitment to reform. But by March 1912, his doubts about Wilson's progressivism had disappeared, and he announced his support. Baker led the pro-Wilson movement in Ohio. When Governor Judson Harmon won the primary there and imposed a unit rule on the Ohio delegation to the Democratic convention in Baltimore (requiring the entire delegation to vote as a unit), Baker won the fight on the floor against the unit rule and delivered nineteen additional delegates to Wilson. He played, in short, a pivotal role in Wilson's nomination. During the fall campaign he undertook speaking tours in Iowa and Wisconsin and welcomed Wilson on his visit to Cleveland. In November, Wilson carried Ohio by an ample margin.[10]

Wilson was eager to bring Baker into his cabinet, but the mayor, who was only a year into his first term, declined an appointment. As he wrote to the new president, "My place in your army is out here where I can interpret you to the virile but somewhat impatient people who are making a wonderful city of Cleveland." Always a localist, Baker believed that great industrial cities such as Cleveland were vital laboratories of social reform. Colonel House, who was helping the president put together his cabinet, was upset by what he viewed as Baker's provincialism and by his refusal "to take a broader view of the situation and do the big work." He was, House concluded, "a high minded fellow, and a man of ability, but I am afraid he is not constructive enough to handle the Interior Department."[11]

During 1913, as the new administration settled in, Baker worked with McAdoo and Tumulty on patronage in Ohio. He made several trips to Washington to confer with the president and secretary of the treasury, and, as his biographer observes, he developed a "closer and more personal" relationship with McAdoo than with any other member of Wilson's cabinet.[12]

In the years before the outbreak of World War I, Baker was upset by the militarism of President Theodore Roosevelt and of the major European powers. "I cannot help believing," he wrote, "that the accumulation of means of war and destruction is both a temptation to their use . . . and a demoralization of the peace-loving and civilized sentiment of our people."

He was a member of a variety of peace organizations and, while not a pacifist, believed that disputes among nations should be settled by diplomatic efforts. When war broke out in August 1914, Baker, despite his admiration of German culture, condemned Germany's invasion of Belgium and praised Wilson's neutrality policies. He supported Wilson's response to the sinking of the *Lusitania*, and in early 1916 even endorsed, without enthusiasm, the president's preparedness program. By then he had become less neutral, convinced that "Germany intended this war, prepared for it, and began it," and also convinced that Germany had become, as one biographer writes, "an outlaw nation that posed a mortal threat to international decency and order."[13]

On January 1, 1916, Baker was out of office, looking forward to building up his new law firm. He was tired of public life and concerned about the financial well-being of his family. But events in Washington would soon change Baker's life. On February 10, 1916, Secretary of War Lindley M. Garrison, bellicose and outspoken, finally resigned. Wilson, who had wanted to bring Baker into his cabinet in 1913, now tried once again. Baker traveled to Washington to discuss the offer with the president, pointing out all the reasons that he should not be secretary of war. When he finished, the president asked, "Are you ready to take the oath?" Baker began his new position on March 9, 1916. He was forty-four years old.[14]

At first glance, Baker seemed unqualified for the position. He had the appearance, one historian notes, of a "detached scholar," and in 1914 he had declared his "utter non-comprehension of military matters." McAdoo remembered how Baker "used to sit at this desk at the War Department with one leg curled up under him on the cushion of his chair. On his desk there was always a fresh pansy, and he continually smoked a pipe. A small man physically, Baker looked boyish in the company of the tall and bulky generals who were usually around him." Raymond Fosdick, however, who knew both Baker and Wilson well, recalled that Baker was "the most satisfactory man to work with whom I have ever known. Endowed with a crisp, incisive mind, he had a power of analysis and a capacity for lucid statement which shown through every letter he wrote and every speech he made." It was hardly surprising that the president and the new secretary of war quickly developed "strong ties of mutual respect and affection."[15]

On May 11, 1916, in a conversation with the journalist Ray Stannard Baker, Wilson revealed how pleased he was with the secretary of war: "I am delighted with your namesake in the Cabinet," Wilson told the reporter. "It is a comfort to have him with me." Baker, Wilson continued, "had a trained mind: an administrative mind & that his experience as Mayor of Cleveland . . . made him especially useful." Unlike Garrison, who "was an intensely argumentative man," Baker accepted a fact, "makes room for it & goes ahead." Even Colonel House initially was impressed with the new secretary of war. After a long talk, he recorded that "I like Baker and we got along famously. . . . I believe Baker is an abler man than Garrison and that time will prove him so." When House urged Wilson to replace Vice President Thomas R. Marshall with Baker, Wilson replied that "he felt that Baker was too good a man to be sacrificed."[16]

Baker realized that he knew nothing about the War Department, a sprawling organization with a wide variety of duties. As he told his chief military adviser, "I am an innocent. I don't know anything about this job. You must treat me as a father would his son. I am going to do what you advise me." Once in office, Baker moved carefully to push legislation through Congress that would bring about a moderate expansion of the regular army. He sought to appease preparedness advocates without offending those who were opposed to any expansion of the American military. The passage of the National Defense Act in May 1916 achieved these goals, while in August 1916, Baker created a Council for National Defense designed to coordinate the purchases of various federal departments.[17]

Baker fervently hoped, however, that the United States could avoid being drawn into the war. As the mayor of Cleveland, he had been a strong supporter of Wilsonian neutrality, and by the time he became secretary of war he had reached a number of conclusions about the conflict. He believed that the Allies "were dealing with an adversary who had abandoned all the conventions and restraints of civilization," that the British blockade was not the same as German U-boat warfare, and that Germany through its violation of international treaties had "debased the coinage of the common thought of the world." Despite his sympathy for the Allies, Baker opposed American intervention until a cabinet meeting on March 20, 1917, when he finally joined his colleagues in advocating a declaration of war. As he later put it, "America is in arms now to vindicate upon the battlefield the right of democracy to exist against the denials of autocracy." On April 3, after Baker reread the president's war message, he wrote to him that "I am willing to have future generations judge your administration by that document."[18]

When Baker entered the cabinet, he received a warm welcome from Secretary of the Navy Daniels. The two men, who were responsible for so much of the American war effort, met often and corresponded frequently. As Daniels remembered, "[Baker] and I were yoke fellows in everything and stimulated the perfect working together of the Army and Navy, which made them invincible in the World War." But he soon clashed with Secretary of the Treasury McAdoo, who viewed American entry into the war—with its great expansion of the powers of the federal government—as a way to expand his own authority. He and Baker would soon differ over the best way to coordinate the purchase of war materials. Most of all, however, Baker sought to be loyal to the president and to try to resolve disputes among his cabinet colleagues before they reached Wilson. Or as he remembered, "I think I knew his mind completely and entirely, not only from what he said to me but because I had come to have a very sensitive appreciation of the way his mind worked."[19]

The president appreciated Baker's efforts, declaring that "[Baker] is one of the most genuine and gifted men that I know." Colonel House, however, had always been skeptical of Baker's abilities, and in late March 1917, when it was certain that the nation would soon enter the war, he had a long talk with the president about wartime leadership, urging him to replace Baker and Daniels. "They were," he asserted, "good men in peace time but did not fit in with war. That even if they were fit, the country did not believe them to be, and the mistakes that were sure to be made would be laid upon his shoulders because of them. I felt that he had taken a gamble that there would be no war and had lost." He needed, in short, "better timber than was generally thought to be in the War and Navy Departments." While Wilson listened "sympathetically" to House's argument, he was determined to keep Baker close to his side. The next day he brushed aside House's suggestion that he dispatch Baker as ambassador to Great Britain.[20]

Prior to April 1917, the administration had engaged in little planning for the mobilization of the nation's industrial resources or moved to create an effective military machine. In 1916, Congress had, at Wilson's urging, approved a substantial expansion of the navy and had also increased the size of the regular army. But as of April 1, 1917, the army was still a tiny force, with only 5,791 officers and 121,797 regulars, along with 80,446 National Guard troops under state control. The army's general staff was weak, its bureau chiefs all-powerful, its officer corps unacquainted with modern war, and American industry unprepared to equip even a small force with adequate weapons.[21]

In the spring of 1917, Baker was a key figure in Wilson's efforts to swiftly mobilize the nation. The secretary of war and the president agreed on the need to raise a large American army through conscription and selected General John J. Pershing as commander of the American Expeditionary Force. In June 1917, they dispatched him to France with instructions to create an independent American force on the Western Front. Baker was, however, reluctant to make widespread changes in the War Department; he was slow to realize, as one historian notes, "that the economy could not meet the combined demands of the army, the Allies, and the American public without sweeping national regulation." By late 1917, discontent was growing over what seemed the weakness of the American war effort. Severe weather in the Northeast created a coal crisis, the nation's rail and shipping lines were close to collapse under the strain of wartime demands, and sickness in hastily constructed army camps aroused critics of the War Department. Republicans, led by Theodore Roosevelt, bitterly attacked the alleged failures of the administration and the apparent confusion and inefficiency of the nation's preparations for war. Baker's critics were un-relenting. As he put it, "these people wouldn't believe I was Secretary of War unless I was six feet tall and had guns strapped around my waist."[22]

During a visit to Washington on January 5, 1918, House realized "that there is a great deal of criticism of Baker's administration of the War Department. He is now compared to Daniels, and to Baker's disadvantage. . . . Baker seems to be getting deeper into the mire, and the President cannot see it. Baker's mind is so sympathetic with that of the President's that the President does not realize that he is no more of an administrator than he is himself."[23]

Some congressional Democrats shared the Republican critique, and on January 10, 1918, the chairman of the Senate's military affairs committee, George E. Chamberlain (D-OR), brought Baker before his committee and grilled him for three days. Baker aggressively defended the War Department, leading the *New York Times* to condemn his "cocksure and airily complaisant attitude." As the pressure on him mounted, Baker on January 21 sent a letter of resignation to the president. Two days later he talked with Daniels, who found him looking "5 years older." The conversation with the secretary of the navy apparently restored Baker's spirits, and on January 28 he once again appeared before Chamberlain's committee. This time, however, Baker was prepared, reviewing the War Department's mobilization programs for over four hours and giving the public the first thorough analysis of the nation's war effort. During the committee's after-noon recess, Senator Ollie James (D-KY) rushed into the president's office and declared: " 'Jesus, you ought to see that little Baker. He's eating 'em up!' " The president stood behind his secretary of war, dismissing Chamberlain's accusations as "an astonishing and absolutely unjustifiable dis-tortion of the truth."[24]

Wilson moved quickly to rally his forces in Congress and to improve the administration's war effort. He gained the authority to reorganize gov-ernment agencies, and he assembled a war cabinet—consisting of Baker, Daniels, McAdoo, and the heads of key wartime agencies—that met every week. Baker also moved to make changes in the War Department, strip-ping the bureaus of much of their autonomy and appointing a new, powerful chief of staff, Peyton C. March. But Baker lost his struggle with McAdoo over the chairmanship of the War Industries Board, an agency designed to set priorities and to coordinate industrial mobilization. McAdoo was convinced that Bernard Baruch was the obvious choice, while Baker opposed his appointment because of his career as "a Wall Street financier." In early March, Wilson sided with McAdoo, selecting Baruch as chairman. Prior to the January crisis, Baker, one biographer notes, had been "only half at war," not fully aware of the urgent need to reorganize his department or of the need to take the public into his confidence. The president's intervention had saved the secretary of war, and by the middle of March much of the confusion and anxiety over the administration's war effort seemed to have passed. When Ray Stannard Baker encountered him in London, he found Baker to be "the same light-footed, active little man as ever—all wires and energy, his eyes very black and his face full of little wrinkles, some of which are assuredly war wrinkles—a kindly, smiling, eager, able man."[25]

Baker had no role in devising the strategy of the AEF. His task was to supervise the training, transportation, and provisioning of the new American army. Once American troops were in France, the secretary of war and the president had delegated sweeping authority over their deployment to General Pershing. On March 10, 1918, Baker reached Paris for an inspection tour of American facilities. Eleven days after his arrival, the German army launched a massive offensive against Britain's Fifth Army, one that threatened to separate British and French forces and drive the BEF toward the northwest and Channel ports. Allied leaders, fearful of a collapse of their armies, now renewed the pressure on Baker and Wilson for the "brigading" of American troops arriving in France. But Pershing was adamant; during the spring crisis he allowed some of his troops to be fed directly into British and French units, while he continued to build up a separate American force. By the end of June, nine hundred thousand American troops were in France. During his stay there Baker had seen firsthand the demands of modern war and, in discussions with Allied leaders, had insisted on maintaining Pershing's independence.[26]

Baker was proud of the AEF, his great army of citizen-soldiers who were, he believed, united in a crusade for democracy. Throughout 1917–18 he sought to improve the morale of American troops, and he was convinced that the AEF was "the *sanest, most sober,* and *least criminalistic* body engaged in the great war, under any flag, or that could be found in any group the same size in civil life." But Baker's army was one dominated by white men. He had always rejected the idea of racial equality and had accepted segregation in civilian life. Of the four hundred thousand Afro-Americans who were drafted, about two hundred thousand served in France. But they served in segregated units and mostly had noncombat roles. As Baker asserted, "there is no intention on the part of the War Department at this time to settle the so-called race question."[27]

As the crisis on the Western Front grew, Allied demands for intervention in Russia and the re-creation of the Eastern Front intensified. Baker remarked that "we have been literally beset, with the Russian question in its various forms." In early June, Wilson agreed to send a small American force to Murmansk and Archangel, and later in the summer of 1918 he also agreed to dispatch seven thousand troops to Siberia. Baker thought that the Archangel expedition was "nonsense from the beginning," and he also opposed sending American troops to Siberia. It was the only serious disagreement with the president that he ever had. But he remained loyal to Wilson and never publicly criticized his decisions.[28]

On July 18, 1918, a massive Allied offensive began on the Western Front, in what became known as the Second Battle of the Marne. American forces were now heavily engaged in the fighting. In September, Baker returned to France and observed American troops in action, but he had no desire—unlike Pershing—to prolong the war and push for the unconditional surrender of Germany. He was aware of the AEF's growing supply problems and also wanted to end the war quickly for humanitarian reasons. Baker supported Wilson's negotiations with German leaders over the terms of surrender and, with the signing of the armistice on November 11, congratulated the AEF for contributing to "the great victory for the forces of civilization and humanity."[29]

* * *

As the war drew to a close, the secretary of war and the president remained close. On the day of the armistice, Baker wrote to his chief that
"your constant support and confidence and forbearance have been at once
my comfort and my courage whenever the task seemed either long or hard,"
while Wilson informed Baker that "I wonder if you know how genuinely
and entirely I have trusted and believed in you and how happy I am that
the trust and belief have been absolutely justified by the result." As one
observer noted, Baker "was the son Wilson never had."[30]

The president had planned to take Baker to Paris as one of the American peace commissioners, but McAdoo's resignation from the cabinet in
mid-November changed his plans. With McAdoo gone, Baker was now
the cabinet's most prominent member, and he felt that he could not leave
Washington at such a critical moment. But McAdoo's resignation annoyed
Baker. He too was worn out and under financial strain at the end of the
war, but he did not desert the administration. Neither Baker nor Wilson
ever forgot McAdoo's behavior.[31]

While Wilson negotiated in Paris, Baker struggled to dismantle the
American war machine, without any guidance from the president. He
moved quickly to cancel army contracts and to close down wartime com-
mittees, and also confronted the complicated task of withdrawing the AEF
from France. He had, however, no larger vision of demobilization, reassuring the president that there was "no necessity for government action . . .
the present problem is not one of reconstruction but of readjustment."[32]

During the winter of 1918–19, Baker's loyalty to the president never
wavered. As a flawed peace treaty emerged in the spring of 1919, he argued
that Wilson had "stuck it out on the theory that with all his disappointments he would get a better thing for the world than would happen if he
were to leave." While the president had been temporarily defeated by the
"vindictiveness" and "parochial zeal" of the Allies, his vision had led to
the creation of the League of Nations, "the most handsome and enduring
idea born."[33]

After Wilson's return from Paris, he and Baker saw little of each other.
In early October, when the president suffered a stroke, Baker, like Edith,
Tumulty, and Grayson, joined what one historian describes as their "con-

spiracy of false optimism about his health and acuity." On October 18, although Baker had not seen Wilson since his collapse, he wrote that he had received memoranda "which show that he is quite his old self so far as clearness of mind and decision of will are concerned." Years later, reflecting on Wilson's illness, Baker argued that there was no need for the president to resign because "Wilson had a better mind at his sickest moment . . . than anyone else at his best." During the winter of 1919–20, as the fight over the ratification of the peace treaty proceeded, Baker, like Daniels, was against making any concessions to Republican opponents of the treaty. Secretary of State Lansing was critical of both men, observing that they were never willing to challenge any of the president's decisions.[34]

In early March 1921, Baker left Washington and returned to Cleveland, where he was eager rejoin his legal practice. Under Baker's direction his law firm thrived, acquiring wealthy individuals and prominent corporations as its clients, and Baker soon gained the reputation as one of the finest lawyers of his generation. Progressives criticized him for becoming too close to the very conservative forces that he had once opposed, but Baker, who was worried about his family's finances, was not troubled by the wealthy clients who sought his legal services.[35]

While Baker traveled to Washington often on business, he seldom visited the ex-president. He was upset by Wilson's physical and mental decline, telling his wife in early 1924 that "unless it is thought that I can be useful I think I will not often call when I come down. It is quite too depressing." Baker had, however, powerful memories of his association with Wilson, writing to him that "I have gathered imperishable recollections of a great man dealing highly with great affairs which will enrich all the rest of my life so that my affectionate wishes for your welfare are also an expression of deep and abiding gratitude." Wilson had a high opinion of his former secretary of war, regretting that he lacked the qualities necessary for political success.[36]

During the 1920s, Baker's great cause was American membership in the League of Nations, and he was even willing to work with sympathetic Republicans to bring it about. He was unenthusiastic about McAdoo's campaign for the Democratic nomination in 1924, in part because he was "wholly without leadership on the question of our foreign affairs." Baker still had doubts about McAdoo's temperament: "From all I have ever seen, I believe his tendencies are really democratic, but he has an unconscious love of power and a fondness for seeing the machine go in response to his urging which makes him restless and unhappy, unless he is doing something that either makes a flash or a loud noise." He would support Mc-Adoo if he won the nomination, "but why," he wrote to his wife, "is it that I feel repelled by the very ardor of his pursuit of the prize?"[37]

Baker attended the 1924 Democratic convention in New York, where his main purpose was to insert a pro–League of Nations plank in the party's platform. When Baker lost in the resolutions committee, he carried the fight to the floor of the convention where he gave, one biographer notes, "a speech that many considered to be the greatest they had ever heard." But Baker's oratorical triumph did not impress the majority of convention delegates, who rejected his pro-League plank by a vote to two to one. In the fall, Baker campaigned for John W. Davis, who was, he believed, "a true internationalist," the ablest man now living in the Democratic Party.[38]

The flood of war memoirs and diaries that appeared during the 1920s upset Baker. He suggested that all the "keepers of diaries should be incarcerated," and was especially indignant when he read the first volume of *The Intimate Papers of Colonel House*, which appeared in 1926. House had written, Baker complained, "the meanest book he had ever read," claiming credit for all the achievements of the Wilson administration. Baker bristled with contempt for "Mr. Smooth-It-Away," relieved that he had never known House well, "part of the general good fortune which has accompanied me through life."[39]

By the late 1920s, Baker was disappointed by the indifference of the Democratic Party to foreign affairs and by its preoccupation with domestic issues such as Prohibition. He gave up his campaign for American membership in the League, but he remained a fervent internationalist on a wide range of issues. As 1928 approached, some prominent Democrats urged Baker to run for the nomination, but he was ambivalent, well aware of the burdens of the presidency. He thought that Al Smith was an impressive candidate, but doubted that he could be elected, and was disappointed with the platform adopted by the Houston convention. "McKinley," he complained, "could have run on the tariff plank, and Lodge on the one on international relations." Smith was "trying to be more Republican than the Republicans."[40]

The economic collapse in 1929 did not surprise Baker, but he was taken aback by the severity and length of what became the Great Depression. He had, however, few ideas about how to combat the crisis. Baker was reluctant to expand the powers of the federal government or to have it engage in centralized economic planning. He believed that private charities and private relief efforts offered the key to recovery, and he became chairman of the National Citizens' Committee, which sought to mobilize local communities to combat the Depression.[41]

Inevitably, given his prominence, Baker was drawn into the 1932 campaign for the Democratic nomination. Some Democrats believed that he was Wilson's legitimate heir, or as Raymond Fosdick had written to him in 1926, "Wilson told me of his prophetic belief that you would one day succeed him." But Baker was an undeclared candidate; he did not want to withdraw and disappoint his friends, but he had few ideas about domestic policy and by the early 1930s had lost much of his reformist reputation. Oswald Garrison Villard, editor of the *Nation*, believed that Baker had betrayed the liberal ideas of his youth, concealing his conservatism behind eloquence and sentimentality. Moreover, McAdoo, now a candidate for the Senate from California, argued that Baker was too conservative. He was determined to block his nomination. Baker's name was never put before the Chicago convention, and California's switch on the fourth ballot from John Nance Garner to Franklin Delano Roosevelt guaranteed the latter's nomination and ended Baker's quasi-candidacy. Baker, who was content with his life in Cleveland, felt an "unbelievable sense of relief and freedom." Or, as he observed in 1936, "the fact is that I never wanted to be president... [and] as I look back over the past four years, I realize what a tremendous responsibility it would have meant and I have never had a moment's regret that I was not chosen."[42]

Baker was eager to get rid of Herbert Hoover and campaigned for FDR, hoping that the Democratic Party would recapture the idealism of 1912 and 1916 and that it would revive Wilson's internationalism. But he was not enthusiastic about FDR as a person: "I have, of course, known him for many years and know the charm of his personality. There is, however, a certain immaturity and impulsiveness about him which Walter Lippmann once summed up in the statement that there was about him 'a fatal touch of the boy scout.' "[43]

Initially Baker admired FDR's courage and optimism and was impressed with the legislation enacted during the Hundred Days. But Baker was a nineteenth-century liberal, one who worried about the expansion of presidential power and the subordination of the individual to the state. His relations with the new administration—which were never close—soon began to deteriorate. He opposed the National Recovery Act and Tennessee Valley Authority, convinced that the New Deal "was too quick to trade individual liberty for collective security." Like many old progressives, he opposed the paternalism and collectivism of the New Deal, and in 1936 was especially upset by FDR's court-packing plan. He would not, however, join conservative opponents of the New Deal in the American Liberty League, but by 1936 his loyalty to the Democratic Party was shaken. He wrote to his daughter that "I find it difficult to be a Democrat and impossible to be a Republican." Certain that FDR would prevail, he cast his vote for his Republican opponent, Alfred M. Landon.[44]

Baker was much more approving of FDR's foreign policy. He liked his choice of Cordell Hull as secretary of state and realized that the president—despite his internationalist inclinations—had to tread carefully because of the power of isolationists in Congress. Through his membership in the Council on Foreign Relations, he worked hard to raise the public's awareness of issues beyond America's borders. The failure of the Senate in 1935 to accept American membership in the World Court, the judicial arm of the League, upset Baker. As the 1930s progressed, he worried about the ambitions of Germany, Italy, Japan, and the Soviet Union, and continued to hope that somehow the League of Nations "may yet save us from catastrophe." But in January 1937, he wrote that "with four aggressive nations loose and bent on world domination, I should be in favor of any war necessary to restrain any one of [them]."[45]

Over the years, Baker, who was never a physically strong man, had worked long hours on complicated tasks. As early as 1889 he had developed a heart murmur, and in 1928, when he was only fifty-six, he had his first heart attack. He now took frequent vacations to ease the strain on his heart, but more attacks followed. In the summer of 1937, he suffered a stroke, and on December 25, 1937, when he was only sixty-six, he died. A few days before his death, Baker wrote a letter to an old friend, explaining that "really I have every reason in the world to feel highly satisfied with what life has been to me most of my years." Baker was always a serene and meditative man, more drawn to his legal practice and to his books than to public service. He had been inspired by Woodrow Wilson and was widely regarded as his legitimate political heir, but Baker had never pursued the presidency with a singleness of purpose. As one historian notes, "to the end of his life Baker remained a scholar in politics, an omnivorous reader and a classicist, haunting the Democratic Party with a promise of leadership never quite fulfilled."[46]

Woodrow seated at his desk with Edith at his side, June 1920. The collapse of Wilson's health in October 1919 left Edith in charge of a triumvirate that included Grayson and Tumulty. Library of Congress, Prints and Photographs Division, LC-DIG-ppmsca-13425. Photo by Harris & Ewing.

Edith Bolling Galt

"My Husband Woodrow Wilson . . . helped me build from the broken timbers of my life a temple wherein are enshrined memories of his great spirit"

Sometime in March 1915, Edith Bolling Galt and Helen Bones, Woodrow Wilson's cousin and White House hostess, went for a walk in Rock Creek Park. After a long outing on muddy paths, Helen insisted that they return to the White House for tea, reassuring Edith that the president and Dr. Grayson were away playing golf. But when the two women got out of the elevator on the second floor, they ran into Woodrow and his physician. They all agreed to have tea together, and Edith recalled, "we met round a glowing fire in the oval sitting room and had an hour of delightful talk." A few days later, on March 23, Edith returned to the White House for dinner. That evening she wrote to her sister-in-law that after a "delightful dinner," the two women found that the president "was full of interesting stories and a fund of information, and finally, at Miss B's request, read us three English poems, and as a reader he is unequalled." Edith and Woodrow soon discovered that they had much in common—their reverence for their fathers, their southern background, and a fondness for dialect jokes that portrayed African Americans in a condescending way.[1] Edith was forty-two, sixteen years younger than Woodrow, a tall, youthful, vibrant woman, with soft hazel eyes, dark brown hair, and a musical southern voice. Or as one Secret Service agent remembered, "she was . . . a fine figure of a woman, somewhat plump by modern American standards, but ideal from the viewpoint of a mature man. Her face was not only lovely but alive. She laughed easily. . . . As I saw her eyes dancing and her lips trembling with the effort to keep laughter back I thought, 'Lordy me, lady! I'll bet you're driving the boss wild!'" Woodrow was smitten, as he had been many years before when he met Ellen Axson, and soon Edith would become the most important person in his life. She devoted herself entirely to him, and after his death in February 1924, Edith worked tirelessly for the next thirty-seven years to shape his historical reputation.[2]

Edith Bolling Galt was born on October 15, 1872, the seventh of eleven children, nine of whom lived into adulthood. Her family lost its plantation in eastern Virginia during the Civil War and at the end of the conflict moved to Wytheville, a prosperous town of around two thousand people in the western part of the state. Her father, a lawyer and circuit court judge, moved his large family to a three-story brick building near the center of town. The extended Bolling family lived on the second and third floors, while the ground floor was filled with shops. Edith's mother, Sallie White, a gentle, deferential woman, was absorbed in raising her many children, while her father, William Holcombe Bolling, was often away on court business. Nevertheless, he was a vivid presence in Edith's life, or, as she remembered, "to everyone of us he was not only a father, but a comrade—who shared our joys and sorrows, who understood our complexities, and taught us all we knew of *fine* principles and real Christianity."[3]

The dominant figure in Edith's childhood, however, was her grandmother Anne Bolling. Edith slept with her grandmother, learned to meet her many demands, and to take care of her twenty-six canaries. Her grandmother, Edith recalled, was "an unusually capable and dominant person, to whom an obstacle only meant something to overcome. She used to say with scorn: 'I hate a *can't*; anyone can do anything they try to.'" And "she was strong in her likes and dislikes as she was in every relation to life. She simply did, or did not, like you—there was an end of it, and no compromise." Edith did not attend school in Wytheville; Grandmother Bolling, with some help from her father, looked after her education.[4]

Edith had a parochial childhood. Not until the age of thirteen did she leave Wytheville, and not until the age of fifteen did she leave for a boarding school, Martha Washington College, in nearby Abington. Edith disliked the harsh regimen at the school and did not return for a second year. Two years later she tried another boarding school, Richmond Female Seminary, but it closed at the end of her first year. Her time there marked the end of Edith's formal schooling. Years later, after she met Woodrow Wilson, she would regret her sketchy education, writing to him, "Never before did I long for the wisdom of a well informed mind half so much for then I could be a staff for you to lean on." In her memoir, published in 1939, Edith gave a somewhat romantic view of her childhood, recalling that "the blue circle of the mountains bounded my world." But her friend and Wilson biographer Ray Stannard Baker viewed growing up in Wytheville differently, observing, "It was a narrow, pinched and difficult existence: no servants, no money, but with a hospitable home crowded with children and relatives," and dominated by the formidable Grandmother Bolling.[5]

Edith's older sister had married Alexander Galt, a member of a prosperous family that owned a fine jewelry and silver store in Washington, DC. In 1889, Edith began the first of several visits to her sister's home. The time that she spent with Gertrude opened a new world of music, theater, and fashion for Edith, who was an ambitious and curious young lady. During one of her visits she met Norman Galt, the handsome cousin of her brother-in-law who lived with his father in a spacious brownstone and who worked in the family business. Norman soon fell in love with Edith, beginning a four-year courtship that finally ended in the spring of 1895 when Edith agreed to marry him. She was twenty-two; Norman, thirty-one. As Edith recalled, while she liked Norman, she was not inclined to marry anyone, but "his patience and persistence overcame me, and after four years of close and delightful friendship we were married." Edith now lived in considerable style, accompanying her husband on several trips to Europe, and in September 1903, she gave birth to a son. But the baby was premature and lived for only three days. Norman was passionately in love with Edith, writing her ardent letters when they were separated. Edith, however, chose to view Norman, as one historian notes, like a "fastidious uncle." Norman Galt died in January 1908 at the age of forty-five; the couple had been married for thirteen years.[6]

Edith inherited her husband's interest in a thriving business, but she had no experience in the world of commerce to draw upon. She proved, however, to be a capable executive, relying on a manager and a lawyer to run the jewelry store. In the years after Norman's death, Edith enjoyed a comfortable, affluent life, driving around Washington in a small electric car and traveling often to Europe, where she bought clothes at Worth's, a famous fashion house in Paris and where, in 1911, she and her young friend Alice Gertrude Gordon stayed for five months.[7]

In the summer of 1912, Edith once again traveled to Europe. "That was," she remembered, "a Presidential election year, but so little was my interest in political affairs that I could hardly have told who the candidates were." But she was pleased that Woodrow Wilson, a fellow southerner, had won, and in early November 1912, when she returned from abroad, Edith, urged on by her sister-in-law, read a compilation of the president-elect's speeches. And on April 8, 1913, she attended Wilson's historic address before a joint session of Congress. She then left for another trip to Europe with Altrude.[8]

Edith spent the summer of 1914 in Maine with Altrude, and when she returned to Washington she found herself recovering from an illness she had contracted there. Cary Grayson, at Altrude's urging, came to check on Edith's health every day. He had already written to Edith about the president's sadness and now spoke of his "heart breaking loneliness." Grayson introduced Edith and Helen Bones, and soon the two women were taking long walks together, and Edith found that her "imagination was fired by the picture Helen gave me of a lonely man, detached from old friends and associations—the fate of official life—uncomplainingly bearing the burden of a great sorrow and keeping his eye single to the responsibilities of a great task."[9]

Within a few weeks after their first meeting, Edith and Woodrow were taking long drives together and eating dinner at the White House, where afterward they would retreat to the president's study for private conversations. On April 28, Woodrow sent his first note to Edith, and soon a torrent of passionate letters followed as the president explored the nature of his love for his new companion. On May 4, less than two months after they had met, Woodrow declared his love and asked Edith to marry him. She gently rebuffed him, but there is no doubt that she was drawn to Woodrow and intrigued by the role she would play if she was to become First Lady. Two days before the sinking of the *Lusitania*, Edith wrote to Woodrow, "How I want to help! What an unspeakable pleasure and privilege I deem it to be *allowed* to share these tense, terrible days of responsibility, how I thrill to my very finger tips when I remember the tremendous thing you said to me tonight [Woodrow had declared his love] and how pitifully poor I am, to have nothing to offer you in return." Woodrow's reassurances of her helpfulness, and his willingness to discuss with her the crisis with Germany, led Edith to write, "And oh! Do you know what a flood of happiness sweeps over me when you say I am really a help, a haven to you and sanctuary for your tired spirit?" Soon Grayson confirmed her new role, telling her that "Well, Mrs. Galt you seem to understand the President, and do him more good than anyone else. You don't *worry* him, and I *wish you would go* whenever they ask you, for he really needs all the diversion he can get."[10]

Despite her fears of inadequacy, Edith was not reluctant, early in her relationship with Woodrow, to offer her opinion on critical issues of the day. In early June, when she read a draft of his second *Lusitania* note to Germany, she thought it "seemed flat and lacking in color." Two days later Woodrow revealed to her that he had worked all evening to improve it. On June 10, after Edith learned of William Jennings Bryan's resignation as secretary of state, she informed Woodrow that she felt "joy that at last you are rid of this awful creature." When she learned that Woodrow had called on Bryan, she was upset that he had gone to see "that awful Deserter," and was convinced that "if anything could make me hate him worse than I did before, this [visit] would accomplish it. And I will be glad when he expires from an overdose of peace or grape juice and I never hear of him again." Woodrow was startled by the strength of Edith's convictions, writing "My how I like you, Edith, my incomparable Darling. And how you can *hate*, too. Whew!" As one of Edith's biographers writes, "one must marvel at how swiftly she gained his trust, how freely she offered her opinions on issues and personalities, and how thoughtfully he pondered those views."[11]

At the end of June, Edith and Woodrow, after a brief separation, were reunited in Cornish, New Hampshire, where they would spend part of the summer together. They relaxed with family and friends at Harlakenden, mixing work with leisure, often sitting on the sunny terrace overlooking the Connecticut River. In the evenings, after reading the latest dispatches and documents that had arrived from Washington, Woodrow would explain each issue to his eager apprentice. As the weeks passed, Edith remembered that "those days in Cornish brought the banishment of any doubt of my love for Woodrow Wilson."[12]

On August 2, Edith left Cornish to visit friends in New York and New Jersey. During her absence she was pleased with the flow of documents that arrived in a big envelope, and was excited by the fact that she now had "all the threads in the tangled fabric of the world's history laid in her hands." Sometimes old doubts about her competence surfaced, but Woodrow dismissed these doubts, pointing out that "I feel about your character and the disinterested loyalty of your friendship just as I have so often told you I felt about House. If I did not love you, I would still utterly trust you and cling to you and value your clear-sighted counsel. . . . You are talking nonsense, dear little girl . . . when you speak of wishing that you had 'the wisdom of a well-informed mind' in order that you might be a 'staff for me to lean on.' I have plenty of well informed minds about me. I can get all the wisdom of [sic] information that I can make use of. That is not what I need. . . . I have not loved you blindly. . . . I know what I say when I say that you are fit to be *any* man's help-mate, the partner of his mind as well as of his heart."[13]

Given Woodrow's remarkable assessment of Edith's capabilities, it is hardly surprising that at the end of August she wrote to him questioning the value of two of his oldest and closest advisers, Tumulty and House. Edith's dismissal of both men prompted Woodrow to write a long response, explaining that a president needed a diverse array of advisers, men whose talents supplemented his own. Edith did not press her case, but she now assumed that she could judge members of his inner circle of advisers and in effect claim that she should be the president's main confidant.[14]

On September 1, Edith and Woodrow were reunited in Washington.

Woodrow and Edith, shortly after their marriage in December 1915. House supported Wilson's remarriage but did not anticipate the extent to which Edith's love for her husband would exclude many of his advisers. Library of Congress, Prints and Photographs Division, LC-USZ62-65032. Photo by Boland.

Some of the president's advisers, especially McAdoo and Tumulty, were worried about the political implications of what they now realized could be an early presidential remarriage. McAdoo's clumsy intervention, however, failed to deter his father-in-law, who confessed to Edith his indiscretions in the letters he had written to Mary Allen Hulbert. Edith, who stayed up all night pondering Woodrow's confession, concluded at the end of her vigil that she finally could see "straight into the heart of things" and promised that she was "ready to follow the road 'where love leads.'" After the official announcement of their engagement on October 6, 1915, Woodrow was ecstatic, writing to Edith that "the old shadows are gone, the old loneliness banished, the new joy let in like a great healing light." In October and November, the two lovers saw each other every day, and sometimes, as Woodrow walked back to the White House from Edith's house near Dupont Circle, the president's Secret Service agent remembered how "he whistled softly, through his teeth, tapping out the rhythm with restless feet: 'Oh, you beautiful doll! You great big beautiful doll! Let me put my arms around you, I can hardly live without you.'" They were married on December 18 in a small ceremony in Edith's home.[15]

For Edith, the transition from Woodrow's fiancée to his First Lady was, she recalled, "a chapter from the life-story of Cinderella." She was a vital, fashionable woman, a gifted mimic, who now organized her day around that of her husband. His interests became her interests, her goal the preservation of Woodrow's health and the success of his policies. In a letter to Altrude Grayson, Edith revealed how intertwined their lives had become: "We are on the sofa in my room—W. W. sitting up straight making notes for 2 speeches . . . and I with my head in the pillows and feet on his knee." At the end of January 1916, when Wilson began his preparedness tour, Edith accompanied him. Reporters found her "stately as a duchess" and were fascinated with her charm and graciousness. As one noted, Edith's presence would "open up the White House" and "let many people know just how winning the President really is."[16]

During the summer of 1916, as the political pressures on Wilson mounted, Edith realized how much her life had changed in the past four years. In 1912 she had never met a president; now she was at the president's side, trying to reduce the pressure on Woodrow so that he could keep going until the conclusion of the campaign. When Wilson took to the road in October, Edith was at his side, all smiles and handshakes. Edith was pessimistic about the results and wondered what she and Woodrow would do if he left the presidency. Instead, after his remarkable victory, she faced four more years in the White House.[17]

Edith soon revealed, however, that her opinions of Woodrow's close advisers had not changed. She tried, unsuccessfully, to remove Tumulty, suggested that House replace Ambassador Walter Hines Page in London, continued to dislike McAdoo as "thoroughly selfish," and for a time was upset with Cary Grayson's efforts to become a rear admiral. But Woodrow was reluctant to make changes; as he prepared for a second term, his inner circle of advisers remained more or less in place.[18]

Edith continued to be nearly always at Woodrow's side. On January 20, 1917, she read his peace note to the belligerents aloud while he copied it on his typewriter. Two days later, she heard him deliver his address to the Senate and concluded that "it is so just and conclusive that more and more I feel that he is inspired and that he must obtain all he is striving for, for the good of the world." But as Wilson's peace initiative failed, and as German U-boats began to sink American ships, Edith realized that "the war is stretching its dark length over our own dear country."[19]

Once the United States entered the conflict, Wilson faced formidable challenges in mobilizing the nation for war and in sending an American army to France. As the demands on the president mounted, Edith believed that her primary mission was to protect Woodrow's health. But she also became a role model for wartime frugality, placing sheep on the White House lawn, pledging to wear simple clothing and buy inexpensive food, and also serving coffee and sandwiches to soldiers passing through Washington at a Red Cross canteen. She had no sympathy, however, for advocates of women's suffrage, who began in early 1917 to picket the White House and to demand that the president lead the fight to give women the right to vote. Edith had no interest in voting, disliked the "detestable suffragettes," and gave Woodrow no support as he gradually shifted his position and in 1918 finally endorsed a constitutional amendment to solve this vexing question.[20]

As Edith reflected on Woodrow's wartime leadership, he seemed to her greater than ever. She was impressed with the "calm poise of the President, and his patient and unfailing optimism," and was also impressed with his techniques for relaxing. Woodrow was light on his feet and could tap dance, imitating the actors he saw at Keith's Theater, and he could also "twist his face about as an actor does in playing character parts." Unlike Woodrow's other advisers, Edith was with him every day, sitting with him, if necessary, far into the night. She had no intention of making changes in an advisory system that placed her in such a key position. In August 1918, when Edith and Woodrow visited House at Magnolia, Massachusetts, the Colonel took Edith aside and spoke to her "about this condition [Woodrow's failing memory] and told her how much I disapproved of the President's method of conducting his work." House wanted the president to delegate more of his work to others, but Edith was unsympathetic. "When he delegated it to others," she responded, "he found it was not well done."[21]

On November 11, 1918, when news of the armistice reached Washington, Edith, she remembered, was stunned, "unable to grasp the full significance of the words!" After she and Woodrow drove in an open car through cheering crowds, they decided to dress up and attend a celebration at the Italian Embassy. Back at the White House, they were too excited to sleep and, before a fire in Edith's room, talked into the early hours of the morning. Woodrow then read a chapter from the Bible and went to bed.[22]

Edith understood that Woodrow must travel to Paris and lead the American peace commission. On December 4, 1918, they left New York on the *George Washington*, and Edith, who felt better and better as the ten-day voyage progressed, impressed many of her fellow passengers with her physical vigor and friendliness. Edith's social secretary, Edith Benham, recorded her impressions of the first couple: "The more I am with the Wilsons the more I am struck with their unrivaled home life. I have never dreamed such sweetness and love could be. One never hears anything between them but just love and understanding, and it is very beautiful to see his face light up and brighten at the very sight of her and to see her turn to him for everything, though she is a woman of a lot of spirit."[23]

Edith was swept away by the reception the president received in France. The cheering crowds in Paris, she wrote to her family, made it seem as if "here the *world* seemed to be waiting to welcome and acclaim my wonderful husband." She was delighted with their first residence in Paris, the palace of Prince Murat, which contained "two enchanting suites for the President and me," and was "breathlessly happy" as she and Woodrow embarked on grand tours of England and Italy. "She rode," her biographer Phyllis Lee Levin continues, "from ceremony to ceremony in flower-filled open carriages, in furs and feathers, proud witness to the resounding applause that paid tribute to her husband wherever he went." Fate seemed to have chosen her, Edith remembered, "for such a Cinderella role."[24]

On January 18, 1919, when the peace conference opened, Edith found that Woodrow's routine was far different from that in Washington. During the day he was absorbed in various meetings, and in the evening the League of Nations Commission, which he chaired, would meet. Edith now filled her days with shopping and visits to hospitals, canteens, and rehabilitation centers for recovering soldiers. After Ray Stannard Baker became the press officer of the American Peace Commission, he would appear every night at seven to learn from the president what had taken place during the day. Edith listened carefully to these conversations. She wrote to her family that she hoped Woodrow could "put through all the splendid things he is striving to do for the world," but she had only a superficial understanding of the issues, dismissing the concerns of Clemenceau, Lloyd George, and Orlando. As the conference progressed, she began to view it as a morality play, with her husband a true idealist and visionary struggling against corrupt European leaders. "Seeing him," Edith remembered, "growing grimmer and graver, day by day, how I longed to be a man so I could be of more help to him. All I could do was to try to 'soothe him with a finer fancy, touch him with a lighter thought.'"[25]

On February 14, Wilson read the draft covenant of the League of Nations to a plenary session of the peace conference. As Edith listened to Woodrow's speech, she was convinced that "[i]t was a great moment in history, and as he stood there—slender, calm, and powerful in his argument— I seemed to see the people of all depressed countries—men, women, and little children—crowding around and waiting upon his words." After the speech, as Edith and Woodrow reunited in their car, she remembered, "Oh, how glad I was to find him and tell him all the things that filled my heart!"[26]

The next day, February 15, Edith and Woodrow boarded the *George Washington* at Brest. On February 24, when their ship arrived at Boston, Edith was impressed with their reception, concluding that "if Boston were a representative nation, the pulse of the Nation beat steady and true for what the President was working to attain." But Edith was overly optimistic, underestimating, as did Woodrow, the depth of the opposition to his conception of the League of Nations and portraying the leader of the Republican opposition in the Senate, Henry Cabot Lodge, as a villain rather than as a legislator with a legitimate point of view.[27]

After returning to France on March 13, Edith recorded in her memoir a dramatic version of Woodrow's encounter with House on the train ride back to Paris. The president was shocked by the compromises House had made during his absence, convinced that he had given away everything. Edith was "bursting with indignation." She made no attempt to understand House's position, viewing him as a scapegoat and blaming him for the collapse of her husband's health. "I look back on that moment," she recalled, "as a crisis in his life, and feel that from it dated the long years of illness, due to overwork, and that with the wreckage of his plans and his life have come these tragic years that have demoralized the world."[28]

On April 3, when Woodrow became "violently ill," he once again had to rely on House to represent him for a few days on the Council of Four. But Edith, along with Grayson, was now completely disenchanted with House. She complained to Woodrow, "Oh, if Colonel House had only stood firm while you were away none of this would have to be done over. I think he is a perfect jellyfish." Woodrow defended House, but he too had lost confidence in his longtime counselor.[29]

While Woodrow was recovering from his illness, Edith, Grayson observed, "was a perfect angel. She was most attentive, her only thought being for the President's comfort." Through the remainder of the peace conference, Edith sought to protect Woodrow's health and restore his vitality. Grayson was filled with admiration for her devotion: "It was most refreshing to see how Mrs. Wilson entertained the President with light enjoyable conversation, detaching his mind from the heavy responsibilities to which he had been subjected during the day. Her attentions and affection for the President are truly touching and beautiful."[30]

On the evening of June 28, Edith and Woodrow left Paris to return to what she viewed as the "simple dignity of the White House." Both were aware of flaws in the peace treaty, but Edith was her husband's most determined defender, convinced that during the deliberations in Paris "never did he turn from the weapons of truth and right."[31]

Once back in the United States, Edith soon became aware of the strength of the opposition to the peace treaty. Or as she wrote to her friend Henry White (who had been a member of the American Peace Commission), "Of course I believe it will all come right in the end, but the partisan spirit seems armed to the teeth, and it may take a long time to conquer." But she was also aware of the frailty of Woodrow's health and, along with Grayson and Tumulty, opposed his western tour.[32]

From the start of the tour, which began on September 3, Edith was worried about Woodrow's condition. While she was proud of his performance and realized that the tour was gathering momentum as the train headed west, she also understood that the heat and the seemingly endless series of lunches, dinners, receptions, and speeches took a frightful toll on her husband. She remembered that "he grew thinner and the headaches increased in duration and in intensity until he was almost blind during the attacks." She knew that "only rest, complete rest, and an escape from the maddening crowds, could restore my husband. But I was trapped." Edith and Grayson resolved to find a way for the president to rest each day, but they were unable to resist the constant pressure. In Los Angeles, toward the end of the tour, Edith finally met Mary Allen Hulbert, who Woodrow had last seen in May 1915. Edith found her a "faded, sweet-looking woman who was absorbed in an only son," while Mary Allen wrote that Edith "was much more junoesque [than her official photo], but handsome, with a charming smile that revealed her strong, white teeth. She was, without question, a woman of strong character."[33]

On the evening of September 25, after the presidential train stopped outside of Pueblo, Colorado, both Edith and Grayson realized that Woodrow's health had broken down. The next day they concluded that the remainder of the tour must be cancelled and that the president must return to Washington as soon as possible. On September 28, the train reached Union Station, and on October 2, Edith awoke to find that Woodrow had suffered a stroke that had paralyzed the left side of his body. Edith felt, understandably, that her primary obligation was to protect her husband's health. She quickly decided to discourage him from resigning, to conceal the nature of his illness from the public, and to become a kind of surrogate, immersing herself in the workings of the government. As Edith explained, "Woodrow Wilson was first my beloved husband whose life I was trying to save, fighting with my back to the wall—after that he was President of the United States." She later claimed that soon after Woodrow's stroke she had a long talk with Dr. Francis X. Dercum, a prominent Philadelphia neurologist. "Madam," Dercum allegedly explained, "it is a grave situation, but I think you can solve it. Have everything come to you; weigh the importance of each matter, and see if it is possible by consultations with the respective heads of the Departments to solve them without the guidance of your husband. In this way you can save him a great deal. But always keep in mind that every time you take him a new anxiety or problem to excite him, you are turning a knife in an open wound. His nerves are crying for rest, and any excitement is torture to him." But the president must not resign, the doctor continued, for that "would have a bad effect on the country, and a serious effect on our patient. . . . If he resigns, the greatest incentive to recovery is gone; and as his mind is as clear as crystal he can still do more with a maimed body than any one else." No doubt Edith wished, in retrospect, that she had had such a conversation with Dr. Dercum to justify the path that she pursued, but historians agree that her account is a confabulation, a recording of fictitious events that she believed to be true.[34]

Thus began Edith's "stewardship." She had faith in her executive ability, explaining that "I had talked with him [Woodrow] so much that I knew pretty well what he thought of things." But as one biographer writes, "the problem . . . was not that a woman was running the country: it was that no one was running the country. Edith did not have a political agenda, she had a personal agenda: her husband's health and happiness were to come before the needs of the country." Documents flowed from Tumulty to Edith, but she decided what the president would read and who he would see. Edith, however, had never acquired more than a superficial understanding of affairs of state; reading documents Woodrow had sent her, or sitting in on his conferences with political leaders, had not prepared her for acting in a thoughtful and decisive manner. At a time of painful transition from war to peace, the nation was adrift.[35]

Nevertheless, some observers were impressed with Edith's performance. In early November 1919, Ray Stannard Baker stopped at the White House to have lunch with the First Lady. "Mrs. Wilson," he recorded, "looks worn & tired after her long vigil, but remains irrepressibly cheerful." Baker spent the entire afternoon talking with Grayson, who described the ordeal of the western trip and asserted that "he did not see how they could have gotten along without her." Baker concluded that "Mrs. Wilson is a woman of much stronger character than people realize. She has no great education . . . but real natural gifts & having common sense. She conducted herself in the highest places in Europe with perfect ease & grace. She watches the President's interests as only a woman of great power could."[36]

Throughout the winter of 1919–20, Edith persisted in her new role. She seldom left Woodrow's side, decided what people and documents would reach her husband, deferred action on critical issues, and pursued some of her personal vendettas. On November 19, Edith, with encouragement from Baruch, urged Woodrow to accept the Lodge reservations, claiming that the long, bitter fight was "eating into my very soul." "For my sake," she asked him, "won't you accept these reservations and get this awful thing settled?" Woodrow replied, "Little girl, don't you desert me; that I cannot stand." It was Edith's last effort to find a compromise. When the treaty was finally defeated on March 19, 1920, Edith blamed Senator Lodge, claiming that "at his door lies the wreckage of human hopes and the peril to human lives that afflict mankind today [1939]."[37]

Throughout the spring of 1920, Edith continued to believe that Woodrow's best chance for recovery was to stay in office, and she even concluded that her husband might have to run for a third term. But Edith was overwhelmed with demands from a husband who was combative and depressed, from critics of her "stewardship," and from the constant need to appear cheerful and hopeful. As Baker observed, "everything must come through one overstrained woman! Dr. Grayson, of course, is very close to the President, but everything of importance is handled by Mrs. Wilson."

Edith continued, however, to be inspired by her contact with Woodrow. "No one," she wrote to a friend, "who has not been in daily, hourly, contact with the struggle he has made against physical suffering, and mental anxiety coupled with disappointments, disloyalty and every possible discouragement can ever fully recognize the greatness of his great spirit." As she wrote to Woodrow, "sometimes you tell me I am strong or, as you put it, 'great'—don't you see little Boy—that it is the contact with you and your greatness that lifts me up and if there is merit in me, it is because I am your mirror in which your fineness is reflected."[38]

At the Democratic convention in San Francisco, which opened on June 28, 1920, Wilson's name was not put in nomination, and he played no part in the 1920 presidential campaign. As the end of his presidency neared, Edith and Woodrow began to contemplate the future. In December, they bought a house on S Street, which Edith believed was an "unpretentious, comfortable, dignified house fitted to the needs of a gentleman's home." Edith managed to ease Woodrow's transition from the White House to his new S Street home, having the furniture in his White House bedroom duplicated and working out a new routine for her lonely and depressed husband. She tried to find some way of giving Woodrow "something definite to accomplish" to challenge and sustain him, but various writing projects failed. Edith, however, remained optimistic, convinced that "there are great things ahead of him [Woodrow]." Some observers, such as Ray Stannard Baker, were impressed with Edith's high spirits. When he stopped at S Street to see Wilson, he found Edith at Woodrow's side while he ate his lunch. "She seems," Baker recorded, "most happy these days & I never saw her looking more beautiful. She goes about the house whistling like a leaf." But Grayson, who visited S Street often, believed that "the situation with Mr. W is very trying and terrible on Miss Edith. She is showing the effects of it—very nervous and more excitable than I imagined [she] would ever become." And some were more critical of Edith. The British statesman Lord Robert Cecil, who visited Wilson in April 1923, found Edith's presence annoying, complaining that "Mrs. Wilson, who seemed to me quite definitely a foolish woman, sat there the whole time interposing banal observations."[39]

Toward the end of August 1923, Edith, badly worn down, left to visit friends in Massachusetts, her first break in caring for Woodrow in almost four years. Edith wrote to Woodrow daily, but he was lonely without her and revealed that "I never before realized so fully how completely my life is intertwined with yours." When Edith returned on September 5, she realized how much Woodrow's health had failed. Throughout the fall of 1923, Edith continued to care for Woodrow, but early in 1924 she began to feel that his energy was fading, and on January 29, when Edith returned from dinner with some friends, she found that Woodrow had grown worse and decided to summon Grayson from his shooting vacation at Baruch's estate in South Carolina. Grayson arrived on January 31, and Edith soon concluded that Woodrow was dying and that his daughters should be summoned. Edith remained at Woodrow's bedside, and on the morning of February 3 she held his hand as his life finally ended.[40]

For the next thirty-seven years, Edith sought to shape Woodrow's legacy. She established her control over his private papers and in early 1925 chose Ray Stannard Baker as his authorized biographer, collaborating closely with Baker on what became a multivolume project stretching from 1927 to 1939. She also sought to protect Woodrow's reputation, challenging those who criticized any aspect of his presidency. When the first two volumes of House's *Intimate Papers* appeared in 1926, Edith was outraged at his treatment of Woodrow, writing to one friend that she "could not stoop from our great task to cross swords with the puny figures" strutting on the stage. The anger she felt after reading House's memoir prompted her to begin writing her own memoir, which was published in 1939. Edith also worked to restore the manse in Staunton, Virginia, where Woodrow was born and which was declared a permanent memorial in 1941. After the publication of the final volume of Baker's biography, the producer Darryl Zanuck proposed a movie based on Wilson's life. Edith agreed, but insisted on revising the original script and worried about the choice of an actor who would portray Woodrow. The movie *Wilson*, which opened in August 1944, was a box office failure but a critical success.[41]

In the 1920s and 1930s, Edith traveled widely, often with Belle Baruch (Bernard Baruch's daughter), who was a close friend, or with her brother Randolph. She made many trips to Europe, always stopping at Geneva so that she could observe the deliberations of the League of Nations, and in August 1929 took a three-month tour of China, Egypt, Turkey, India, Hong Kong, and Japan. Edith traveled in style and, everywhere she went, received a warm welcome.[42]

As the years passed, Edith became a kind of grande dame, one who appeared at important events and one who was celebrated as the Democratic Party's first lady. On December 8, 1941, when Franklin Roosevelt delivered his war message after the Japanese attack on Pearl Harbor, Edith was present at the joint session of Congress. Josephus Daniels's son described her as "a well-preserved, still elegantly dressed widow of sixty-nine." During the postwar years, Edith was a familiar figure at the White House, and in 1960 she was a fervent supporter of John F. Kennedy, eager for the Democrats to recapture the presidency. She found the election "thrilling" and especially admired Jacqueline Kennedy, who was "so cultivated and charming" and would be a great help to her husband. In January 1961, Edith sat on the platform at JFK's inauguration.[43]

Edith lived longer than most of those who had been important in her life. Of Woodrow's three daughters, only Eleanor McAdoo outlived her. Ray Stannard Baker died in 1946; her brother Randolph, in 1951. All of the other members of Woodrow's inner circle of advisers—with the exception of Bernard Baruch—were gone. But Edith labored on, active until the end. She died on December 28, 1961 (Woodrow's birthday), at the age of eighty-nine. She was buried in the Washington National Cathedral next to her husband, where the service was conducted by Woodrow's grandson, the Reverend Francis B. Sayre Jr. Edith's devotion to Woodrow, during his life and after his death, had been complete. But as one biographer sadly concludes, "on her vigorous temperament, introspection never cast its ripening light."[44]

Baruch at the racetrack in May 1920. A tall, elegant Wall Street speculator, Baruch became, after America's entry into the war in April 1917, a key figure in the mobilization of the American economy. Baruch also became one of Wilson's most trusted companions and remained close to Edith until her death in 1965. Library of Congress, Prints and Photographs Division, LC-DIG-ggbain-30486. Photo by Bain News Service.

CHAPTER TEN

Bernard M. Baruch

"[C]ountless millions will always be thankful to God for having given us Woodrow Wilson in . . . the greatest crisis of all times"

On October 12, 1912, Bernard M. Baruch, a forty-two-year-old Wall Street "speculator," traveled to the Plaza Hotel in New York City to meet Woodrow Wilson. Baruch had admired Wilson for his fight against the eating clubs at Princeton, and now he had a chance to meet the Democratic presidential candidate. Baruch remembered that "from the moment I clasped Wilson's hand, I was taken with him. His lean, somewhat ascetic face was dominated by sparkling clear eyes. He was cordial and forthright and I was quickly impressed by his keen mind." The two men discussed issues of the day, especially Wilson's New Freedom, and then went their separate ways. "Although I did not then realize it," Baruch recalled, "I had met a man I would soon regard as one of the greatest in the world." Baruch played a minor role in the first Wilson administration, but with America's entry into the war in April 1917 he became a key figure in the mobilization of the American economy, and by the time of the Paris Peace, he had become one of the president's most trusted companions.[1]

Baruch was born on August 19, 1870, in Camden, South Carolina, the second of four children of Simon and Belle Baruch. Simon had immigrated to the United States in 1855 to avoid conscription in the Prussian army. He had gone to Camden, a small city of around two thousand people, where he knew the proprietor of the general store. Mannes Baum became his patron, sending him to medical school, first in Charleston, then to Richmond, Virginia. Upon his graduation in April 1862, he joined the Confederate army as an assistant surgeon, fought at the battles of Antietam and Gettysburg, and was taken prisoner twice. At the end of the war, he returned to Camden, where he became a successful country physician, treating both whites and Blacks and becoming a prominent local citizen.[2]

In 1867, Simon married Isabelle Wolfe, the daughter of a wealthy slaveholder whose plantations had been destroyed by Union troops as they marched through South Carolina. The Baruchs and their four children had a warm family life. Simon was six feet tall, erect, with a dark beard and soft voice. Belle was a talented amateur actress who played the piano, sang, and looked after her four boys. Despite the turmoil of Reconstruction in South Carolina, the Baruch family never suffered any real economic adversity. The family lived in a large, comfortable house, and Bernard grew up with a Black nanny. He had a happy childhood, with brothers to play with and with the freedom to live an outdoor life during the summer, fishing, swimming, and hunting. The Baruch boys were "rarely disciplined" by their parents, and Bernard would sometimes ride with his father in a buggy as he made his rounds in the countryside. The young Bernard admired his father. While Simon belonged to the Ku Klux Klan and opposed carpetbag rule in South Carolina, Bernard claimed years later that his father had no prejudices against Blacks or bitterness toward the North. But he was an ambitious man who was upset by the violence in South Carolina and who aspired to become more than a country doctor. Belle urged Simon to take the family to New York City, where there would be more opportunities. In the winter of 1880, Simon sold his house and practice and made the move. Bernard was ten years old.[3]

New York was, Bernard remembered, a "strange new world." Initially the Baruch family lived in two rooms in a boardinghouse on West Fifty-Seventh Street. While Bernard and his brothers adjusted to urban life, Simon's medical practice prospered, and he also became a leader in the movement to build municipal bathhouses and an international authority on hydrotherapy. The family soon moved to a house on 157th Street, where

Belle established a comfortable home. She joined a wide variety of clubs and organizations, encouraged the ambitions of her four sons, and also plotted their careers.

In New York, Bernard first encountered prejudice against Jews. His father regarded himself as an American rather than a Jew, while his mother was more devout, observing Jewish holidays. As a boy Bernard studied Hebrew, attended synagogue and Sunday schools, and, until his graduation from college, kept every Jewish holy day. But Bernard would eventually become, like his father, an assimilated Jew, an agnostic who rejected Zionism and who disliked those whom he regarded as "professional Jews."[4]

Bernard wanted to attend Yale University. But his mother decided that he was "too young to leave home" and instead, in the fall of 1884, when he was only fourteen, he entered City College of New York, then a small institution with a rigid curriculum. He was a good, but not an outstanding, student and failed to develop the ability to express himself well either verbally or on paper. Although he was rejected by fraternities because of his Jewishness, he was popular with his classmates and elected president of the senior class. Bernard was a good-natured, handsome young man, six feet four, 170 pounds, with a broad chest and slender legs. He was a talented athlete, became a skilled boxer, developed a lifelong fascination with prizefighting, and enjoyed gambling on any situation that tested his nerve and his knowledge.

Initially Belle thought that her second son ought to become a doctor, but by the time of his graduation from City College in 1889 she had changed her mind and decided that a business career would be more appropriate. In the fall of that year, through his father's connections, he became an office boy in a wholesale glass company, then became an apprentice in a Wall Street firm that specialized in arbitrage. In 1891, he made his "real start in Wall Street" in the brokerage firm of A. A. Housman & Company.[5]

Although Bernard was only an office boy, he was also a bright and ambitious young man who studied the industrial geography of the United States. Soon he began to speculate on stocks, and initially he made mistakes and lost money, including $8,000 that his father had given him to invest. Gradually, however, he built up a circle of Wall Street friends and learned how to assess the corporations he planned to invest in. Baruch established a presence on Wall Street; he was the "Lone Eagle," "tall, aquiline, smiling, but uncommunicative among excited stock dealers." In the late 1890s, he became a wealthy man, who, through careful study and self-discipline, one biographer writes, "made money quite simply and naturally as other men might have composed music or painted pictures." In October 1897, he married Annie Griffen, an Episcopalian, and the young couple developed a lavish lifestyle, with a townhouse in New York and a summer home in New Jersey. Three children, two girls and a boy, followed, but Baruch was an absent husband and father. He worked long hours, attended horse races and prizefights, and enjoyed show people and the theater. Baruch was not an introspective or particularly well-read man, but he was a superb companion, charming, gregarious, and generous, one who learned largely through conversation with others. He became a dashing figure, tall, lean, and handsome, fascinated with boxing, gambling, and hunting. Throughout his life women were drawn to him.[6]

In the summer of 1900, when Baruch was thirty years old, he proudly told his father that he was worth a million dollars. Simon Baruch was unimpressed—a "quizzical expression" appeared on his face; he wondered what his son planned to do with all this money. Simon had, after all, built a career serving the community and pursuing medical research. His question troubled his son, who now began to compare his own career with that of his father. Bernard knew that his father, who would turn sixty in July 1900, was worn down by his medical practice and lacked sufficient time for his own research. He decided to set up an income for Simon so that he could retire and pursue his research interests full-time. Bernard's generosity, however, did not quiet doubts he felt about his own career, or, as he remembered, feelings of "emptiness" and "stirrings of discontent."[7]

Baruch decided that he no longer wanted to handle other people's money, and in 1903, he left A. A. Housman & Co. and opened his own office on Wall Street. He now turned "toward new horizons, in which constructive enterprise and investment took more and more of my time." Baruch understood the importance of finding new sources of supply for copper and rubber, and in 1904 traveled to Mexico in a private railroad car to explore the possibilities of a new method of rubber production. Baruch had entered the exciting and highly profitable world of raw materials.[8]

In 1897, Baruch began to search for a southern retreat where he could recover from the stress of life on Wall Street. In 1905, he finally found the ideal place, Hobcaw Barony, an inaccessible, seventeen thousand–acre coastal plantation near Georgetown, South Carolina. The main house, which lacked a telephone, could only be approached by a boat trip across Winyah Bay and then by a four and one-half mile drive through virgin forest and cypress swamp. Mail and telegrams were brought twice a day. For fifty years, Baruch would retreat there, fishing and hunting and relishing memories of his South Carolina boyhood. Over the years he would entertain many famous guests—including Winston Churchill and Franklin D. Roosevelt—and develop a reputation as a man with a genius for friendship.

Baruch took a paternalistic attitude toward the African Americans who lived at Hobcaw. He restored his plantation, building cabins, schools, and a church for his plantation Blacks, and making sure that they received proper medical care. He was impressed with the progress they had made after the turn of the century and also with the "warmth and richness of Negro life." But there were limits to Baruch's paternalism. He would not socialize with African Americans and viewed those who lived on his plantation as "simple, lovable, [and] irresponsible." He had one friend, a frequent visitor to Hobcaw, driven around the plantation to visit with Blacks, and after her tour had ended remarked, "Now you see how silly you are to go around beating your breast. They're happy the way they are. No sense in stirring them up."[9]

In the early years of the twentieth century, Baruch felt a "gradual awakening of his social consciousness." Although he was raised a Democrat, he never voted for William Jennings Bryan and was drawn to Theodore Roosevelt's reform agenda and "dynamic personality." In 1912, however, Baruch attended the Democratic convention in Baltimore, where he planned to vote for the party's nominee, Woodrow Wilson. Baruch's meeting with Wilson in October only confirmed his earlier decision.

Baruch was not, however, deeply involved in the 1912 campaign or in the early years of Wilson's presidency. He approved of New Freedom legislation and carried out a variety of chores for advisers such as McAdoo and House, but it was the outbreak of war in August 1914 that changed Baruch's relationship to the president and his administration. "As the war," he remembered, "catapulted America out of her isolation, it lifted me out of the narrow canyon of Wall Street onto the stage of national and international affairs." At the start of the conflict, Baruch, although sympathetic with the Allies, believed that the United States should stay out of the struggle. But he also supported the efforts of Theodore Roosevelt and of other prominent Republicans to prepare the nation for war. As Baruch observed events in Europe, he concluded that "modern war meant total war" and that, if the American economy was to be mobilized for war, it would require "a centralized government organization."[10]

In September 1915, Baruch called at the White House for the first time. As he explained his ideas for preparing American industry for war, he remembered noticing the "keen, perceptive face of Woodrow Wilson." Baruch now began to promote his preparedness program with members of Wilson's inner circle, and in August 1916, when the president created a Council of National Defense, he made Baruch a member of its advisory commission. The speculator was becoming an important adviser, and his generous contributions to Wilson's 1916 campaign further emphasized his value to the administration.

Throughout the winter of 1916–17, Baruch often visited the White House. He was in the gallery when Wilson delivered his war message to Congress on April 2, 1917; afterward Baruch wrote to the president that "to those of us who had followed you like crusaders through the toil and trouble of the last few years, it is but the expression expected from our leader." But the nation's entry into the war only increased the problems of mobilization, and conflicts persisted between military and civilian authorities. In May 1917, Wilson created the War Industries Board, but it too lacked the authority to coordinate the American war effort.[11]

In January 1918, the administration finally began to respond to the crisis in military production and procurement. Tumulty, McAdoo, and Daniels all urged the president to appoint Baruch chairman of a more powerful WIB. Tumulty informed the president that "one thing is certain,—that we know where Baruch stands because he has been with us from the start. We are sure of Baruch's vision, loyalty, and generous sympathies." McAdoo, who had sponsored Baruch from early in the administration, insisted that "he is by all odds the most capable man for the position." Daniels wrote that "in capacity to do the work and in loyalty Baruch is the best man, but whether under all the conditions and prejudices it would be wise to name him now is debatable."[12]

But Newton Baker saw little need for any further centralization of the war effort; he wanted the WIB to be led by "a great industrial captain" and "doubted whether the country would accept as an ideal appointment a man whose success in life had been largely that of a Wall Street financier." Colonel House agreed. From early in the administration he had used Baruch for a variety of political errands, but he did not want him to move into the president's inner circle of advisers. On March 4, 1918, after some hesitation, Wilson appointed Baruch chairman and gave him broad authority over production and procurement. For the purchases of both American and Allied armed forces Baruch was to be, the president wrote, "the general eye of all supply departments in the field of industry."[13]

By early 1918, Wilson had come to trust and admire the financier and had decided that he "liked to have Baruch near him," while Edith regretted that she and Woodrow had not met him earlier. Wilson appreciated Baruch's charm and amiability, and also realized that he had an encyclopedic knowledge of American industry and a view of the whole of the nation's economy. In return, Baruch gave the president friendship and loyalty. He found him "warm and human" and believed that Wilson was "one of the great war leaders of all time," that he was a man of "vision and high purpose" who also "provided hard, practical leadership." Looking back, he concluded that "it was a great crusade, and I count it the finest privilege of my life to have been a part of it." Baruch did not, however, always like the president's decisions. Occasionally he would say, "I don't agree with you Mr. President. Sorry sir." Wilson would respond, "I'll listen to your reason." In Baruch's experience, the president never demanded a complete agreement with his policies; rather, he "constantly sought the advice and the opinion of others before making decisions." But once those decisions were made, Wilson expected his advisers to carry them out loyally.[14]

While Baruch reported directly to the president, the jurisdiction of the WIB over the nation's economy was ambiguous, and he had to rely heavily on persuasion and the voluntary cooperation of business leaders. Nevertheless, the WIB now assumed economic functions that would have been unimaginable before American entry into the war. Under Baruch's leadership the WIB fixed prices, set industrial production quotas, determined wages and hours, and established priorities for the use of raw materials. In fact, Baruch had never managed a large organization, and he was bored by day-to-day administration. But he had a talent for picking capable assistants and emerged as a skilled impresario, one who focused on the broad aspects of policymaking and one who knew how to thrive in the bureaucratic politics of wartime Washington.[15]

The chairmanship of the WIB allowed Baruch to transform himself from a Wall Street speculator into a wartime statesman. The war gave him a kind of celebrity status as Wilson's adviser and as the benevolent director of the American economy. Baruch, his critics now observed, had an insatiable vanity and publicized himself relentlessly. He appeared regularly in newspapers and in newsreels, the tall, handsome, omnipotent "Dr. Facts" who had, so it seemed, transformed the American war effort.[16]

In March 1918, Wilson had also formed a War Cabinet, where powerful managers such as Baruch and Herbert Hoover could meet with the president and deal with a variety of wartime issues. The members of the War Cabinet fought bureaucratic battles among themselves, but Baruch subordinated his ambitions to those of his patron, Secretary of the Treasury McAdoo. In a letter to House, Baruch portrayed himself as a selfless team player, as someone who was trying "to keep everything I can from the President."[17]

In the fall of 1918, as the war moved toward an end, Baruch and Mc-

Adoo believed that the government should withdraw from the economy and that "reconstruction would take care of itself." When McAdoo resigned as secretary of the treasury in November, Baruch turned down the offer to replace him. During the war he had discovered that he liked short-term positions, not a lengthy commitment with onerous day-to-day responsibilities. Public service appealed to Baruch, but he needed something that would allow him to continue his migratory lifestyle. He wintered in New York and Washington, traveled to Hobcaw in the spring, and was accustomed to summer trips to Europe, where he rented a castle in Scotland and mingled with influential people. Like Colonel House, Baruch's way of life precluded formal administrative positions.[18]

In late November 1918, Baruch resigned as chairman of the WIB. He longed to go to Paris, where the peace conference would soon open, and where he could be at the president's side and perhaps achieve international fame. Wilson seemed determined to find a place for Baruch. He wrote to him that "I do not mean to let you go yet if I can help it, because there is much remaining to be done." Wilson wanted Baruch in Paris both as an adviser and friend, and on December 18 he instructed him to leave for France as soon as possible. Baruch arrived in Paris on January 11, 1919, excited to be at this great event. As he remembered, "in the air was a mingling of hope, excitement, and uncertain anticipation."[19]

Baruch quickly established himself in style. He had a suite at the Ritz Hotel and rented a villa at St. Cloud, where he could retreat on weekends and entertain friends. Paris was expensive, but Baruch could afford to wine and dine those he wanted to impress. Away from the conference table, he attended dinners and dances and went to the racetrack with Cary Grayson. One American journalist remembered his first encounter with Baruch. Arthur Krock found him in "a sumptuous apartment overlooking the Ritz Gardens, clad in a purple dressing gown. There a magnificent human creature, rose from a reclining chair to his lean height of six feet five or so and greeted me with an aristocratic charm. . . . Our introduction over, the Babylonian king then sank back into his reclining chair and his minions resumed their operations: a pretty girl manicured his nails, a barber shaved his face and trimmed his hair, a chasseur shined his boots, while over him hovered his valet, Lacy, to perform any final touches to Baruch's toilet." Baruch was instantly attracted to Clemenceau, "one of the truly great men I have met," and tried without success to impress an important member of the British delegation, Lord Robert Cecil. "Baruch," he recorded in his diary, "spent the whole evening in explaining what a great man he was, and how he had had the complete dictatorship of American industry throughout the war. A man of great power but not attractive."[20]

Initially, Baruch was uncertain of his role. As he recalled, "I just sat around; nobody paid any attention to me." He was, in fact, one of the five economic advisers to the American Peace Commission, and he soon found a place for himself on the Supreme Economic Council and the Reparations Commission. Like the president, Baruch sought a moderate peace. He opposed the continuing economic blockade of Germany and French demands for the annexation of the Saar and the separation of the Rhineland from Germany. And he especially resisted extreme British and French demands on reparations. Baruch wanted a fixed sum that Germany would be able to pay. After Wilson returned to the peace conference on March 13, he agreed that the Allies could include the costs of the war in their reparations demands. Baruch warned the president that his concession was a serious mistake, that if Germany's postwar economy was not rebuilt, all of Europe would suffer. But Wilson refused to reconsider his decision.[21]

The growing distance between Wilson and House, particularly evident after the president returned to Paris, benefited Baruch. Grayson and Edith, keenly aware of Woodrow's need for relaxation and male companionship, encouraged the friendship between the two men. Sometimes, on Sundays, Woodrow and Edith drove to St. Cloud, where they would enjoy lunch in the garden of Baruch's villa and talk in a relaxed way. "The President," Grayson noted in his diary, "has shown a genuine affection for Mr. Baruch and greatly admires him for his ability." Later in the peace conference, Grayson concluded that Baruch "is making a great hit over here with the President, Miss E & everyone except Colonel House."[22]

Despite Wilson's concessions on reparations, Baruch continued to be proud of his courage, writing that "the new world dawning for all needs

Left to right: Cary Grayson, Joseph Tumulty, and Bernard Baruch. All three were part of the president's inner circle of advisers and were proof of the diverse talents that he assembled. Library of Congress, Prints and Photographs Division, LC-USZ62-138651.

this fearless frank leadership and while you are with us it will never be wanting." Baruch realized that the final results fell short of what he and the president wanted, but he believed that the settlement would have been far harsher if Wilson had not been there, and he expected the new League of Nations to correct some of the imperfections of the Versailles settlement. Baruch was certain the peace treaty would be approved by the Senate, confiding to one colleague that when the president returned with the treaty in his pocket "our troubles will be over and the opposition [will] fade away."[23]

Once back in Washington, Baruch quickly realized the depth of the opposition and "threw himself into the fight for ratification of the Treaty." He gave money to the League to Enforce Peace, testified in favor of the treaty before the Senate Foreign Relations Committee, and realized, toward the end of the summer of 1919, that the president was too worn down to embark on a speaking tour. A few days before Wilson headed west, Baruch asked him, "Mr. President, if anything happens to you, what will we do?" Wilson replied, "What is one life in a great cause?"[24]

By mid-October 1919, Baruch concluded that reservations were essential if the Senate was to approve the peace treaty. He sought to act as a channel between the president and his opponents, and in early February 1920, he urged Wilson to accept a compromise. Baruch had not seen his mentor since he had left on his speaking tour. "Then," he recalled, "I had been disturbed by his evident exhaustion; now I was shocked by his drawn and wasted appearance." But Wilson refused to compromise: "No. They are not reservations, they are nullifications." Baruch left empty-handed, worried that it appeared as if he had deserted the president. But Edith silently "took my hand between hers in sympathy," and a few days later she informed him that Woodrow told her, "You know, Baruch is true to the bone. He told me what he believed, not what he knew I wanted him to say."[25]

At the end of the Wilson administration, Baruch, who was forty-nine, was adrift. The war, and Woodrow Wilson, had transformed his life, and Baruch assured Wilson that he would be eternally grateful "for your having pointed to me the finer and better things that men should be happy to live for, and if necessary, to suffer for . . . victory for your ideals is merely deferred." For Baruch, Wilson had, one historian observes, "assumed a Christlike significance"; he was a disciple who would carry the torch far into the future. On February 4, 1924, the day after Wilson's death, Baruch wrote that "the greatest figure of the century has passed, but no man of any age has left a richer, truer heritage for mankind."[26]

* * *

Baruch had hoped that McAdoo would succeed his father-in-law in 1920, and he was discouraged by the defeat of the Democrats in November and by the nation's retreat from the high plateau of "Wilsonian idealism" into what he termed was a "stony valley of disillusion, cynicism, and materialism." In the early 1920s he continued to support McAdoo for the presidency, convinced that "besides my personal affection for this peppery, courageous fighter for good causes, I believed he deserved the Democratic nomination on the basis of ability and past performance." Baruch was deeply involved in McAdoo's campaign, giving him constant advice and crucial financial support and occasionally trying to restrain his impulsiveness. When McAdoo became involved in the Teapot Dome scandal, Baruch urged him to withdraw and hoped that in the end the Democratic Party would turn to him. McAdoo rejected Baruch's advice and failed to receive the nomination.[27]

The massive defeat of John W. Davis in November 1924 discouraged Baruch. He wrote to McAdoo that "as far as politics is concerned, I don't even let anybody come into my office and talk about it to me." Baruch wanted to be valued for his advice as well as for his money, and in the mid-1920s he decided to invest in Democratic Senate leaders. Baruch met with them often, entertained them at Hobcaw, and concluded that he could achieve more influence through them than by supporting weak Democratic presidential candidates.

Nevertheless, Baruch could not stay out of the 1928 presidential campaign. He supported Governor Albert Ritchie of Maryland—a conservative who emphasized states' rights—for the nomination, and when the Ritchie boom faltered, he turned to Al Smith. Baruch had known Smith for many years, admired his achievements as governor of New York, and gave his campaign financial support. Baruch believed, until the end, that he had a good chance of winning. Smith's defeat left Baruch dismayed by the "exploitation of religious prejudice" in the campaign.[28]

During the Wilson years Baruch had developed a reputation as an economic wizard, and by the early 1920s, he had decided to enhance his public image. He now viewed himself no longer as a Wall Street speculator but as a high-minded statesman who was dedicated to the legacy of Woodrow Wilson. Baruch cultivated Washington correspondents and gathered around him an entourage—led by the noted *New York World* journalist Herbert Bayard Swope—who wrote his articles and speeches. Baruch was a poor writer. As he once put it, "When I try to be intellectual which means talking a lot of hooey I just flop." Baruch was especially generous with those people and causes associated with Woodrow Wilson. He loaned money to Cary Grayson and McAdoo, helped to finance the purchase of Wilson's S Street house, and was especially attentive to Edith. Baruch praised her conduct during Wilson's last years, describing her as "a ministering angel every hour of the day, always bright and cheerful, ever present at his side." Edith had always admired Baruch, referring to him as "My dear Baron," and in the years after Woodrow's death she valued their "delightful little talks." Edith traveled to Europe with Baruch's daughter Belle, enjoyed his gift of a trip to Japan, and accepted his advice on a wide range of personal and financial matters. He shared her loathing for Colonel House and commiserated with her over the publication of *The Intimate Papers* by "Judas and his charlatan biographer." Baruch and Edith were bound together in what both regarded as a sacred cause.[29]

Baruch was skeptical of the "much-trumpeted prosperity of the 1920s." He wanted more government supervision and regulation of the economy, became an expert on the agricultural crisis of the decade, and spoke out often on war debts and reparations. Baruch was an ardent internationalist, arguing that only the United States could restore the German economy and restrain French ambitions. In 1923, he asserted that "there will be no peace in the world until America takes the position to which her power and wealth obligate her." Baruch traveled widely, meeting with European leaders and urging American membership in the League of Nations and the necessity of reducing the reparations burden on Germany. But as long as Republicans controlled the White House, Baruch was an outsider whose views were largely ignored by those in power.[30]

* * *

Toward the end of the summer of 1929, Baruch, who was in Europe, became concerned about the instability of the stock market and returned to the United States. Worried that a major downturn of the market was imminent, he sold many of his holdings and, when Black Thursday came on October 24, 1929, he was not, like many of his friends, financially wiped out. Baruch, however, thought the Depression would end quickly; he did not foresee how "deep and terrible" it would be. And he saw the impact of the economic collapse in South Carolina, writing in 1931 that "never have I witnessed such despair and hopelessness."[31]

As the Depression deepened, Baruch realized that the nation needed action and that federal leadership was essential. Baruch, however, wanted recovery efforts to be based on what he regarded as sound economic principles. He believed in a balanced budget and urged cuts in unnecessary government spending. Baruch was a powerful Democrat, but his center of gravity lay with senior Democrats in the Congress, and he was not active in the battle for the Democratic nomination in 1932. Baruch had known Franklin D. Roosevelt since he was a youthful state senator in New York, but he was not impressed with FDR's record as governor, and he did not join his pre-convention campaign. Nevertheless, during the general election Baruch sent a steady stream of memoranda to FDR, and after the election he was invited to Warm Springs, Georgia, to consult with the president-elect.[32]

Baruch quickly developed mixed feelings about the New Deal. By January 1934, he worried that it had "broken down the morale and character of our people and whether, when it is all finished, they will be able again to fend for themselves." But Baruch did not want an open break with the president; he liked his status as the elder statesman of the Democratic Party and craved access to the White House. He would not join conservative Democrats in an open break with FDR, although by 1935 Baruch was upset by the New Deal's tax policies and by much of its social legislation. While he had a tense relationship with the president and his "Brain Trust," he developed a warm friendship with Eleanor Roosevelt, who had, he believed, a "rare combination of intelligence and great heart." He even offered financial support for one of her planned communities in West Virginia.[33]

During the 1930s, Baruch carefully observed events in Europe. He had no illusions about Hitler and his rise to power, writing in 1935, "Hitler and peace! The very terms are antithetical. He is today the greatest menace to world safety." In 1937, Baruch returned from a trip to Europe convinced that the continent was a "tinderbox." Britain and France, he believed, were unprepared to deal with the German menace, and he was also well-aware of the deficiencies of the American military. Baruch now pressed for American rearmament and also urged FDR to heed the lessons of World War I and to set up a proper organization for the mobilization of the nation's economy. The president, however, wanted no mobilization tsar who would undercut his own authority and, aware of the power of isolationist sentiment, moved slowly, from Baruch's perspective, to prepare the nation for war.[34]

After American entry into the war in December 1941, Baruch devoted all of his time to improving the nation's war effort. He became a trouble-shooter in defense programs, a "free-lancer without portfolio." Baruch relished this role, since it gave him considerable influence without the day-to-day responsibilities of an official position. By 1942, he had become the sage of Lafayette Square, the "park bench statesman," a wise and charming old man who drew on his experience in World War I. As before, Baruch, through a variety of surrogates, orchestrated his publicity campaign, one that portrayed him as a great patriot and adviser to presidents. One longtime friend remembered him as the "Oracle of the Obvious." "Never one to run out of breath when blowing his own trumpet, he saw himself as an iconic father figure to the nation." He also looked the part, "with his erect carriage and proud bearing, thick white hair, a strong aquiline nose, crafty blue eyes. . . . He had a deep voice, and a flattering grace of manner, his courtly, old-school Southern gentleman pose."[35]

FDR was ambivalent about Baruch. He valued his skills and experience and gave him an open door to the White House but believed that the financier was a conniver who was motivated by his own personal aggrandizement. He also needed him. In 1944, the president, whose health was declining, spent the whole month of April recuperating at Hobcaw. During the rest of the year, the two men remained in touch, and on January 21, 1945, the day before FDR left for the Yalta conference, Baruch saw the president, reminded him of the need for an effective international organization, and also reminded him of Wilson's tragic experience in 1919. On his return from Yalta, FDR asked Baruch to travel to London to consult with Prime Minister Churchill about a variety of postwar issues. On April 12, Baruch was in London when he learned of FDR's death. As he flew home the next day, he recalled first meeting him in Albany in 1911 and also recalled his zest for living and his humor and courage. "Like Wilson," Baruch remembered, "he had the capacity to raise men's hopes, strengthen their wills, and call forth the best that was within them."[36]

Baruch aged during the war. His deafness in one ear worsened, making conversation difficult; his energy level dropped; and his speech patterns were often hard to follow. Baruch remained, however, a powerful figure in Washington and a popular figure with the public. As one journalist noted, "Baruch today is without doubt the most respected individual in the country."

In March 1946, President Truman appointed Baruch the American representative on the United Nations Atomic Energy Commission. The task of the commission was to figure out a way to establish international control of nuclear energy. After months of study, Baruch and his team recommended that the United States should not end its production of bombs or dismantle its existing nuclear stockpile until an effective system of controls was put in place. But Soviet leaders would not accept international controls, and in January 1947, Baruch resigned his position, realizing that his work was over.[37]

By early 1947, Baruch understood that the United States was now in what he called a Cold War, and he urged the Truman administration to mobilize the nation's economic, political, and spiritual resources. But Baruch did not get along with Truman and his advisers. Increasingly he found the president a "rude, uncouth and ignorant man," while Truman regarded the elder statesman as devious and egocentric. As the president complained to an aide who urged him to consult with Baruch, "I'm just *not* going to do it. I'm not going to spend hours and hours on that old goat, come what may. If you take his advice, then you have him on your hands for hours and hours, and it is *his* policy. I'm just not going to do it." After 1948, Baruch was no longer welcome in the White House. He now felt alienated from the Democratic Party that he had supported for so many years. In October 1952, Baruch endorsed Dwight D. Eisenhower for the presidency, and in May 1953, he entered the White House for the first time in five years. Eisenhower, he concluded, "is a very decent, high-minded man, who is such an improvement over the last."[38]

In the 1950s, Baruch remained popular. In the spring of 1953, he attended a show starring the comedian Danny Kaye at the Palace Theater in New York. Kaye, when he discovered that Baruch was in the audience, walked down to the footlights, raised his hand for silence, and announced: "Ladies and gentlemen. We have in our midst one of the great Americans of all time, an elder statesman, whose name will go ringing down the corridors of history. I give you Bernard M. Baruch." Baruch stood for the next ten minutes while the crowd cheered and clapped. Despite his popularity, however, Baruch seemed in some ways out of step with his times. In politics he took a series of conservative positions, complaining about the civil rights movement that "I think we talk too much of rights and not enough of obligations." He admired the anticommunist agenda of the House Committee on Un-American Activities and believed that Senator Joseph R. McCarthy (R-WI) was alerting the nation to serious internal dangers. Baruch was, in fact, distrustful of popular crusades and wanted basic political and economic policies designed by a small elite. He hoped that an advisory council of elder statesmen would impose whatever policies were necessary to ensure that a stable and prosperous United States would lead the world.[39]

During 1956, the year of Woodrow Wilson's centenary, Baruch often wrote about Wilson's legacy and his rightful place in history. Wilson was, he believed, a "luminous figure," a "truly civilized man," who proved through his political career that idealism and realism were not in conflict. Baruch concluded that "all the qualities that account for Wilson's greatness—his strength of character, his imagination and intelligence, his courage and realism and idealism—were brought into sharpest focus by the war and the quest for peace. Here was the challenge of history. He met it. Here was the test of greatness. He passed it." The president realized that in the "modern world war could no longer be isolated," and that a reign of law must be established through the League of Nations, one that included the use of force if necessary to maintain it. History, Baruch concluded, had "vindicated" Wilson, for the United States, through the Western alliance, now led the "free world." No doubt Baruch felt that his place in history was linked to that of his great mentor. He gave his personal papers to Princeton University, where they would reside next to those of Wilson, and in 1957, and again in 1960, published memoirs that explained the central role that Wilson had played in his life.

In his early nineties, Baruch remained physically active, surprising those who met him with his strong voice and clear mind. He sat out the 1960 presidential campaign but was impressed with John F. Kennedy's inaugural address and pleased that the new president invited him to the White House. Lyndon B. Johnson continued to court Baruch, who now supported the Voting Rights Act of 1965 and in the spring of that year endorsed LBJ's escalation of the war in Vietnam. It was his fifth American war.

Baruch did not live to see the outcome of the war in Vietnam. He died on June 20, 1965, fifty-three years after he had met Woodrow Wilson. He was the last Wilsonian.[40]

Ray Stannard Baker, a half-length portrait. Baker, a brilliant journalist, grew close to the president over the years and, as press secretary of the American Peace Commission, saw Wilson nearly every day. He became the president's authorized biographer and his defender before the bar of history. Library of Congress, Prints and Photographs Division, LC-USZ62-36754.

CHAPTER ELEVEN

Ray Stannard Baker

"[T]he kind of man who has . . . divided men into bitter opponents, or worshipful admirers, and so it will be to the end of time"

On January 21, 1910, Ray Stannard Baker, one of the most famous journalists of his era, heard the president of Princeton University, Woodrow Wilson, speak in the ballroom of the Hotel Astor in New York City. "No other speaker," Baker remembered, "I had ever heard made an impression quite so vivid and clear cut as he. I felt that here was the kind of thinking statesman the country needed and could trust." Later in the year, Baker, eager to meet Wilson, traveled to Princeton, New Jersey, where he had a long talk with him at Prospect House. Once again Baker was conscious of the "extraordinary sense of sincerity and conviction I had felt at the Astor dinner," and he left convinced "that I had met the finest mind in the field of statesmanship to be found in American public life." But Baker doubted that Wilson, who lacked any practical political experience, could ever achieve the presidency. He watched with fascination Wilson's meteoric rise in New Jersey politics and his successful presidential campaign in 1912. Over the years Baker drew closer to the president, and at the Paris Peace Conference, where he was the press secretary of the American Peace Commission, Baker saw Wilson nearly every day. He was so drawn into the drama surrounding the president that he eventually convinced both Woodrow and Edith that he was the best man to tell the story of his life. For fourteen years he labored on his great task; he became, more than anyone else, the keeper of the flame, the writer who sought to shape Wilson's legacy.[1]

* * *

In the spring of 1875, Alice Potter Baker brought her three sons to St. Croix Falls, a small frontier village in northern Wisconsin. The eldest of her sons, Ray Stannard, had been born on April 17, 1870. Baker's mother, his "poor, gentle, beautiful, sensitive mother," disliked her new home and longed for the family and friends she had left behind in Michigan. She died when her eldest son was only thirteen. Baker's father, Joseph Stannard Baker, was born in western New York on March 20, 1838. Early in the Civil War, he worked with the Secret Service in Washington, and he remembered meeting Abraham Lincoln. Later in the war—when he was only twenty-four—he became the commander of a cavalry regiment and fought in some of the fierce battles on the Virginia front. After the war, he moved to Lansing, Michigan, and four years later he migrated to northern Wisconsin, where he was the agent for those who had large landholdings in the northern part of the state. Everyone knew Major Baker, a formidable figure, with his erect military bearing, side whiskers, and white hair. He thrived in the task of opening up new country for settlement. His business required that he take long trips into the up-country, and often he took his eldest son with him. Like his father, Ray was fascinated with these expeditions into largely uninhabited terrain, and he found his father to be a compelling figure, one who was a gifted storyteller, a strict Presbyterian, and a collector of books. His father, he recalled, was "the greatest influence and joy of my boyhood."[2]

Ray attended a one-room schoolhouse in St. Croix Falls and at the age of fifteen left home to attend Michigan Agriculture College near Lansing, Michigan. There he met an inspired teacher, William J. Beal (and eventually would marry his daughter), and in general prospered during his four years at the school. While he was a serious student, he also joined a fraternity, became editor of the college paper, and was the class orator his final year. And he took long "tramps" in the countryside surrounding Lansing.[3]

After his graduation in 1889, Ray returned to St. Croix Falls. His father, who had become totally deaf, needed help with his business. His son now disliked his life there, which he found suffocating and lacking in the sort of stimulation that he had become accustomed to in college. He decided that he would study the law, and in January 1892 entered the law school of the University of Michigan at Ann Arbor. While Ray found the intellectual atmosphere of the university exciting, he was bored with the law and decided to take English literature seminars taught by another great teacher, Fred Newton Scott. Scott also gave a course in journalistic writing, one in which students followed a particular issue in a daily newspaper. Soon Ray decided to become a writer. In June 1892, at the age of twenty-two, he left for Chicago to find newspaper work.[4]

Baker found a job with the *Record*, and soon took long walks exploring Chicago and reporting on conditions there. Beyond the prosperous facade, he found a city in turmoil. As he wrote to his father, "there are thousands of homeless and starving men in the streets. I have seen more misery in this last week than I ever saw in my life before." In March 1894, the *Record* assigned the young reporter to join "General" Jacob Coxey's Army on its march to Washington to demand a government sponsored public works program. Later in the year, he reported on the strike in Pullman, Illinois—the model town founded by the industrialist George M. Pullman—which became the center of one of the great industrial conflicts of the late nineteenth century. Reporting on these events gave Baker an education in the strife between labor and capital, and he became sympathetic to Eugene Debs and the members of his American Railway Union. In 1896, he attended the Democratic convention in Chicago, where he heard William Jennings Bryan deliver his "Cross of Gold Speech." Bryan, he recalled, was a handsome man, "young, tall, powerfully built, clear eyed, with a mane of black hair. . . . He had a beautiful, deeply modulated voice, and he talked to them [men] with an intimacy of feeling . . . of complete dedication to a sacred cause." Baker concluded that Bryan, while he was a "great popular orator," gave his followers little "to get hold of." Looking back, he realized that the Great Commoner was very different from Woodrow Wilson, who "swayed people's heads, often without reaching their hearts."[5]

Baker soon realized the limitations of a reporter's life, or, as he wrote to his father in early 1898, "I have seen that newspaper work would not do to grow old in." He now had a wife and children, and he hoped for a larger salary and a job that would give him more time to think and to write. He began writing stories for popular magazines and did this so well that in February 1898 he left Chicago for New York and a position on the staff of *McClure's Magazine*.[6]

Baker was nearly twenty-eight years old. He was a handsome man, five foot ten, mild-mannered, rather quiet, with an intense, wide-ranging curiosity and an ability to work well with other writers. Baker was fascinated with his new life at *McClure's*, which had become, under the leadership of its flamboyant leader, one of the most popular and progressive magazines in the country. Samuel S. McClure allowed his reporters to write long and carefully researched articles on vital issues of the day, and Baker found that he was now part of an "intoxicating editorial atmosphere." He worked with other talented writers—Ida Tarbell, Lincoln Steffens, William Allen White—and "suddenly and joyously," he remembered, he was transported to a world "full of strange and wonderful new things," and he was "at the heart of it, especially commissioned to look at it, hear about it, and above all, to write about it."[7]

In the spring of 1900, Baker traveled to Europe to report on the political developments in France, Germany, and Great Britain. He returned to the United States depressed, dissatisfied with his life in New York, which, for all of its excitement, did not give him the time he needed to think. In the winter of 1900 he moved, with his wife and daughter, to a remote ranch in Arizona, where he restored his health and concluded that he needed to be free to search for his "dominating passion." He realized that the kind of men he liked were "all devoted to noble objectives outside themselves: all deeply sincere. Men not possessing, but possessed. And finally, all had creative imaginations, or if it seems a better word—vision, to which they were unselfishly devoted."[8]

Baker left Arizona determined to find a way to do his own work. In April 1902, he moved his family to East Lansing, Michigan, where they would be near relatives and friends and where Baker could lead a more relaxed life. He retained, however, his ties to *McClure's Magazine*, and in the early years of the twentieth century he wrote a series of pathbreaking articles on capital and labor. He wrote on the captains of industry, on union corruption, and on a miners' strike in Pennsylvania. Along with Tarbell and Steffens, he became a new breed of investigative reporter, "muckrakers" who produced a "literature of exposure." These articles achieved a tremendous popular response. As Baker recalled, "I doubt whether any other magazine published in America ever achieved such sudden and overwhelming recognition. . . . We had put our fingers on the sorest spots in American life." It seemed to many observers that Baker had become "the greatest reporter" in the nation.[9]

In the fall of 1906, Baker began research for a series of articles for *McClure's Magazine* on racial problems in the South, articles that were collected in 1908 in a popular book titled *Following the Color Line*. As one biographer notes, Baker "brought to the problem a curious mixture of ignorance, idealism, and prejudice." He had never known an African American until he went to college; nor, in later years, had he devoted much attention to the plight of Blacks in American society. The articles he wrote for *McClure's* were based on interviews and extensive travel, but they were full of contradictions. Baker approved of Jim Crow laws, but he also emphasized the hostile environment in which Blacks had to live. He argued that separate schools were good for Blacks, but that African Americans were not innately inferior and that they were in the process of awakening to a new "democratic spirit." Years later he was critical of the president's willingness to let Burleson and McAdoo segregate their departments, but he would only criticize Wilson in private, not in public; in his biography he would defend his hero's inaction on the question of race.[10]

Inevitably, Baker's path crossed with that of Theodore Roosevelt, especially after he began to work on the tangled question of railroad regulation. Baker had first met TR in 1898, when the Rough Rider returned a war hero from Cuba. He was attracted by Roosevelt's energy and "concentration of purpose," convinced, he wrote to his father in 1904, "that he is a very great man, greater than his generation realizes." By early 1905, however, Baker, who was deep into his research on railroad regulation, concluded that the nation's railroads should be owned by the federal government. In the fall of that year, Baker and TR—who was moving toward a more modest form of regulation embodied in the Hepburn Act of 1906—engaged in a heated exchange of letters. The president was growing tired of the "new journalism," and in April 1906, he condemned "gross and reckless assaults on character" and compared journalists who made such attacks to "the man with the muckrake" in John Bunyan's *Pilgrim's Progress*. TR's attack on all reform journalists led Baker to lose confidence in the man he had once admired so much: "I met the President many times afterward and there were numerous exchanges of letters, but while I could wonder at his remarkable versatility of mind, and admire his many robust human qualities, I would never again give him my full confidence, nor follow his leadership." Roosevelt, Baker concluded, "left little of vision or of creative statesmanship to his successors. Young men are not likely to look back to him . . . for inspiration as to Thomas Jefferson, Abraham Lincoln, Woodrow Wilson."[11]

Baker adored his life in East Lansing, where he could live close to nature and escape many of the tensions of big-city existence. In 1906, he began to publish articles about the experiences of David Grayson, his nom de plume. These stories were an instant hit, and over the next thirty-five years Baker would publish nine volumes that would eventually sell over two million copies. David Grayson, an educated man who lived with his sister in the countryside, found fulfillment in simple things and celebrated the richness of a quiet rural life. Grayson's collected stories bore titles such as *Adventures in Contentment* and *Adventures in Friendship*, which resonated with those Americans who felt the strain of a rapidly urbanizing nation.[12]

Baker liked William Howard Taft and in 1908 voted for him rather than for Bryan. But he soon concluded that Taft was no reformer and that he had lost the progressive wing of the Republican Party. As he wrote to his father, "a real revolution is underway, and it will not stop until government by trusts & special interests is wiped out." Baker realized that Theodore Roosevelt, after his return to the United States in mid-June 1910, remained "the most interesting, amusing, thrilling figure in America." But TR's overwhelming personality, he believed, "obscures everything," and in

1912, rather than join the Bull Moose movement, Baker turned to Woodrow Wilson, a new personality in the nation's public life. "As for me, I shall vote for Wilson. I distrust the old party behind him & some of the things he stands for, but I have great confidence in the man and in the faction of the party (the progressive—Bryan faction) which he represents. And I like his clear, calm way of putting things."[13]

Initially Baker was uncertain about the progressivism of the new administration and critical of some of Wilson's appointments to his cabinet —such as Josephus Daniels and Albert Burleson (a Texas congressman who became postmaster general). But Baker remained convinced that Wilson was "a thinker in the White House." In early September 1914, he had a long talk with the president, who "looked very well, clear-eyed, confident, cheerful. . . . I was pleased not only with the President's clear exposition of his policies, but more than ever before with the man himself—his forthrightness, the sense of inner discipline he gave, the kind of self-confidence in the leader that convinces and inspires his followers." By the spring of 1916, Baker had become much more committed to Wilson and his administration. In May of that year, he interviewed Wilson from eight to ten o'clock in the evening in the library upstairs at the White House. The president came in "stepping quickly and lightly," and Baker was once again impressed with the power and suppleness of Wilson's mind. As he recalled, "He pounces upon things half said and consumes them before they are well out of one's mind. And his pounce is sure, accurate, and complete." By 1916, Baker was impressed with the legislative achievements of the president and his party and became active in his campaign for reelection. After Wilson's triumph, Baker admitted in his journal that during the campaign "such doubts and suspense I have never known."[14]

The outbreak of war in August 1914 upset Baker, who believed that if the United States entered the conflict, many of the advances of recent years would be wiped out. At the start of the war he was inclined toward pacifism, and he was sometimes critical of the president's neutrality policies. Not until the spring of 1916 did he conclude that "Wilson grows in power and esteem." His speech on May 27, 1916, in which he advocated the creation of a "universal association of nations," deepened Baker's commitment to the administration, as did Wilson's "Peace without Victory Speech" on January 22, 1917. Baker believed that the president had seized "the moral leadership of liberals the world over. . . . His address seems to me the greatest and most daring act of statesmanship I have known in my time." On April 3, 1917, the day after Wilson asked Congress for a declaration of war, Baker recorded that "I follow him wholeheartedly, and now that we are getting in I want to see the war carried forward with energy, but without passion and hatred, as a duty to be done. . . . It is a great time we live in."[15]

During the winter of 1917–18, rumors spread of growing unrest in Allied nations and of the emergence of a peace-by-negotiation movement. The president, who felt that his diplomats were not keeping him properly informed, decided to send Baker to Europe to report on sentiment in Britain, France, and Italy. In early February 1918, Baker left for London, and during the ensuing months he traveled through Allied nations, talking with a wide range of leaders. Like many progressives, he was convinced of Wilson's support among the masses of the people, asserting that "the only leader in the world today who in any way touches or inspires these masses in England, France and Italy is Mr. Wilson." He concluded that if the Allies won the war with their present governments, they would impose an old-fashioned peace and make no effort to realize Wilson's ideals. Baker oversimplified, exaggerating the president's following among liberal and labor groups and ignoring the popular support for the governments of David Lloyd George, Georges Clemenceau, and Sidney Sonnino. In early December 1918, on the eve of the peace conference, Baker was uncertain how Wilson could work with what he termed "old imperialist governments" and seemed pessimistic about the president's fate. "I have," he recorded, "curiously, a feeling of doom in the coming to Europe of Woodrow Wilson. He occupies a pinnacle too high: the earth forces are too strong. He is now approaching the supreme test of his triumph and his popularity. They are dizzy heights he stands upon: no man has long breathed such a rarified atmosphere and lived. All the old, ugly depths—hating change, hating light—will suck him down."[16]

* * *

Just before the armistice, Baker arrived in Paris, eager to return to his home in Amherst, Massachusetts (where he had moved in 1910). But on December 18, the president, a few days after his own arrival in Paris, asked Baker to stay and to become the press secretary of the American Peace Commission. He now had to organize the press department and to give American correspondents—who were clamoring for news—summaries of every day's negotiations. Despite the burdens of his new position, however, he realized that he would now be in daily contact with Wilson and that it would give him, in short, a special insight into a great, historic event.

When the president left Brest on February 15 to return to America, Baker accompanied him. During the voyage home, he urged Wilson to give the public a much fuller explanation of the deliberations in Paris, to engage, in fact, in more public diplomacy. He also had long talks with Cary Grayson, who gave him a full account of the history of his patient's health. Baker concluded that Grayson had performed, "a wonderful service in preserving the precious life of the president."[17]

Baker realized that Wilson's real difficulties would begin after he returned to France on March 13. Many issues that had been put off now had to be confronted. But the president, he observed, was badly overworked, and on April 3 he recorded in his diary that his chief was "growing grayer and grimmer all the time, standing upon principles of justice and right." That day Wilson's health collapsed and, even after he returned to work, Baker was pessimistic about the prospects for the peace conference. He was dejected: "ached with longing for time to live, to think, to feel." Baker was "imprisoned" at the peace conference.[18]

Earlier in the peace conference Baker had been impressed with Colonel House, recording that "without Colonel House this Peace Commission work could not go on. He is the universal conciliator, smoother-over, connector! He is a kind of super-secretary—a glorified secretary. He is the only man who keeps closely in touch with the President—constantly informing and advising him, getting people together, helping along publicity by seeing the correspondents—a busy, useful, kindly, liberal, lively little man. He can't make a speech, uses rather poor English, but is indefatigable in his service and, so far as I can see, is without personal ambition." But when Woodrow, Edith, and Grayson turned against House, so did Baker, who now dismissed him as a "dilettante," a lover of the game without any real responsibilities. Baker—with more access to Wilson than anyone except Edith and Grayson—had become a member of the president's inner circle of advisers.[19]

In early May, when Baker read the peace treaty, he concluded that it "is a terrible document; a document of retribution to the verge of revenge. . . . I can see no real peace in it." Baker now tried to "clarify my mind" about Wilson and to decide whether or not he could support the treaty. "Never was I more in doubt," he recorded, "as to my own course. This Treaty seems to me, in many particulars, abominable. How can I go home and support it, support the League of Nations founded upon it, support Wilson?" But he also believed that Wilson had worked in a terrible atmosphere and that he had been forced to pay a high price for the League. He hoped, as did the president, that "new liberal governments" would spring up everywhere and dominate the new organization. But Baker could not, in the end, abandon "the only great man here." "I do not," he observed, "see him perfect. He is not a man I love as I love some men, but he is a man I respect and admire enormously. . . . What a man he is! As lonely as God! . . . When all is said, a great man, a Titan struggling with forces too great for him."[20]

On May 30, Baker traveled with the president to Suresnes, where Wilson gave a speech dedicating the new cemetery for American soldiers. Baker was swept away by his friend's oratory, convinced that it was the greatest speech he had ever heard. It gave him, he realized, a deeper understanding of Wilson, "a glimpse of a great soul struggling against the forces of time and space." He resolved to help him in what was sure to be a bitter battle for the ratification of the peace treaty.[21]

Baker returned to the United States with Edith and Woodrow on the *George Washington*. On July 8, when the ship arrived in New York, he said goodbye to the president, whom he had talked to daily for many months. But Wilson did not respond to the occasion, "[N]ot one word did he say about it, either commentating or otherwise—or intimate that he even cared to see me again. He said good-bye to me just as he would have said it to a visitor of an hour." Baker was disappointed but not surprised by the president's behavior. In earlier years, he observed, Wilson seemed a cold, aloof man, but more and more he seemed "intensely engrossed, absorbed, concentrated." Baker returned to Amherst still "deeply moved by a solicitude for the man himself."[22]

During the summer of 1919, Baker watched with dismay Wilson's struggle with Senate Republicans and his decision to embark on his ill-fated western tour. He was astonished at the president's courage, believed the attacks on him were shameful, and in November 1919 published a small book, *What Wilson Did at Paris*. Baker now believed that the peace treaty was the best that could be obtained under difficult circumstances, that compromise with its opponents was inevitable.[23]

In early November 1919, Baker traveled to Washington, where he had lunch with Edith and Cary Grayson. Edith, he recorded, "looks worn & tired after her long vigil but remains irrepressibly cheerful," while Grayson was eager for his friend's approval. He was no doubt relieved to learn that Baker believed that he had done the right thing. "The president's physician was," Baker concluded, "a fine, brave simple man if ever there was one." He also concluded that "the President will be much longer in getting up & about than anyone knows—& he may never get up." After years of observing Wilson, Baker decided that "the plain fact is that the President has a 600 horse-power motor in a frail, light, delicate chassis. A great, powerful driving will directed by an intellect so ambitious to achieve that no physical body could bear the strain for long at a time—especially if the hills are high and rugged, as they were at Paris. So he keeps breaking down: Dr. Grayson, the clever mechanician always at his side to watch the machine." Baker also stopped in New York to visit Colonel House, whose stock, he wrote, "has fallen to zero." Baker liked House—despite his loss of influence—and also observed that he had a "genius for appealing to men's vanity." The president knew that his counselor possessed skills that he lacked, for he was a man "stark in his simplicity, directness, his want of artifice: but those qualities—his true greatness—will not be regarded until he is dead."[24]

On January, 22, 1920, Baker once again lunched at the White House (and once again did not see the president). After a long talk with Edith, he was impressed with "her sound good sense, her real understanding of the difficulties of the present situation & her eagerness to help." Baker wanted Wilson to compromise, convinced that, if he had not been ill, he would have found a way to "save the situation." But Edith could not move her husband, who "still has in mind the reception he got in the west, and he believes the people are with him."[25]

Baker realized that the president did not know what was going on and that Senate Democrats would have to accept the Lodge reservations if they wanted a peace treaty and a League of Nations. Wilson, he concluded, needed to make a "large gesture" to break through the deadlock, but he also understood that he was unlikely to do so: "The poor President! So nearly a friendless man. Yet beyond all of this yelping pack he is the only man who has had truly constructive ideas: & it is to him & to him alone that the world will owe the League of Nations—*if ever it gets it*. There is something indescribably tragic in the sight of this sick man, now willing to kill his own child rather than to have it misborn in the world! . . . It is the old tragedy of a man's dearest desire thwarted by the defects of his own temperament, and his own physical weakness."[26]

For Baker, the president was a flawed hero, but the journalist, who was now transforming himself into a historian, was eager to tell the story of Wilson at the peace conference: "The great thing is not to excuse or defend every act of the President: which I have never done: but to present this strong, able, fallible man struggling with vast events, in a torn world." In January 1921, Baker traveled to Washington to begin work on his peace conference book. Initially, he read documents at the White House, then, after Woodrow and Edith moved to S Street, he had a room there, and in late May he took all the documents with him to Amherst. Baker praised Edith, recording that "Mrs. Wilson is splendid. Good sense, a fine spirit, devotion! What has she not gone through these last months. The President could not have lived without her—literally. The relationships between them are beautiful!" On this trip Baker found Woodrow far better than he was in November, but later in March he described him as "looking inconceivably old, gray, worn, tired. His hair seemed unusually thin: & his face a kind of parchment yellow. . . . Only the eyes seemed undimmed very bright, clear, piercing: burning like living coals in the ashes of a spent fire."[27]

Once again, while he was on the East Coast, Baker stopped in New York to visit with Colonel House. The Colonel, he discovered, was seeing lots of people and was eager to talk about his break with Wilson. Although Baker was now critical of House, he still liked him "very much." "I never meet the Colonel," he wrote, "without a new sense of personal liking such as I have never at any time felt for the President. He is a human soul. . . . His intellectual equipment is small: he has no real mind of his own. . . . He compromises everything away in order to preserve 'harmony' & keep people liking one another."[28]

On May 25, 1921, Baker had a long talk with Edith, who now told him at length about Woodrow's break with his counselor. House, Baker observed, understood Wilson better than most men, realizing that "the President always hated to bother with human arrangements." "The President," he continued, "had vast labor to do, great legislative plans to work out, many speeches to make: and he was always at the edge of his physical capacity, always having to conserve his energy—and he let the cultivation of these ordinary human relationships . . . slip by." And yet, Baker wrote, the president "had a strange power—a veritable genius—for presenting these ideas so that they stole away men's hearts. I remember well the profound impression he made upon me the first time I heard him speak. He seemed to be everything I desired in a leader! And so he charmed, elevated, persuaded the whole world in 1917 & 1918." Wilson, Baker concluded, should be seen as "a distant high peak, cold, snow-capped, with a kind of glittering beauty & power, reaching toward the stars—distant, distant! Men may hate him bitterly, as many do, or admire him, or try to explain him—but they can't get around him. There he is! And he will always be discussed, fought over, hated, admired, speculated about." As for Wilson and House, Baker now saw clearly that "[i]t was perhaps because these two men were at opposite poles of temperament: one cold & negative, the other warm &

positive, that they so flew together, each recognizing in the other what he lacked. . . . People love House . . . and he loves his friends: and is to-day, as he was in Paris, cheery, optimistic—yes, happy! He lives always in a kind of warm haze of good-feeling. What a contrast with the grim, bitter, tragic lonely old man there in S Street!" House, he predicted, "will be utterly forgotten" in twenty years—except as "a friend, a helper of the President."[29]

By October 1921, Baker's book on Wilson and the peace conference was nearly finished, and in January 1922 newspapers began the serialization of the manuscript. The actual book, titled *Woodrow Wilson and the World Settlement*, appeared later in the year in three volumes, two of narrative and one of documents. Baker told the story of America's encounter with world affairs, drawing a sharp distinction between the New World versus the Old. He now defended Wilson and discarded many of his earlier criticisms of the peace treaty, although he did point out Wilson's ignorance of economics and his failure in human relationships. "Finally," he concluded, "we see in high relief the figure of an extraordinary human being, with supreme qualities of many kinds, with temperamental and physical limitations, who will never cease to fascinate the historian and biographer of representative and decisive characters."[30]

By the time *Woodrow Wilson and the World Settlement* appeared, Baker hoped to become the president's official biographer, and in early 1924 he wrote to Wilson, admitting that it was his "great ambition" to write a "complete study of your whole career." Wilson put him off, but after his death Baker renewed his campaign, with help from Cary Grayson. On January 5, 1925, Baker met with Edith, who now showed him a letter that Woodrow had written on January 25, 1924, making the journalist his "preferred creditor" with first access to his papers. Edith insisted on only one condition, that she would be able to read the manuscript of each volume before it was sent to the publisher. Edith became, in fact, an enthusiastic collaborator, listening to Baker's many doubts and frustrations over the years and encouraging him, despite fatigue and ill-health, to complete his great task.[31]

In early March 1925, Baker, if he had had any illusions, realized the magnitude of his challenge when a moving van brought five tons of Wilson's papers to his house in Amherst. During the first few years of the project he collected additional material, conducting extensive interviews with those who knew Wilson and visiting many of the sites where he had lived. Baker was excited by the challenge he confronted, writing to Edith, "I wonder if any biographer ever before came into the possession of such unexpected riches." In his introduction to the first volume, Baker admitted "that I have written with sympathy goes without saying: who would have the courage to undertake such a task in cold blood? And how, without sympathy, could there be understanding?" Between 1927 and 1931, he published the first four volumes, but poor health and financial worries slowed him down, and volumes seven and eight did not appear until 1939. Baker's work on Wilson—which had extended over fourteen years and consumed 4,037 pages—was finally done. In May 1940, he won the Pulitzer Prize for his achievement.[32]

During the 1920s, Baker was discouraged by Republican dominance of national politics. He regarded the presidencies of Warren Harding and Calvin Coolidge as "one of the darkest, most hopeless periods in recent American history." But he was also discouraged by Democratic presidential candidates and voted, unenthusiastically, for James Cox in 1920 and John Davis in 1924. Four years later he actively supported Al Smith, and in 1932 he hoped that Newton Baker would win the nomination. Baker finally came out for Franklin Roosevelt, "but with no great enthusiasm." Once FDR was in office, Baker felt some of the early excitement of the New Deal, but he disliked many of its specific measures and soon became disillusioned with FDR's broker state. In an April 1935 interview with the president, Baker emphasized the need for vision, recording that "I did not come away glowing with confidence as I came sometimes in the old days from talks with Wilson." In 1936, Baker voted for FDR, but he was depressed by the fact that "in this dreary campaign there was almost no call to any kind of unselfish service; everywhere group demands for special favors, and career politicians promising to grant them." A few years later he made a final judgment on FDR, who was, he concluded, "a highly capable work-a-day statesman [but] . . . he will never be remembered with Lincoln and Wilson."[33]

* * *

Throughout the 1940s, Baker remained devoted to Wilson's legacy, spending months in Hollywood in the winter of 1943–44 as a consultant to Darryl Zanuck's movie *Wilson*. But his main literary effort, now that the president's biography was concluded, was to tell the story of how he had been brought up on the American frontier, of how he had become a famous journalist, and of how he had eventually dedicated himself to a great leader and his cause. *Native American: The Book of My Youth*, appeared in 1941, while *American Chronicle: The Autobiography of Ray Stannard Baker* was published in 1945. At the end of the second volume, Baker concluded that "I think the deepest satisfaction of the later years of my life has been to see Woodrow Wilson coming into his own, being recognized for the pre-eminent man he was, as the true inheritor and prophet of the great American tradition." He ended with a coda:

> Curious, in time, I stand, noting the efforts of heroes:
> Is the deferment long? Bitter the slander, poverty, death?
> Lies the seed unreck'd for centuries in the ground?
> Lo! To God's due occasion,
> Uprising in the night, it sprouts, blooms,
> And fills the earth with use and beauty.

Baker died on July 12, 1946, at the age of seventy-six.[34]

Guardians of the Legacy

Aside from Ellen Wilson, who died in August 1914, all of the members of
Woodrow Wilson's inner circle lived for years beyond the president, giv-
ing them time to reflect on their association with him. Cary Grayson died
prematurely in February 1938 at the age of fifty-nine, but all of the others—
Tumulty, Daniels, McAdoo, House, Edith, Newton Baker, Baruch, and Ray
Stannard Baker—lived long lives. All had the opportunity, if they were
so inclined, to write a memoir explaining how they had been drawn into
Wilson's inner circle and what the president had accomplished.

In 1921—before his hero's death—Tumulty published first, a hastily written, hagiographic memoir (which the president disliked) titled *Woodrow
Wilson as I Know Him*. Grayson was more discreet. Three years later,
upset by some of the criticisms of the president, he wrote his recollections
of their association, published posthumously in 1961 as *Woodrow Wilson:
An Intimate Memoir*. Colonel House was eager to make a case for his own
importance, publishing the first two volumes of his edited diary, *The Intimate Papers of Colonel House*, in 1926 (volumes 3 and 4 followed in 1928).
House had no doubts about Wilson's greatness as a political leader, but
he also emphasized the president's shortcomings and portrayed himself
as the dominant partner in the relationship. Nor would House admit that
Wilson—disappointed with his counselor's behavior—had ended their
friendship. House simply would not explore the reasons for the break be-

tween the two men. Nor would McAdoo, in his 1931 memoir, *Crowded Years: The Reminiscences of William G. McAdoo*, address his gradual estrangement from the man he hoped to succeed in the presidency. Edith disliked both House and McAdoo, but it was only after she read House's *Intimate Papers* that she decided to pen her own account of her years with the president. Full of resentment toward House, and urged on by Baruch, she wrote *My Memoir*, published in 1939. The book was full of detail—some inaccurate—but left no doubt that her husband was the dominant figure of his era.

Only one of the president's intimates, Newton Baker, refused to write about his own role in the administration. Baker disliked the flood of memoirs and diaries that appeared in the 1920s and was particularly contemptuous of House's claim to fame. Absorbed in his highly successful law practice, he was content to let future historians sort through the claims of the president's friends and foes.

Despite his admiration for Wilson, Josephus Daniels was slow to record his own memories of his association with the president. Daniels was close to his onetime protégé, Franklin Roosevelt, and from 1933 until 1941 served as his ambassador to Mexico. Not until 1944 did he publish the first of two detailed volumes, *The Wilson Era: Years of Peace*, and two years later *The Wilson Era: Years of War and After*.

Bernard Baruch also delayed the publication of his memoirs, in part because of his service to FDR's administration, in part because of his unceasing efforts to burnish his own reputation. Baruch lived long enough to participate in Wilson's centenary in 1956, and finally, in 1957 and 1960, he published *Baruch: My Own Story* and *Baruch: The Public Years*, the memoirs of the last Wilsonian.

All of these men and women admired Wilson, believed in his greatness, and believed that their service to him was the high point of their lives. All wrote books filled with interesting detail, but they also seemed unable to move beneath the surface of the Wilson presidency. It was left to Ray Stannard Baker, a skilled observer of men and events, to probe the deepest into Wilson's personality and to explain better than the other observers the qualities that led to his great political success. Baker wrote two volumes of memoirs, the first, *Native American: The Book of My Youth*, appeared in 1941; the second, *American Chronicle: The Autobiography of Ray Stannard Baker*, in 1945, a year before his death. They were, one reviewer noted, "the story of a man who found a leader and a cause, who devoted his whole life to them and burned himself out in their service." Baker's Wilson was a tragic figure, a flawed hero, a leader with both extraordinary gifts and disturbing weaknesses. Baker knew that the struggle over Wilson's legacy, despite his own efforts, would last decades into the future. He would not have been surprised, I think, to see the flood of books assessing Wilson and his legacy that has appeared nearly one hundred years after his death.[1]

Prologue

1. Michael Kazin, "A Most Controversial President," *New York Times*, June 24, 2018; Jennifer Schuessler, "A President's Legacy Gets Complicated," *New York Times*, Nov. 29, 2015; John Milton Cooper Jr., *Woodrow Wilson: A Biography* (New York, 2009), 410–11; A. Scott Berg, *Wilson* (New York, 2013), 5; Baker Diary, May 25, 1921, in Arthur S. Link, ed., *The Papers of Woodrow Wilson* [*PWW*], 69 vols. (Princeton, NJ, 1966–93), 67:293.

2. "A Talk with the President," by Samuel G. Blythe, Dec. 5, 1914, *PWW*, 31:390–403; Wilson to Edith Galt, Aug. 28, 1915, *PWW*, 34:352.

3. Edith Gittings Reid, *Woodrow Wilson: The Caricature, the Myth, and the Man* (New York, 1934), 22; Wilson quoted in William E. Leuchtenburg, *The American President: From Teddy Roosevelt to Bill Clinton* (New York, 2015), 79; John Milton Cooper Jr., "American Sphinx: Woodrow Wilson and Race," in John Milton Cooper Jr. and Thomas J. Knock, eds., *Jefferson, Lincoln, and Wilson: The American Dilemma of Race and Democracy* (Charlottesville, VA, 2010), 145–62.

Acknowledgments

1. Robert K. Massie, "Parting Words," *New York Times Book Review*, Mar. 4, 2012.

2. Ray Stannard Baker, *American Chronicle: The Autobiography of Ray Stannard Baker* (New York, 1945), 514.

Chapter 1 · Woodrow Wilson

Chapter subtitle: Wilson to Ellen Axson, Feb. 24, 1885, in Arthur S. Link, ed., *The Papers of Woodrow Wilson* [*PWW*], 69 vols. (Princeton, NJ, 1966–93), 4:287.

1. A. Scott Berg, *Wilson* (New York, 2013), 87; Margaret Axson Elliot, *My Aunt Louisa and Woodrow Wilson* (Chapel Hill, NC, 1944), 156–57; Editorial note, "Wilson's Introduction to Ellen Axson," *PWW*, 2:333–35; Stockton Axson, *Brother Woodrow: A Memoir of Woodrow Wilson*, ed. Arthur S. Link (Princeton, NJ, 1993), 91; Eleanor Wilson McAdoo with the collaboration of Margaret Y. Gaffey, *The Woodrow Wilsons* (New York, 1937), 300; Ray Stannard Baker, *Woodrow Wilson: Youth, 1856–1890* (New York, 1927), 162.

2. Edwin A. Weinstein, *Woodrow Wilson: A Medical and Psychological Biography* (Princeton, NJ, 1981), 3–20; Berg, *Wilson*, 36; Eleanor Wilson McAdoo, *The Priceless Gift* (New York, 1962), 69.

3. John Milton Cooper Jr., *Woodrow Wilson: A Biography* (New York, 2009), 22–25; Malcolm D. Magee, *What the World Should Be: Woodrow Wilson and the Crafting of a Faith-Based Foreign Policy* (Waco, TX, 2008), 1–7; Woodrow Wilson, "An Address on Robert E. Lee at the University of North Carolina," Jan. 19, 1909, *PWW*, 18I:631.

4. Stockton Axson, *Brother Woodrow*, 15; Cooper, *Woodrow Wilson*, 25–32.

5. Cooper, *Woodrow Wilson*, 33–41; Wilson to Charles Andrew Talcott, May 20, 1880, *PWW*, 1:655; Wilson to Robert Bridges, Oct. 28, 1882, May 13, 1883, *PWW*, 2:148, 358; Ray Stannard Baker, *Woodrow Wilson: Youth, 1856–1890* (New York, 1927), 118.

6. Wilson to Ellen Louise Axson, Feb. 24, 1885, *PWW*, 4:287; Cooper, *Woodrow Wilson*, 45–55.

7. Wilson to Charles Andrew Talcott, Nov. 14, 1886, *PWW*, 5:389; Ray Stannard Baker, *Woodrow Wilson, Life and Letters, Youth, 1856–1890* (Garden City, NY, 1927), 289.

8. Wilson to Ellen Axson Wilson, Mar. 9, 1889, *PWW*, 6:139.

9. Arthur S. Link, *Wilson: The Road to the White House* (Princeton, NJ., 1947), 29–30; Weinstein, *Woodrow Wilson*, 127.

10. Eleanor Wilson McAdoo, *The Woodrow Wilsons*, 3–51; Ray Stannard Baker, *Woodrow Wilson, Life and Letters, Princeton, 1890–1910* (Garden City, NY, 1927), 1–74; David Milne, *Worldmaking: The Art and Science of American Diplomacy* (New York, 2015), 74–75.

11. Baker, *Woodrow Wilson*, 57–62; W. Barksdale Maynard, *Woodrow Wilson: Princeton to the Presidency* (New Haven, CT, 2008), 52–53; Berg, *Wilson*, 119–20.

12. Cooper, *Woodrow Wilson*, 71, 75; Weinstein, *Woodrow Wilson*, 141–49.

13. Maynard, *Woodrow Wilson*, 56–61; Wilson to Ellen Axson Wilson, July 19, 1902, *PWW*, 14:27.

14. Maynard, *Woodrow Wilson*, 65–109; James Axtell, *The Making of Princeton University: From Woodrow Wilson to the Present* (Princeton, NJ, 2006), 241–42.

15. Maynard, *Woodrow Wilson*, 71–82.

16. Henry Wilkinson Bragdon, *Woodrow Wilson: The Academic Years* (Cambridge, MA, 1967), 220, 302.

17. Weinstein, *Woodrow Wilson*, 141–49; Ellen Axson Wilson to Florence Stevens Hoyt, June 27, 1906, *PWW*, 16:430; Frances Wright Saunders, *First Lady between Two Worlds: Ellen Axson Wilson* (Chapel Hill, NC, 1985), 168.

18. Cooper, *Woodrow Wilson*, 89; Maynard, *Woodrow Wilson*, 113–53; Andrew Fleming West to Wilson, July 10, 1907, *PWW*, 17:271.

19. Maynard, *Woodrow Wilson*, 152–63; Wilson to Cleveland Hoadley Dodge, June 9, 1911, *PWW*, 23:139; Wilson to Mary Allen Hulbert Peck, Feb. 12, 1911, *PWW*, 22:426.

20. Maynard, *Woodrow Wilson*, 195–99; Wilson to Mary Peck, *PWW*, 22:325; Mary Allen Hulbert, *The Story of Mrs. Peck: An Autobiography* (New York, 1933), 143–44, 158–79; Wilson, "A Salutation," ca. Feb. 1, 1908, *PWW*, 17:611; Wilson to Mary Allen Hulbert, Dec. 22, 1912, *PWW*, 25:616. Wilson's recent biographers doubt that his infatuation with Mary Peck involved physical intimacy. Berg, *Wilson*, 6, 176–77; Cooper, *Woodrow Wilson*, 99–101.

21. Cooper, *Woodrow Wilson*, 102–19; Eleanor Wilson McAdoo, *The Woodrow Wilsons*, 101; Wilson to Mary Allen Hulbert Peck, June 5, 1910, *PWW*, 20:501.

22. Wilson to Mary Allen Hulbert Peck, Sept. 5, 1909, *PWW*, 19:358; Wilson to Ellen Axson Wilson, Feb. 21, 1910, *PWW*, 20:146; Cooper, *Woodrow Wilson*, 123.

23. Wilson to Ellen Louise Axson, Dec. 18, 1884, *PWW*, 3:553; Robert Alexander Kraig, *Woodrow Wilson and the Lost World of the Oratorical Statesman* (College Station, TX, 2004), 11–140; David Greenberg, *Republic of Spin: An Inside History of the American Presidency* (New York, 2016), 78–79.

24. Raymond Fosdick, *Chronicle of a Generation: An Autobiography* (New York, 1958), 43–47; Stockton Axson, *Brother Woodrow*, 53; Edmund W. Starling, *Starling of the White House* (New York, 1946), 37, 85; William G. McAdoo, *Crowded Years: The Reminiscences of William G. McAdoo* (Boston, 1931), 511.

25. Wilson to Mary Allen Hulbert, July 21, 1912, *PWW*, 24:562; Wilson to Ellen Louise Axson,

Mar. 11, 1885, *PWW*, 4:352; Ellen Axson Wilson to Anna Harris, Jan. 31, 1899, *PWW*, 11:102; Weinstein, *Woodrow Wilson*, 81, 87, 115–16.

26. Wilson to Mary Allen Hulbert Peck, June 2, 1912, *PWW*, 24:451; Wilson to Mary Allen Hulbert Peck, May 11, 1912, *PWW*, 24:392.

27. Charles E. Neu, *Colonel House: A Biography of Woodrow Wilson's Silent Partner* (New York, 2015), 58, 79–81, 105–6.

28. August Heckscher, *Woodrow Wilson* (New York, 1991), 275–82; Arthur S. Link, *Wilson: The New Freedom* (Princeton, NJ, 1956), 70–73; John Reed to Joseph Patrick Tumulty, with enclosure, June 30, 1914, *PWW*, 30:231–38.

29. William Leuchtenburg, *The American President: From Teddy Roosevelt to Bill Clinton* (New York, 2015), 72–79; Wilson to Mary Allen Hulbert, June 29, 1913, *PWW*, 28:12.

30. Berg, *Wilson*, 271, 332–38; Wilson to Mary Allen Hulbert, Aug. 7, 1914, *PWW*, 30:357.

31. Wilson to Mary Allen Hulbert, Aug. 23, 1914, *PWW*, 30:437; House Diary, Nov. 6, 1914, Jan. 13, 1915, Edward Mandell House Papers, Yale University Library.

32. Cooper, *Woodrow Wilson*, 279; Berg, *Wilson*, 355–61; Wilson to Edith Galt, May 5, 1915, *PWW*, 33:111–12.

33. Wilson to Edith Galt, July 20, 1915, *PWW*, 33:539; Edith Galt to Wilson, Aug. 3, 1915, *PWW*, 34:77–78; Edith Galt to Wilson, June 18, 1915, *PWW*, 33:421; Edith Galt to Wilson, Aug. 7, 1915, *PWW*, 34:130–31; Wilson to Edith Galt, Aug. 15, 1915, *PWW*, 34:207–10; Phyllis Lee Levin, *Edith and Woodrow: The Wilson White House* (New York, 2001), 99; Edith Galt to Wilson, *PWW*, 34:91.

34. Edith Galt to Wilson, Aug. 25, 26, 1915, *PWW*, 34:326–29, 336–39; Wilson to Edith Galt, Aug. 28, 1915, *PWW*, 34:350–55.

35. Neu, *Colonel House*, 209–11; House Diary, Sept. 24, 1915, House Papers.

36. Cooper, *Woodrow Wilson*, 306–7, 328–30.

37. House Diary, Mar. 6, 1916, House Papers; Tom Shactman, *Edith and Woodrow: A Presidential Romance* (New York, 1981), 125–33; Kristie Miller, *Ellen and Edith: Woodrow Wilson's First Ladies* (Lawrence, KS, 2010), 133–37.

38. House Diary, Apr. 11, 1916, House Papers; "A Memorandum by Ray Stannard Baker of a Conversation at the White House," May 12, 1916, *PWW*, 37:31–38.

39. "A Memorandum by Homer S. Cummings," Aug. 7, 1916, *PWW*, 38:5–8.

40. Wilson to Cleveland Hoadley Dodge, Sept. 7, 1916, *PWW*, 38:157–58; Edith Bolling Wilson, *My Memoir* (New York, 1939), 103–8.

41. Arthur S. Link, *Wilson: Campaigns for Progressivism and Peace, 1916–1917* (Princeton, NJ, 1965), 108–64.

42. "An Address to the Senate," Jan. 22, 1917, *PWW*, 40:533–39.

43. Neu, *Colonel House*, 302.

44. Cooper, *Woodrow Wilson*, 415–16; Wilson to Jessie Sayre, July 21, 1917, *PWW*, 43:240–42; Edith Bolling Wilson, *My Memoir*, 116, 134–41.

45. Neu, *Colonel House*, 331–34.

46. House Diary, Aug. 15, 16, 17, 18, 19, 1918, House Papers; William Wiseman to Lord Reading, Sept. 5, 1918, *PWW*, 49:454–55; Cooper, *Woodrow Wilson*, 440–41.

47. Neu, *Colonel House*, 372–79.

48. Cooper, *Woodrow Wilson*, 454–88; Grayson Diary, April 3, 4, 1919, *PWW*, 56:554–58, 584; Grayson to Tumulty, April 7, 1919, *PWW*, 57:235–36.

49. Cooper, *Woodrow Wilson*, 498–500; Baker Diary, Apr. 3, 1919, *PWW*, 56:577–78.

50. Neu, *Colonel House*, 405–6; Edith Bolling Wilson, *My Memoir*, 245–46; Note, *PWW*, 55:488.

51. Neu, *Colonel House*, 413–14; Grayson to Alice Gordon Grayson, Apr. 16–17, 27, May 9–10, 15, 1919, Grayson Papers, Woodrow Wilson Presidential Library and Museum, Staunton, VA.

52. Berg, *Wilson*, 615; Cooper, *Woodrow Wilson*, 508–20; Kraig, *Woodrow Wilson*, 141–85.

53. Cooper, *Woodrow Wilson*, 520–31.

54. Cooper, *Woodrow Wilson*, 520-42; Grayson Diary, Sept. 6, 26, 1919, *PWW*, 63:63–66, 519; Levin, *Edith and Woodrow*, 337–57; Thomas J. Knock, "One Long Wilderness of Despair: Woodrow Wilson's Stroke and the League of Nations," in Jeffrey A. Engel and Thomas J. Knock, eds., *When Life Strikes the President: Scandal, Death, and Illness in the White House* (New York, 2017), 105–28.

55. Cooper, *Woodrow Wilson*, 540–50; Grayson memorandum, Nov. 17, 1919, *PWW*, 64:43–45, n. 1; "A Statement," Dec. 14, 1919, *PWW*, 64:187; John Milton Cooper Jr., *Breaking the Heart of the World: Woodrow Wilson and the Fight for the League of Nations* (New York, 2001), 283–89; House to Edith Wilson, Nov. 24, 27, 1919, House Papers.

56. Cooper, *Woodrow Wilson*, 550–78; Grayson memorandum, Mar. 25, 1920, *PWW*, 65:123–25; John Milton Cooper Jr., *Pivotal Decades: The United States, 1900–1920* (New York, 1990), 372; Baker Diary, Nov. 28, 1920, *PWW*, 66:435–36; Ray Stannard Baker, *American Chronicle: The Autobiography of Ray Stannard Baker* (New York, 1945), 481–82.

57. Baker Diary, Mar. 22, 1921, *PWW*, 67:237–38; Cooper, *Woodrow Wilson*, 591; Wilson to Ray Stannard Baker, Dec. 13, 1923, *PWW*, 68:499; Four News Reports, Feb. 2, 1924, *PWW*, 68:553–55.

Chapter 2 · Ellen Axson Wilson

Chapter subtitle: Ellen Axson, quoted in Stockton Axson, *Brother Woodrow: A Memoir of Woodrow Wilson*, ed. Arthur S. Link (Princeton, NJ, 1993), 91.

1. Kristie Miller, *Ellen and Edith: Woodrow Wilson's First Ladies* (Lawrence, KS, 2010), 6–10; Ellen Axson to Woodrow Wilson, Nov. 5, 1883, in Arthur S. Link, ed., *The Papers of Woodrow Wilson [PWW]*, 69 vols. (Princeton, NJ), 1966–93, 2:517.

2. Ellen Axson to Woodrow Wilson, Nov. 17, 1883, *PWW*, 2:532; Frances Wright Saunders, *First Lady between Two Worlds: Ellen Axson Wilson* (Chapel Hill, NC, 1985), 15–25.

3. Saunders, *First Lady between Two Worlds*, 26–55.

4. An edited version of their correspondence is in Eleanor Wilson McAdoo, ed., *The Priceless Gift: The Love Letters of Woodrow Wilson and Ellen Axson Wilson* (New York, 1962); Ellen Axson to Woodrow Wilson, Apr. 3, 11, June 17, 1885, *PWW*, 4:448, 475, 723; Saunders, *First Lady between Two Worlds*, 58.

5. Saunders, *First Lady between Two Worlds*, 79; Eleanor Wilson McAdoo, *The Priceless Gift*, 183–86; Ellen Wilson to Woodrow Wilson, May 18, 1886, *PWW*, 5:238.

6. Woodrow Wilson to Ellen Wilson, Mar. 11, 1889, *PWW*, 6:142; Saunders, *First Lady between Two Worlds*, 96–117; Margaret Axson Elliott, *My Aunt Louisa and Woodrow Wilson* (Chapel Hill, NC, 1944), 157, 176–77; Stockton Axson, *Brother Woodrow*, 104.

7. Eleanor Wilson McAdoo, *The Priceless Gift*, 186, 201–2.

8. Eleanor Wilson McAdoo, *The Priceless Gift*, 206, 210, 217–18; Ellen Wilson to Woodrow Wilson, Aug. 14, 1899, *PWW*, 2:229; Saunders, *First Lady between Two Worlds*, 124–25; Ellen Wilson to Woodrow Wilson, *PWW*, 11:229.

9. Eleanor Wilson McAdoo, *The Priceless Gift*, 225; Ellen Wilson to Florence Hoyt, June 28, 1902, *PWW*, 12:464.

10. Saunders, *First Lady between Two Worlds*, 139–46; W. Barksdale Maynard, *Woodrow Wilson: Princeton to the Presidency* (New Haven, CT, 2008), 34.

11. Woodrow Wilson to Ellen Wilson, Apr. 22, 1903, *PWW*, 14:422; Ellen Wilson to Woodrow Wilson, Apr. 10, 1904, *PWW*, 15:241; Saunders, *First Lady between Two Worlds*, 145.

12. Saunders, *First Lady between Two Worlds*, 157–64.

13. Eleanor Wilson McAdoo, *The Priceless Gift*, 241–43.

14. Saunders, *First Lady between Two Worlds*, 181–82; John Grier Hibben to Woodrow Wilson, July 8, 1907, *PWW*, 17:263–64.

15. Edwin A. Weinstein, *Woodrow Wilson: A Medical and Psychological Biography* (Princeton, NJ, 1981), 181–89; Woodrow Wilson to Ellen Wilson, July 20, Aug. 3, 20, 1908, *PWW*, 18:372, 388, 408; Saunders, *First Lady between Two Worlds*, 187–93.

16. Woodrow Wilson to Mary Allen Hulbert Peck, Sept. 12, 1909, *PWW*, 19:384; Miller, *Ellen and Edith*, 40–46.

17. Margret Axson Elliott, *My Aunt Louisa and Woodrow Wilson*, 252; Miller, *Ellen and Edith*, 47; Saunders, *First Lady between Two Worlds*, 203, 209–12.

18. Miller, *Ellen and Edith*, 49–52; Saunders, *First Lady between Two Worlds*, 214–15; Ellen Wilson to John Wescott, Feb. 23, 1912, *PWW*, 24:190.

19. Ellen Wilson to Woodrow Wilson, May 22, 1911, *PWW*, 23:81; Eleanor Wilson McAdoo, *The Woodrow Wilsons* (New York, 1937), 149, 180–81; News Report, Nov. 5, 1912, *PWW*, 25:518.

20. Ellen Wilson to William Howard Taft, Jan. 10, 1913, *PWW*, 27:28; Frank J. Aucella and Patricia A. Piorkowski Hobbs, *Ellen Axson Wilson: First Lady and Artist* (Washington, DC, 1993), 5–8; Eleanor Wilson McAdoo, *The Woodrow Wilsons*, 205.

21. Shelley Sallee, "Ellen Louise Axson Wilson," in Lewis L. Gould, ed., *American First Ladies: Their Lives and Their Legacy*, 2nd ed. (New York, 2001), 232–36; Betty Boyd Caroli, *First Ladies: From Martha Washington to Michelle Obama* (New York, 2010), 142–45; A. Scott Berg, *Wilson* (New York, 2013), 301–2.

22. John M. Blum, *Joe Tumulty and the Wilson Era* (Boston, 1951), 31–32; Charles E. Neu, *Colonel House: A Biography of Woodrow Wilson's Silent Partner* (New York, 2015), 87, 200; Rear Admiral Cary T. Grayson, *Woodrow Wilson: An Intimate Memoir* (New York, 1960), 27–28; Josephus Daniels, *The Wilson Era: Years of Peace—1910–1917* (Chapel Hill, NC, 1944), 479–89; William G. McAdoo, *Crowded Years: The Reminiscences of William G. McAdoo* (Boston, 1931), 285.

23. Eleanor Wilson McAdoo, *The Priceless Gift*, 314; Jessie quoted in Ray Stannard Baker, *Woodrow Wilson: Youth, 1856–1890* (New York, 1927), 244; Miller, *Ellen and Edith*, 74–80; Saunders, *First Lady between Two Worlds*, 241–48; Eric S. Yellin, *Racism in the Nation's Service: Government Workers and the Color Line in Woodrow Wilson's America* (Chapel Hill, NC, 2013), 103.

24. Woodrow Wilson to Ellen Wilson, Oct. 12, 1913, *PWW*, 28:393; Ellen Wilson to Woodrow Wilson, Oct. 5, 1913, *PWW*, 28:364.

25. Saunders, *First Lady between Two Worlds*, 264, 270.

26. Saunders, *First Lady between Two Worlds*, 273–76; John Milton Cooper Jr., *Woodrow Wilson: A Biography* (New York, 2009), 260–61.

27. Eleanor Wilson McAdoo, *The Priceless Gift*, 314–16; Saunders, *First Lady between Two Worlds*, 277–79.

Chapter 3 · Josephus Daniels

Chapter subtitle: Josephus Daniels, *The Wilson Era: Years of War and After, 1917–1923* (Chapel Hill, NC, 1946), viii.

1. Josephus Daniels, *The Wilson Era: Years of Peace, 1910–1917* (Chapel Hill, NC, 1944), 3–9; Daniels, *The Wilson Era: Years of War and After*, ix.

2. Lee A. Craig, *Josephus Daniels: His Life and Times* (Chapel Hill, NC, 2013), 1–22; Josephus Daniels, *Tar Heel Editor* (Chapel Hill, NC, 1939), 30.

3. Daniels, *Tar Heel Editor*, 104; Larry G. Gerber, *The Limits of Liberalism: Josephus Daniels, Henry Stimson, Bernard Baruch, Donald Richberg, Felix Frankfurter, and the Development of the Modern American Political Economy* (New York, 1983), 14–16.

4. Craig, *Josephus Daniels*, 26–39.

5. Craig, *Josephus Daniels*, 31–61; Gerber, *The Limits of Liberalism*, 17.

6. Craig, *Josephus Daniels*, 61–89; Daniels, *Tar Heel Editor*, 262.

7. Craig, *Josephus Daniels*, 70–80, 99.

8. Craig, *Josephus Daniels*, 89–98.

9. Craig, *Josephus Daniels*, 104–9; Daniels, *Tar Heel Editor*, 500.

10. Daniels, *Tar Heel Editor*, 497; Craig, *Josephus Daniels*, 108, 110–22, 134.

11. Craig, *Josephus Daniels*, 133–46.

12. Craig, *Josephus Daniels*, 146–53.

13. Daniels, *Tar Heel Editor*, 510; Michael Kazin, *A Godly Hero: The Life of William Jennings Bryan* (New York, 2006), 148–49, 204–6; Josephus Daniels, *Editor in Politics* (Chapel Hill, NC, 1941), 163–65; Craig, *Josephus Daniels*, 173–78.

14. Craig, *Josephus Daniels*, 178–89; Kazin, *A Godly Hero*, 205; Adriane Lentz-Smith, *Freedom Struggles: Afro-Americans and World War One* (Cambridge, MA, 2009), 17–18. Years later Daniels admitted that "the paper was cruel in its flagellations. In the perspective of time, I think it was too cruel" (Daniels, *Editor in Politics*, 145).

15. Craig, *Josephus Daniels*, 190–91; Daniels, *Editor in Politics*, 422.

16. Craig, *Josephus Daniels*, 207–11; Joseph L. Morrison, *Josephus Daniels: The Small-d Democrat* (Chapel Hill, NC, 1966), 10; Kazin, *A Godly Hero*, 205.

17. Craig, *Josephus Daniels*, 213–19.

18. Craig, *Josephus Daniels*, 220–24; Wilson to Thomas Dixon Jr., Dec. 3, 1912, in Arthur S. Link, ed., *The Papers of Woodrow Wilson* [*PWW*], 69 vols. (Princeton, NJ, 1966–93), 25:578; Wilson to Daniels, Feb. 23, 1913, *PWW*, 27:128; Daniels to Wilson, Feb. 25, 1913, *PWW*, 27:135. Colonel House opposed putting Daniels in the cabinet. House Diary, Jan. 8, 24, Feb. 24, 1913, House Papers, Yale University Library.

19. Arthur S. Link, *Wilson: The New Freedom* (Princeton, NJ, 1956), 122–25; Wilson to Daniels, Dec. 26, 1914, *PWW*, 31:533.

20. Daniels, *The Wilson Era: Years of Peace*, 452–55, 481–89.

21. Daniels, *The Wilson Era: Years of Peace*, 94, 115, 568–73; Daniels, *The Wilson Era: Years of War and After*, 533–41; Jonathan Daniels, *The End of Innocence* (New York, 1954), 88–89, 180–93, 249; Daniels to House, Sept. 14, 1917, House Papers; House Diary, Jan. 8, 1913, April 26, 1914, April 6, 1916, Dec. 14, 1916, March 27, 1917. In his memoir, Daniels described House as a "yes-yes man until he was given position beyond his merits or ability" (Daniels, *The Wilson Years: Years of War and After*, 521).

22. Link, *Wilson: The New Freedom*, 122.

23. Link, *Wilson: The New Freedom*, 122–35; George W. Baer, *One Hundred Years of Sea Power: The U. S. Navy, 1890–1990* (Stanford, CA, 1994), 52–62; Diary of Nancy Saunders Toy, Jan. 5, 1915, *PWW*, 32:21.

24. Frank Freidel, *Franklin D. Roosevelt: The Apprenticeship* (Boston, 1952), 157–73; Craig, *Josephus Daniels*, 247–52; Daniels, *The Wilson Era: Years of Peace*, 124–35; Jonathan Daniels, *The End of Innocence*, 54.

25. Kazin, *A Godly Hero*, 205; Craig, *Josephus Daniels*, 70, 367; Bernard M. Baruch, *Baruch: The Public Years* (New York, 1960), 81.

26. A. Scott Berg, *Wilson* (New York, 2013), 307, 347–50; E. David Cronon, ed., *The Cabinet Diaries of Josephus Daniels, 1913–1921* (Lincoln, NE, 1963), 33; Craig, *Josephus Daniels*, 375–77; Lentz-Smith, *Freedom Struggles*, 32–34.

27. Craig, *Josephus Daniels*, 257–61, 267–73; Cronon, *The Cabinet Diaries of Josephus Daniels*, 40–46.

28. Craig, *Josephus Daniels*, 261–67, 273–76; Freidel, *Roosevelt: The Apprenticeship*, 271.

29. Freidel, *Roosevelt: The Apprenticeship*, 237; Craig, *Josephus Daniels*, 289–304.

30. Craig, *Josephus Daniels*, 305–11; Daniels, *The Wilson Era: Years of Peace*, 427; Jonathan Daniels, *The End of Innocence*, 174.

31. Craig, *Josephus Daniels*, 312–24; Daniels, *The Wilson Era: Years of Peace*, 583; "A Memorandum by Robert Lansing," Mar. 20, 1917, *PWW*, 41:442; Cronon, *The Cabinet Diaries of Josephus Daniels*, Mar. 20, 1917, Apr. 18, 1913, 117–18.

32. Baer, *One Hundred Years of Sea Power*, 59–82; Craig, *Josephus Daniels*, 325–47; Daniels, *The Wilson Era: Years of War and After*, 335.

33. Craig, *Josephus Daniels*, 352–62; Margaret MacMillan, *Paris 1919: Six Months That Changed the World* (New York, 2001), 176–79.

34. Cronon, *The Cabinet Diaries of Josephus Daniels*, Apr. 14, June 9, July 16, Oct. 3, 1919; Craig, *Josephus Daniels*, 363; Daniels, *The Wilson Era: Years of War and After*, 473, 481, 512.

35. Cronon, *The Cabinet Diaries of Josephus Daniels*, Dec. 22, 1919, Jan. 9, 12, Feb. 28, Mar. 2, 1920; "A Memorandum by Robert Lansing," Dec. 16, 1919, *PWW*, 64:193.

36. Daniels, *The Wilson Era: Years of War and After*, 555–61.

37. Daniels to Wilson, Mar. 5, 1921, *PWW*, 67:229.

38. Daniels, *The Wilson Era: Years of War and After*, 592–94; Craig, *Josephus Daniels*, 368–86; Gerber, *The Limits of Liberalism*, 192–94.

39. Craig, *Josephus Daniels*, 397–98; Gerber, *The Limits of Liberalism*, 275; Morrison, *Josephus Daniels*, 166, 169; Frank Freidel, *Franklin D. Roosevelt: The Triumph* (Boston, 1956), 4.

40. Josephus Daniels, *Shirt Sleeve Diplomat* (Chapel Hill, NC, 1947), 15–24; E. David Cronon, *Josephus Daniels in Mexico* (Madison, WI, 1960), 3–29; Otis L. Graham Jr., *An Encore for Reform: The Old Progressives and the New Deal* (New York, 1967), 118–19; Gerber, *The Limits of Liberalism*, 255–64.

41. Craig, *Josephus Daniels*, 399–411; Morrison, *Josephus Daniels*, 196, 216; Mark T. Gilderhus, *The Second Century: U.S.-Latin American Relations since 1889* (Wilmington, DE, 2000), 86–90; Helen M. Lilienthal, ed., *The Journals of David E. Lilienthal: The TVA Years, 1939–1945* (New York, 1964), 247.

42. Jonathan Daniels, *The End of Innocence*, 338–39.

Chapter 4 · William Gibbs McAdoo

Chapter subtitle: William Gibbs McAdoo, *Crowded Years: The Reminiscences of William G. McAdoo* (New York, 1931), 511.

1. McAdoo, *Crowded Years*, 109–10.

2. McAdoo, *Crowded Years*, 1–19; Douglas B. Craig, *Progressives at War: William G. McAdoo and Newton D. Baker, 1883–1941* (Baltimore, MD, 2013), 14–15.

3. McAdoo, *Crowded Years*, 24–54; Craig, *Progressives at War*, 14–17.

4. McAdoo, *Crowded Years*, 53–64; Craig, *Progressives at War*, 17–18; John J. Broesamle, *William Gibbs McAdoo: A Passion for Change, 1863–1917* (Port Washington, NY, 1973), 12–14.

5. McAdoo, *Crowded Years*, 64; Craig, *Progressives at War*, 18, 26.

6. McAdoo, *Crowded Years*, 71–108; Craig, *Progressives at War*, 26–30.

7. Craig, *Progressives at War*, 30–34.

8. *New York Herald* quoted in Craig, *Progressives at War*, 35–36; Broesamle, *William Gibbs McAdoo*, 31.

9. Craig, *Progressives at War*, 36–38, 67–68.

10. McAdoo, *Crowded Years*, 37–40; Craig, *Progressives at War*, 68–71.

11. McAdoo, *Crowded Years*, 109–76; Craig, *Progressives at War*, 71–76; Arthur S. Link, *Wilson: The Road to the White House* (Princeton, NJ, 1947), 330–31, 416–17, 451, 481–86, 523; Arthur S. Link, *Wilson: The New Freedom* (Princeton, NJ. 1956), 4.

12. Margaret L. Coit, *Mr. Baruch* (Boston, 1957), 132–33; Link, *Wilson: The New Freedom*,

114–15; "Interview with Newton D. Baker . . . , " Ray Stannard Baker Papers, Library of Congress; McAdoo, *Crowded Years*, 58.

13. Broesamle, *William Gibbs McAdoo*, 138; Brandeis quoted in Link, *Wilson: The New Freedom*, 115–16; Hamlin quoted in Craig, *Progressives at War*, 105–6.

14. Broesamle, *William Gibbs McAdoo*, 158–65; Craig, *Progressives at War*, 119–23; Adriane Lentz-Smith, *Freedom Struggles: African Americans and World War I* (Cambridge, MA, 2009), 33; Eric S. Yellin, *Racism in the Nation's Service: Government Workers and the Color Line in Woodrow Wilson's America* (Chapel Hill, NC, 2013), 81–122; Kathleen L. Wolgemuth, "Woodrow Wilson and Federal Segregation," *Journal of Negro History* 44, no. 2 (April 1959): 167.

15. Craig, *Progressives at War*, 126–32; Roger Lowenstein, *America's Bank: The Epic Struggle to Create the Federal Reserve* (New York, 2015), 206–54.

16. Broesamle, *William Gibbs McAdoo*, 138–40; John Milton Cooper Jr., *Woodrow Wilson: A Biography* (New York, 2009), 69; McAdoo, *Crowded Years*, 271–77.

17. Wilson to Mary Allen Hulbert, Mar. 15, 1914, in Arthur S. Link, ed., *The Papers of Woodrow Wilson* [*PWW*], 69 vols. (Princeton, NJ, 1966–93), 29:346; McAdoo to House, Mar. 3, 1914, Edward M. House Papers, Yale University Library.

18. Wilson to Mary Allen Hulbert, May 10, 1914, *PWW*, 30:12–13; House Diary, Apr. 15, 1914, House Papers.

19. August Heckscher, *Woodrow Wilson* (New York, 1991), 322–23; House Diary, Sept. 26, Oct. 20, 27, 29, 30, 1914, House Papers; Charles E. Neu, *Colonel House: A Biography of Woodrow Wilson's Silent Partner* (New York, 2015), 150–52.

20. Stockton Axson, *Brother Woodrow: A Memoir of Woodrow Wilson*, ed. Arthur S. Link (Princeton, NJ, 1993), 217–18; Admiral Cary T. Grayson, "The Colonel's Folly and the President's Distress," *American Heritage* (Oct. 1964): 4–7, 94–101.

21. House Diary, Aug. 18, 1913, Nov. 6, 1914, House Papers; David F. Houston, *Eight Years with Wilson's Cabinet*, 2 vols. (New York, 1926), 1:68.

22. Neu, *Colonel House*, 209–10; House Diary, Mar. 3, 1917, House Papers.

23. Craig, *Progressives at War*, 146–47; House Diary, Mar. 28, 1917, House Papers.

24. Craig, *Progressives at War*, 164–83.

25. Craig, *Progressives at War*, 196–209.

26. Craig, *Progressives at War*, 210–11; House Diary, Aug. 7, 1917, May 2, 17, 19, 1918, House Papers; Neu, *Colonel House*, 346–47.

27. "A Memorandum by Stockton Axson," Aug. 1919, *PWW*, 67:606.

28. Craig, *Progressives at War*, 223–29; David Burner, *The Politics of Provincialism: The Democratic Party in Transition, 1918–1932* (New York, 1968), 110; Walter Lippmann, *Men of Destiny* (New York, 1927), 113–16.

29. Craig, *Progressives at War*, 229–35; Eleanor McAdoo to Woodrow Wilson, Mar. 2, 1922, *PWW*, 67:562.

30. Quoted in Craig, *Progressives at War*, 261–79.

31. Craig, *Progressives at War*, 261–79; Douglas B. Craig, *After Wilson: The Struggle for the Democratic Party, 1920–1934* (Chapel Hill, NC, 1992), 36; McAdoo to House, Mar. 4, 27, 1924, House Papers.

32. Craig, *Progressives at War*, 279–85; House Diary, Nov. 8, 1925, House Papers.

33. Quoted in Craig, *Progressives at War*, 252–58.

34. Craig, *After Wilson*, 94–111; Craig, *Progressives at War*, 295–311; McAdoo to House, Jan. 10, 1931, House Papers.

35. Craig, *Progressives at War*, 312–25.

36. Craig, *Progressives at War*, 298, 343–61; Jordan A. Schwarz, *The New Dealers: Power Politics in the Age of Roosevelt* (New York, 1993), 3–31.

37. Craig, *Progressives at War*, 363–69; Thomas M. Storke, *California Editor* (Los Angeles, 1958), 308–9.

38. Craig, *Progressives at War*, 362–63, 368–69, 393–94.

39. Craig, *Progressives at War*, 394–402; George Creel, *Rebel at Large: Recollections of Fifty Crowded Years* (New York, 1947), 270.

40. McAdoo, *Crowded Years*, 511–29. On March 31, 1922, House, in an interview with the historian Charles Seymour, reflected on the differences between Wilson and McAdoo. The president, he recalled, "was much quicker at catching an idea. It was never necessary to argue with Wilson in order to show him a point. Almost before a sentence was finished, he had caught its significance. His mind ran right along. McAdoo, on the other hand, would argue at great length and sometimes needed a great deal of persuasion. He was brilliant and imaginative, more so than Wilson, but unstable and apt always to make mistakes" (Charles Seymour Papers, Manuscript and Archives, Yale University Library).

Chapter 5 · Joseph Patrick Tumulty

Chapter subtitle: Tumulty to James Kerney, Mar. 2, 1921, in Arthur S. Link, ed., *The Papers of Woodrow Wilson* [*PWW*], 69 vols. (Princeton, NJ, 1966–93), 67:203.

1. Arthur S. Link, *Wilson: The Road to the White House* (Princeton, NJ, 1947), 167–68; Joseph P. Tumulty, *Woodrow Wilson as I Know Him* (Garden City, NY, 1921), 19–22.

2. John M. Blum, *Joe Tumulty and the Wilson Era* (Boston, 1951), 3–9; Tumulty, *Woodrow Wilson*, 1–5.

3. Blum, *Joe Tumulty*, 9–12; Link, *Wilson: The Road to the White House*, 133–40.

4. Blum, *Joe Tumulty*, 12–19; Dan Fellows Platt to Wilson, Sept. 19, 1910, *PWW*, 21:141; Tumulty, *Woodrow Wilson*, 27.

5. Tumulty, *Woodrow Wilson*, 27–45; Blum, *Joe Tumulty*, 20–24.

6. Wilson to Mary Allen Hulbert Peck, Mar. 19, 1911, *PWW*, 22:510; Blum, *Joe Tumulty*, 24–37; John Milton Cooper Jr., *Woodrow Wilson: A Biography* (New York, 2009), 130–39.

7. Blum, *Joe Tumulty*, 30–32; Kristie Miller, *Ellen and Edith: Woodrow Wilson's First Ladies* (Lawrence, KS, 2010), 50–51.

8. Blum, *Joe Tumulty*, 37–49.

9. House Diary, Dec. 15, 18, 1912, Edward M. House Papers, Yale University Library.

10. Arthur S. Link, *Wilson: The New Freedom* (Princeton, NJ, 1956), 20–21; Tumulty to House, Jan. 30, 1913, House Papers.

11. Wilson to Ellen Wilson, July 24, 1913, *PWW*, 28:67.

12. Eleanor Wilson McAdoo, *The Woodrow Wilsons* (New York, 1937), 120–21; Phyllis Lee Levin, *Edith and Woodrow: The Wilson White House* (New York, 2001), 170–71; Blum, *Joe Tumulty*, 55–67; David Greenberg, *Republic of Spin: An Inside History of the American Presidency* (New York, 2016), 84.

13. Blum, *Joe Tumulty*, 60; Ray Stannard Baker, *American Chronicle: The Autobiography of Ray Stannard Baker* (New York, 1945), 285.

14. Link, *Wilson: The New Freedom*, 140–43; Blum, *Joe Tumulty*, 68–87; House Diary, July 18–20, 1913, Jan. 22, 1914, House Papers; Charles E. Neu, *Colonel House: A Biography of Woodrow Wilson's Silent Partner* (New York, 2015), 109–10.

15. Hugh Wallace to House, Feb. 17, 18, 1914, House Papers; House Diary, May 11, 1914, House Papers.

16. Blum, *Joe Tumulty*, 84–87; Eleanor Wilson McAdoo, *The Woodrow Wilsons*, 120.

17. Blum, *Joe Tumulty*, 94–105; Tumulty to Wilson, Nov. 19, 1915, Jan. 17, 1916, *PWW*, 35:222, 492; Neu, *Colonel House*, 232.

18. Blum, *Joe Tumulty*, 116–17; Neu, *Colonel House*, 195, 200; Wilson to Edith Bolling Galt,

Aug. 23, 1915, *PWW*, 34:302–3; Edith Bolling Galt to Wilson, Aug. 25, 1915, *PWW*, 34:327; Wilson to Edith Bolling Galt, Aug. 28, 1915, *PWW*, 34:351–52.

19. House Diary, Sept. 24, 1915.

20. Blum, *Joe Tumulty*, 117–20; House Diary, April 6, 1916, House Papers.

21. Blum, *Joe Tumulty*, 120–22; House Diary, Nov. 15, 1916, House Papers; Tumulty to Wilson, Nov. 18, 1916, *PWW*, 38:674; David Lawrence, *The True Story of Woodrow Wilson* (New York, 1924), 333–34.

22. Blum, *Joe Tumulty*, 130–31.

23. Blum, *Joe Tumulty*, 132–39; Tumulty to Wilson, May 31, 1917, *PWW*, 37:427.

24. Blum, *Joe Tumulty*, 146–50.

25. Blum, *Joe Tumulty*, 159–68; Tumulty to Wilson, Oct. 8, 1918, *PWW*, 51:265; "An Appeal for a Democratic Congress," Oct. 19, 1918, *PWW*, 51:381.

26. Blum, *Joe Tumulty*, 169–75; Tumulty to Wilson, Nov. 21, 1918, *PWW*, 53:156; Tumulty to Wilson, Jan. 13, 30, 1919, *PWW*, 59:53, 390–93; Robert C. Hilderbrand, *Power and the People: Executive Management of Public Opinion in Foreign Affairs* (Chapel Hill, NC, 1981), 166–69.

27. Blum, *Joe Tumulty*, 181–85; Tumulty to Wilson, June 3, 4, 1919, *PWW*, 60:112, 147; Tumulty to Wilson, June 3, 1919, in Joseph P. Tumulty, *Woodrow Wilson*, 365; Tumulty to Wilson, June 4, 1919, in James Kerney, *The Political Education of Woodrow Wilson* (New York, 1926), 446.

28. Blum, *Joe Tumulty*, 200–207; Tumulty to Wilson, Aug. 6, 1919, *PWW*, 62:180.

29. Blum, *Joe Tumulty*, 207–10; Cooper, *Woodrow Wilson*, 518–20; Tumulty, *Woodrow Wilson*, 435.

30. Blum, *Joe Tumulty*, 210–13; "Memorandum for the President," Sept. 12, 1919, *PWW*, 63:221–23.

31. John Milton Cooper Jr., *Breaking the Heart of the World: Woodrow Wilson and the Fight for the League of Nations* (New York, 2001), 186–89; Grayson Diary, *PWW*, 63:518–19.

32. Cooper, *Breaking the Heart of the World*, 205–6; Editorial Note, *PWW*, 63:547–48; Lansing memorandum, Feb. 23, 1920, *PWW*, 64:454–58; Tumulty, *Woodrow Wilson*, 444.

33. Blum, *Joe Tumulty*, 213–18, 223–29; Cooper, *Breaking the Heart of the World*, 200–212; Levin, *Edith and Woodrow*, 350–65; Thomas J. Knock, "'One Long Wilderness of Despair': Woodrow Wilson's Stroke and the League of Nations," in Jeffrey A. Engel and Thomas J. Knock, eds., *When Life Strikes the President: Scandal, Death, and Illness in the White House* (New York, 2017), 107–11.

34. Tumulty to Wilson, Dec. 28, 1919, *PWW*, 64:233; E. David Cronon, ed., *The Cabinet Diaries of Josephus Daniels, 1913–1921* (Lincoln, NE, 1963), Dec. 22, 1919, 474; Cooper, *Breaking the Heart of the World*, 314–20; Tumulty to Edith Wilson, Jan. 15, 1920, with draft of letter from Wilson to Senator Hitchcock, *PWW*, 64:276–82.

35. Tumulty to Wilson, Feb. 27, 1920, *PWW*, 64:479–80.

36. Blum, *Joe Tumulty*, 239–55; Grayson memorandum, Mar. 25, 1920, *PWW*, 65:123–25; Cary Travers Grayson, *Woodrow Wilson: An Intimate Memoir* (New York, 1960), 109; Tumulty to Edith Wilson, July 4, 1920, *PWW*, 65:493–95; Tumulty to Edith Wilson, Nov. 1, 1920, *PWW*, 66:298–99; John Milton Cooper Jr., *Pivotal Decades: The United States, 1900–1920* (New York, 1990), 272; John Blum, *Joe Tumulty and the Wilson Era* (Boston, 1951), 255.

37. Blum, *Joe Tumulty*, 255–59; Cooper, *Woodrow Wilson*, 573–78.

38. Blum, *Joe Tumulty*, 260–62; A. Scott Berg, *Wilson* (New York, 2013), 718.

39. Berg, *Wilson*, 718–21; Tumulty to Wilson, Apr. 5, 6, 1922, *PWW*, 67:602; Edith Bolling Wilson, *My Memoir* (New York, 1938), 334; Tumulty to Wilson, Apr. 12, 13, 1922, *PWW*, 68:14–15,

20–23; Tumulty to Wilson, Apr. 13, 1922, in William Allen White, *Woodrow Wilson: The Man, His Times, and His Task* (New York, 1924), 506; Grayson memorandum, May 22, 1922, *PWW*, 68:59–60; Wilson to James Kerney, Oct. 30, 1923, *PWW*, 68:459.

40. Blum, *Joe Tumulty*, 264–67.

41. Douglas B. Craig, *After Wilson: The Struggle for the Democratic Party, 1920–1934* (Chapel Hill, NC, 1992), 246.

42. Blum, *Joe Tumulty*, 265–66; Otis L. Graham Jr., *An Encore for Reform: The Old Progressives and the New Deal* (New York, 1967), 28.

43. Blum, *Joe Tumulty*, 267.

Chapter 6 · Colonel Edward M. House

Chapter subtitle: House's tribute to Wilson, printed in the *New York Times*, Feb. 10, 1924.

1. House to Mezes, Nov. 25, 1911, to Culberson, Nov. 27, 1911, Edward M. House Papers, Yale University Library. House wrote two memoirs, *Reminiscences*, in 1916, and *Memories*, in 1929. Both are in the House Papers.

2. Arthur D. Howden Smith, *Mr. House of Texas* (New York, 1940), 33–35; House, *Reminiscences*, 51.

3. Charles E. Neu, *Colonel House: A Biography of Woodrow Wilson's Silent Partner* (New York, 2015), 3–6; House, *Memories*, 3–5.

4. Neu, *Colonel House*, 8–12; House, *Reminiscences*, 7–11, 39–41; House, *Memories*, 10–22.

5. House, *Reminiscences*, 39–41.

6. House, *Reminiscences*, 35–38; House, *Memories*, 29–33.

7. Neu, *Colonel House*, 14–19; House, *Reminiscences*, 12; Rupert Norval Richardson, *Colonel Edward M. House: The Texas Years, 1858–1912* (Abilene, TX, 1964), 317.

8. Neu, *Colonel House*, 20–25.

9. Neu, *Colonel House*, 20–25; House, *Reminiscences*, 12–19.

10. House, *Reminiscences*, 19.

11. Neu, *Colonel House*, 29–39.

12. Neu, *Colonel House*, 29–39; House, *Reminiscences*, 16–17.

13. Neu, *Colonel House*, 32.

14. Neu, *Colonel House*, 32–38.

15. P. A. Fitzhugh to House, Dec. 25, 1896, House Papers.

16. Neu, *Colonel House*, 39–52; House, *Reminiscences*, 27–35.

17. Neu, *Colonel House*, 53–68; House to Sidney Mezes, Apr. 15, 1912, to Frank Andrews, Sept. 17, 1912, House Papers.

18. Neu, *Colonel House*, 78–85.

19. Neu, *Colonel House*, 78–85; House Diary, Dec. 11, 23, 1912, Jan. 8, 1913, House Papers.

20. Neu, *Colonel House*, 85–87; House Diary, Mar. 25, Apr. 14, 1913, House Papers.

21. Neu, *Colonel House*, 85–87; House Diary, Mar. 25, Apr. 14, 1913, House Papers; Raymond Fosdick, *Chronicle of a Generation: An Autobiography* (New York, 1958), 44–47, 195–97.

22. Neu, *Colonel House*, 87–89; House to Wilson, Apr. 23, 1913, House Papers; Peter Clark MacFarlene, "The President's Silent Partner," *Collier's Magazine*, April 30, 1913.

23. House Diary, May 21–27, 1913, House Papers.

24. Neu, *Colonel House*, 101–2; House, *Philip Dru: Administrator, A Story of Tomorrow, 1920–1935* (New York, 1912), 284.

25. Neu, *Colonel House*, 107–10; Wilson to House, Sept. 4, 1913, House to Wilson, Sept. 10, 1913, House Papers.

26. House Diary, Aug. 18, Nov. 26, 1913, House Papers.

27. Neu, *Colonel House*, 107–10; Wilson to House, Sept. 4, 1913, House to Wilson, Sept. 10, 1913, House Papers; House Diary, Aug. 18, Nov. 26, 1913, House Papers.

28. Neu, *Colonel House*, 115, 118–20.

29. Neu, *Colonel House*, 115, 118–20; House Diary, Mar. 25, Apr. 15, 1914, House Papers.

30. Neu, *Colonel House*, 141–42; House to Wilson, Aug. 7, 1914, House Papers; House Diary, Aug. 30, 1914, House Papers.

31. Neu, *Colonel House*, 150–52.

32. Neu, *Colonel House*, 150–52; House Diary, Sept. 28, Nov. 4, 5, 6, 1914, House Papers.

33. Neu, *Colonel House*, 169; House Diary, Jan. 25, 1915, House Papers.

34. House Diary, Apr. 28, 29, 1915, House Papers; House to Gordon Auchincloss, Apr. 30, 1915, House Papers; Wilson to House, June 1, 1915, House Papers.

35. Neu, *Colonel House*, 193–96; Phyllis Lee Levin, *Edith and Woodrow: The Wilson White House* (New York, 2001), 95–97; House Diary, June 16, 24, 1915, House Papers.

36. Wilson to House, July 21, 1915, House Papers; House Diary, July 30, 31, 1915, House Papers.

37. Edith Galt to Wilson, Aug. 26, 28, 1915, Wilson to Edith Galt, Aug. 28, 1915, *PWW*, 34:336–39, 350–55, 355–58.

38. House Diary, Sept. 22, 1915, House Papers.

39. House Diary, Sept. 22, 23, 24, 1915, House Papers; Wilson to Edith Galt, Sept. 23, 1915, *PWW*, 34:510–11.

40. House Diary, Oct. 21, 31, Nov. 27, Dec. 15, 1915, House Papers.

41. Edith Galt to House, Oct. 18, 1915, House Papers; House Diary, Nov. 4, 5, 22, 30, House Papers; House Diary, Nov. 4, 1915, *PWW*, 35:175; Edith Galt to Wilson, Nov. 30, 1915, *PWW*, 35:275–76; Edwin A. Weinstein, *Woodrow Wilson: A Medical and Psychological Biography* (Princeton, NJ, 1981), 294–95.

42. House Diary, Sept. 15, 1915, House Papers.

43. Neu, *Colonel House*, 220–21; House Diary, Dec. 15, 1915, House Papers.

44. House Diary, Mar. 6, 1916, House Papers.

45. House to Wilson, May 28, 1916, Wilson to House, May 29, June 22, 1916, House Papers; McAdoo to House, July 17, Aug. 30, 1916, House Papers; House Diary, Aug. 27, 1916, House Papers.

46. House to Wilson, Nov. 4, 1916, House Papers; House Diary, Nov. 12, 1916, House Papers.

47. Neu, *Colonel House*, 270–75; House Diary, Dec. 20, 1916, House Papers.

48. Levin, *Edith and Woodrow*, 166–75.

49. House Diary, Jan. 3, 1917, House Papers.

50. House Diary, Jan. 3, 12, 17, Feb. 1, 1917, House Papers.

51. House Diary, Jan. 12, Feb. 4, Mar. 3, 28, 1917, House Papers.

52. Neu, *Colonel House*, 289–90; House Diary, March 27, 28, Apr. 2, 1917, House Papers; House to Fanny Denton, Apr. 2, 1917, House Papers.

53. Neu, *Colonel House*, 295–302; House Diary, Apr. 5, May 19, 27, 28, 30, 31, 1917, House Papers.

54. House Diary, Sept. 9, 10, 12, 13, Oct. 13, 1917, House Papers.

55. House Diary, Jan. 9, 1918, House Papers; William Wiseman, "Notes on Interview with the President," Jan. 23, 1918, *PWW*, 46:85–88.

56. House Diary, June 14, 1918, House Papers; House to Wilson, Sept. 3, 1918, House Papers. Magnolia was the North Shore village where House often rented a summer cottage.

57. "A Memorandum by Sir William Wiseman, Oct. 16, 1918, *PWW*, 51:347–52.

58. Neu, *Colonel House*, 367–74; House to Wilson, Nov. 5, 1918, House Papers.

59. Neu, *Colonel House*, 378.

60. Neu, *Colonel House*, 389–403.

61. Neu, Colonel House, 389–403; House to Wilson, Feb. 14, 1919, House Papers; House Diary, March 6, 7, 1919, House Papers.

62. August Heckscher, *Woodrow Wilson* (New York, 1991), 546.

63. Neu, *Colonel House*, 405–11.

64. Baker Diary, Apr. 3, 1919, *PWW*, 56:577–78.

65. Neu, *Colonel House*, 412–13; House Diary, May 30, 1919, House Papers.

66. House Diary, June 28, 1919, House Papers.

67. House Diary, Nov. 20, 27, Dec. 2, 1919, House Papers.

68. House Diary, Feb. 3, 9, 18, 22, March 2, 1913, House Papers.

69. House Diary, May 11, 27, 1920, House Papers.

70. Neu, *Colonel House*, 456–57; House Diary, Feb. 9, 1924, House Papers; *New York Times*, Feb. 7, 10, 1924.

71. Neu, *Colonel House*, 467–68; *New York Times*, May 7, 1926.

72. Charles Seymour, *The Intimate Papers of Colonel House*, 4 vols. (Boston, 1926–28), 1:viii, 114–50; 2:470; 4:3–12, 512–18.

73. Neu, *Colonel House*, 480–84, 486, 488–90, 492–95.

74. House to James C. McReynolds, Feb. 1, 1933, to Brand Whitlock, March 4, 1933, to Daniel Roper, Nov. 12, 1933, House Papers.

75. Neu, *Colonel House*, 496, 507–8; Seymour memorandum, Jan. 5, 1938, Seymour Papers, Yale University Library.

Chapter 7 · Cary T. Grayson

Chapter subtitle: Rear Admiral Cary T. Grayson, *Woodrow Wilson: An Intimate Memoir* (New York, 1960), xi, appraising Wilson's ultimate place in history.

1. A. Scott Berg, *Wilson* (New York, 2013), 273–77; Ray Stannard Baker, *Woodrow Wilson, 1913–1914* (New York, 1939), 16; Eleanor Wilson McAdoo, *The Woodrow Wilsons* (New York, 1937), 210–11.

2. Josephus Daniels, *The Wilson Era: Years of Peace—1910–1917* (Chapel Hill, NC, 1944), 514; "Miscellaneous Notes and Memoranda by Dr. Grayson," in Arthur S. Link, ed., *The Papers of Woodrow Wilson [PWW]*, 64:485–86.

3. Draft for *National Cyclopedia of American Biography*, 1927, 2–4, Cary T. Grayson Papers, Woodrow Wilson Presidential Library, Staunton, VA.

4. Draft for *National Cyclopedia of American Biography*, 4–6, Cary T. Grayson Papers; Ludwig M. Deppisch, MD, *The White House Physician: A History from Washington to George W. Bush* (Jefferson, NC, 2007), 90–95; Rear Admiral William C. Braisted and Captain William Hemphill Bell, *The Life Story of Presley Marion Rixey, Surgeon General, U. S. Navy, 1902–1910* (Strasburg, VA, 1930), 132–34.

5. Bert E. Park, *The Impact of Illness on World Leaders* (Philadelphia, PA, 1986), 7–8; Bert E. Park, *Ailing, Aging, Addicted: Studies of Compromised Leadership* (Lexington, KY, 1993), 96–98; Berg, *Wilson*, 284–85; Grayson, *Woodrow Wilson*, 2–3.

6. William G. McAdoo, *Crowded Years: The Reminiscences of William G. McAdoo* (Boston, 1931), 271; Admiral Cary T. Grayson, "The Colonel's Folly and the President's Distress," *American Heritage Magazine* (Oct. 1964), 6; House Diary, Mar. 25, 1914, House Papers, Yale University Library; Ray Stannard Baker, *Woodrow Wilson, 1913–1914* (New York, 1939), 78, 178.

7. Berg, *Wilson*, 320, 333–35; Grayson, *Woodrow Wilson*, 33–35.

8. Grayson to House, Aug. 20, 1914, House Papers; Edwin A. Weinstein, *Woodrow Wilson: A Medical and Psychological Biography* (Princeton, NJ, 1981), 255–56.

9. Charles E. Neu, *Colonel House: A Biography of Woodrow Wilson's Silent Partner* (New York, 2015), 141–43, 150–51; House Diary, Aug. 30, Sept. 26, 1914, House Papers.

10. Edith Bolling Wilson, *My Memoir* (Indianapolis, IN, 1938), 29, 51–56; Tom Shachtman, *Edith & Woodrow: A Presidential Romance* (New York, 1981), 20, 53–54, 72–73; Grayson to Alice Gordon Grayson, Aug. 30, Sept. 12, 1915, Grayson Papers; Grayson to Edith Galt, Aug. 25, 1914, *PWW*, 31:564.

11. Berg, *Wilson*, 355–61.

12. Edith Galt to Wilson, May 27, June 4, 1915, *PWW*, 33:274, 339.

13. House Diary, July 30, 31, 1915, House Papers.

14. Edith Galt to Wilson, Aug. 25, 26, 1915, *PWW*, 34:327, 338; Edith Galt to Cary Grayson, June 28, July 19, 1915, Grayson Papers.

15. Wilson to Edith Galt, Aug. 13, 29, 1915, *PWW*, 34:193, 360.

16. Neu, *Colonel House*, 210–12, 220–21; House Diary, Sept. 22, Dec. 15, 1915, *PWW*, 35:360; Wilson to Alice Gordon Grayson, Oct. 3, 1915, Grayson Papers.

17. Grayson to Alice Gertrude Gordon, Jan. 6, 1916, Grayson Papers; Berg, *Wilson*, 406–16.

18. Wilson to Josephus Daniels, July 2, 1915, *PWW*, 33:465; Daniels, *The Wilson Era, Years of Peace*, 513–18; Phyllis Lee Levin, *Edith and Woodrow: The Wilson White House* (New York, 2001), 160–61; House Diary, Jan. 3, 12, 1917, *PWW*, 35:463.

19. Berg, *Wilson*, 429–30, 500–502; Grayson to House, Oct. 28, 1917, House Papers.

20. House Diary, Feb. 27, 1918, *PWW*, 46:485; George Frost Kennan, *Russia Leaves the War* (Princeton, NJ, 1956), 29.

21. House Diary, May 17, 19, 20, 1918, House Papers; McAdoo, *Crowded Years*, 493–95.

22. House Diary, Aug. 16, 18, 1918, *PWW*, 49:276, 298.

23. Berg, *Wilson*, 515–16; Grayson to Alice Gordon Grayson, Dec. 8–9, 1918, Grayson Papers; Grayson Diary, Dec. 25, 1918, Jan. 3, 1919, *PWW*, 53:502–5, 595–97; Grayson Diary, Jan. 12, 1919, *PWW*, 54:4–6; Grayson Diary, Jan. 19, 1919, *PWW*, 54:150; Grayson Diary, Jan. 28, 1919, *PWW*, 54:308–9; Grayson Diary, Jan. 29, 1919, *PWW*, 54:334; Grayson Diary, Feb. 4, 1919, *PWW*, 54:473; Grayson to Alice Gordon Grayson, Jan. 13, 1919, Grayson Papers; Grayson, *Woodrow Wilson*, 58.

24. Grayson Diary, Mar. 4, 1919, *PWW*, 55:410; Ray Stannard Baker Diary, Mar. 8, 1919, *PWW*, 55:465.

25. Neu, *Colonel House*, 405–6; Grayson Diary, Mar. 13, 1919, *PWW*, 55:488; Levin, *Edith and Woodrow*, 243–304.

26. Grayson Diary, Mar. 29, 1919, *PWW*, 56:406–8.

27. Berg, *Wilson*, 568–69; Grayson Diary, Apr. 3, 7, 1919, *PWW*, 56:554–58; Grayson to Tumulty, Apr. 10, 1919, *PWW*, 57:62–67.

28. Grayson to McAdoo, Apr. 12, 1919, *PWW*, 57:304–5; Grayson to Tumulty, Apr. 30, 1919, *PWW*, 58:248; Joseph P. Tumulty, *Woodrow Wilson as I Know Him* (Garden City, NY, 1921), 545.

29. Grayson Diary, Apr. 24, 27, 1919, *PWW*, 58:53–56, 170–71; Grayson to Alice Gordon Grayson, June 6, 1919, Grayson Papers.

30. Grayson Diary, May 3, 1919, *PWW*, 58:367–68.

31. Grayson Diary, May 7, 1919, *PWW*, 58:499–504; Grayson to Alice Gordon Grayson, May 14, 1919, Grayson Papers.

32. Grayson Diary, May 22, 1919, *PWW*, 59:527–30; Grayson Diary, July 1, 1919, *PWW*, 61:360–62.

33. Berg, *Wilson*, 603–20; Note, *PWW*, 62:507–8; Bert E. Park, "Wilson's Neurologic Illness during the Summer of 1919," *PWW*, 62:628–38; Grayson, *Woodrow Wilson*, 95.

34. Grayson Diary, Sept. 6, 1919, *PWW*, 63:63–66; Grayson Diary, Sept. 15, 1919, *PWW*, 63:274–76; Edith Bolling Wilson, *My Memoir*, 275.

35. Grayson Diary, Sept. 25, 26, 1919, *PWW*, 63:487–90, 518–21.

36. Grayson Diary, Sept. 28, 1919, *PWW*, 63:532–33; Berg, *Wilson*, 638–47; Robert Lansing

to Frank Polk, Oct. 1, 4, 1919, *PWW*, 63:539–41; Grayson memorandum, Oct. 6, 1919, *PWW*, 64:496; Lansing memorandum, Feb. 23, 1920, *PWW*, 64:454–58.

37. Neu, *Colonel House*, 429–30; Berg, *Wilson*, 644–49; Josephus Daniels, *The Wilson Era: Years of War and After, 1917–1923* (Chapel Hill, NC, 1946), 512; Note, *PWW*, 64:507; Thomas J. Knock, "One Long Wilderness of Despair": Woodrow Wilson's Stroke and the League of Nations," in Jeffrey A. Engel and Thomas J. Knock, eds., *When Life Strikes the President: Scandal, Death, and Illness in the White House* (New York, 2017), 107–11.

38. Berg, *Wilson*, 649–50; Baker Diary, Nov. 5, 1919, *PWW*, 63:619–22.

39. Note, *PWW*, 64:363; Berg, *Wilson*, 663–78; Grayson, *Woodrow Wilson*, 106.

40. Neu, *Colonel House*, 441–42; Berg, *Wilson*, 680–90; Grayson memorandum, Mar. 25, 1920, *PWW*, 65:123–25; Carter Glass memorandum, June 16, 19, 1920, *PWW*, 65:400, 435–36.

41. Berg, *Wilson*, 694; From the Shorthand Diary of Charles Lee Swem, Jan. 30, 1921, *PWW*, 67:104; Baker Diary, Dec. 1, 1920, *PWW*, 66:451.

42. Berg, *Wilson*, 703–37; Note 3, *PWW*, 67:137–38; John Bolling memorandum, *PWW*, 68:548–50.

43. Berg, *Wilson*, 742.

44. McAdoo, *Crowded Years*, 271; James Grant, *Bernard M. Baruch: The Adventures of a Wall Street Legend* (New York, 1997), 174–75, 264; Bernard M. Baruch, *Baruch: The Public Years* (New York, 1960), 47, 119, 205, 224; Baruch, "Foreword," in Grayson, *Woodrow Wilson*, vi; Grayson to Baker, June 17, 1925, Grayson Papers; Baker to Grayson, June 15, 1929, Grayson Papers.

45. Baruch, "Foreword," in Grayson, *Woodrow Wilson*, vii; Grayson, "The Colonel's Folly and the President's Distress," 6, 96; draft for *National Cyclopedia of American Biography*, 16, Cary T. Grayson Papers.

Chapter 8 · Newton D. Baker

Chapter subtitle: Newton Baker about Wilson, quoted in C. H. Cramer, *Newton D. Baker: A Biography* (Cleveland, OH, 1961), 219. In its larger context, the quotation reads: "He [Wilson] is standing at the throne of God whose approval he won and received. As he looks down from there I say to him, 'I did my best. I am doing it now. You are still the captain of my soul.'"

1. Douglas B. Craig, *Progressives at War: William G. McAdoo and Newton D. Baker, 1863–1941* (Baltimore, MD, 2013), 11–20; Cramer, *Newton D. Baker*, 13–18.

2. Craig, *Progressives at War*, 20.

3. Craig, *Progressives at War*, 21–23, 326–28.

4. Craig, *Progressives at War*, 23–46.

5. Tom L. Johnson, *My Story* (Kent, OH, 1993), 173.

6. Cramer, *Newton D. Baker*, 36–44.

7. Cramer, *Newton D. Baker*, 18–19, 70–75; Raymond B. Fosdick, *Chronicle of a Generation: An Autobiography* (New York, 1958), 241.

8. Craig, *Progressives at War*, 51–60; Cramer, *Newton D. Baker*, 46–63.

9. Craig, *Progressives at War*, 47–48, 60–61.

10. Craig, *Progressives at War*, 61–63; Cramer, *Newton D. Baker*, 64–65.

11. Craig, *Progressives at War*, 63; Newton D. Baker to Woodrow Wilson, Nov. 15, 1912, in Arthur S. Link, ed., *The Papers of Woodrow Wilson* [*PWW*], 69 vols. (Princeton, NJ, 1966–93), 25:549; House Diary, Feb. 18, 1913, Edward M. House Papers, Yale University Library.

12. Craig, *Progressives at War*, 63.

13. Craig, *Progressives at War*, 47, 63–65.

14. Craig, *Progressives at War*, 65–66; Ray Stannard Baker, *Woodrow Wilson: Life and Letters, Facing War, 1915–1917* (New York, 1937), 37–38.

15. Daniel R. Beaver, *Newton D. Baker and the American War Effort, 1917–1919* (Lincoln, NE,

1966), 8; Craig, *Progressives at War*, 66; William G. McAdoo, *Crowded Years: The Reminiscences of William G. McAdoo* (Boston, 1931), 342; Fosdick, *Chronicle of a Generation*, 136, 158–61.

16. "A Memorandum by Ray Stannard Baker of a Conversation at the White House," May 11, 1916, *PWW*, 37:33; Ray Stannard Baker, *American Chronicle: An Autobiography* (New York, 1945), 283, 316, 478; House Diary, April 6, May 24, 1916, *PWW*, 36:19, 424.

17. Craig, *Progressives at War*, 141–46; Beaver, *Newton D. Baker*, 12–16; David R. Woodward, *The American Army and the First World War* (Cambridge, UK, 2014), 27–33.

18. Craig, *Progressives at War*, 147–49; "A Memorandum by Robert Lansing," Mar. 20, 1917, *PWW*, 41:439; Baker to Wilson, Apr. 3, 1917, *PWW*, 41:541.

19. Craig, *Progressives at War*, 109–14.

20. Wilson to Sadler, May 19, 1916, *PWW*, 37:74; Willis Thornton, *Newton D. Baker and His Books* (Cleveland, OH, 1954), 18; Josephus Daniels, *The Wilson Era: Years of Peace, 1910–1917* (Chapel Hill, NC, 1944); House Diary, Mar. 27, 28, 1917, House Papers.

21. Robert H. Zieger, *America's Great War: World War I and the American Experience* (New York, 2000), 64–70; Edward M. Coffman, *The War to End All Wars: The American Military Experience in World War I* (New York, 1968), 5–53; David R. Woodward, *Trial by Friendship: Anglo-American Relations, 1917–1918* (Lexington, KY, 1993), 33.

22. Beaver, *Newton D. Baker*, 50–78; Craig, *Progressives at War*, 150–78; Edward M. Coffman, *The Hilt of the Sword: The Career of Peyton C. March* (Madison, WI, 1966), 148; Meirion Harries and Susie Harries, *The Last Days of Innocence: America at War, 1917–1918* (New York, 1997), 193–204.

23. House Diary, Jan. 9, 1918, House Papers.

24. Beaver, *Newton D. Baker*, 79–104; *New York Times*, Jan. 13, 1918; Daniels Diary, Jan. 23, 1918, in E. David Cronon, ed., *The Cabinet Diaries of Josephus Daniels, 1913–1921* (Lincoln, NE, 1963), 271; Baker to Wilson, Jan. 21, 1918, *PWW*, 46:56–57; Ray Stannard Baker, *Woodrow Wilson: Life and Letters, War Leader, April 6, 1917–Feb. 28, 1918* (New York, 1939), 503–4; "A Press Release," Jan. 21, 1918, *PWW*, 46:55–56.

25. Beaver, *Newton D. Baker*, 104–9; Craig, *Progressives at War*, 181–85; McAdoo to Wilson, Jan. 18, 1918, *PWW*, 46:17; John Maxwell Hamilton and Robert Mann, eds., *A Journalist's Diplomatic Mission: Ray Stannard Baker's World War One Diary* (Baton Rouge, LA, 2012), 34.

26. Craig, *Progressives at War*, 192–96; Beaver, *Newton D. Baker*, 110–50; David Stevenson, *With Our Backs to the Wall: Victory and Defeat in 1918* (Cambridge, MA, 2011), 42–44, 244–55.

27. Craig, *Progressives at War*, 161, 185–90; Baker to Wilson, July 18, 1919, *PWW*, 61:53; Adriane Lentz-Smith, *Freedom Struggles: African Americans and World War I* (Cambridge, MA, 2009), 4; Edward M. Coffman, *The Regulars: The American Army, 1898–1941* (Cambridge, MA, 2004), 216–18.

28. Craig, *Progressives at War*, 215–16; Woodward, *Trial by Friendship*, 178–81.

29. Craig, *Progressives at War*, 194–96, 207–8.

30. Baker to Wilson, Nov. 11, 1918, *PWW*, 53:46; Wilson to Baker, Nov. 12, 1918, *PWW*, 53:54; Craig, *Progressives at War*, 212; Steve Neal, *Happy Days Are Here Again* (New York, 2004), 66.

31. Baker to Wilson, Nov. 23, 1918, *PWW*, 53:182; Craig, *Progressives at War*, 211.

32. Baker to Wilson, Nov. 30, 1918, *PWW*, 53:252–53.

33. Craig, *Progressives at War*, 213, 217.

34. Craig, *Progressives at War*, 216–17; "A Memorandum by Robert Lansing," Dec. 16, 1919, *PWW*, 64:193.

35. Craig, *Progressives at War*, 239–46.

36. Craig, *Progressives at War*, 234; Baker to Wilson, Dec. 24, 1920, *PWW*, 67:3–4; Stockton Axson, *Brother Woodrow: A Memoir of Woodrow Wilson*, ed. Arthur S. Link (Princeton, NJ, 1993), 197.

37. Craig, *Progressives at War*, 263–66, 276–77.

38. Cramer, *Newton D. Baker*, 217–20; Craig, *Progressives at War*, 279–81.

39. Cramer, *Newton D. Baker*, 166–67; Josephus Daniels, *The Wilson Era: Years of War and After, 1917–1923* (Chapel Hill, NC, 1946), 540.

40. Craig, *Progressives at War*, 290–94.

41. Craig, *Progressives at War*, 295–304; Otis L. Graham Jr., *An Encore for Reform: The Old Progressives and the New Deal* (New York, 1967), 26, 50, 162.

42. Craig, *Progressives at War*, 304–9, 315–21; Fosdick to Newton D. Baker, Aug. 31, 1926, Baker MSS, in Craig, *Progressives at War*, 291–92; Oswald Garrison Villard, *Fighting Years: Memoirs of a Liberal Editor* (New York, 1939), 249.

43. Craig, *Progressives at War*, 321; Douglas B. Craig, *After Wilson: The Struggle for the Democratic Party, 1920–1934* (Chapel Hill, NC, 1992), 233.

44. Cramer, *Newton D. Baker*, 259–71; Craig, *Progressives at War*, 367–78, 382–85.

45. Craig, *Progressives at War*, 378–82.

46. Craig, *Progressives at War*, 386–90; Cramer, *Newton D. Baker*, 272–77; August Heckscher, *Woodrow Wilson* (New York, 1991), 380.

Chapter 9 · Edith Bolling Galt

Chapter subtitle: Edith Bolling Wilson, *My Memoir* (Indianapolis, IN, 1939), 360. In its larger context, the quotation reads: "To My Husband Woodrow Wilson who helped me build from the broken timbers of my life a temple wherein are enshrined memories of his great spirit which was dedicated to the service of his God and humanity."

1. Arthur S. Link, ed., *The Papers of Woodrow Wilson* [*PWW*], 69 vols. (Princeton, NJ, 1966–93), 32:424; Edith Wilson, *My Memoir*, 56–58; Edith Galt to Annie Bolling, *PWW*, 32:423.

2. Kristie Miller, *Ellen and Edith: Woodrow Wilson's First Ladies* (Lawrence, KS, 2010), 109; Edmund W. Starling, *Starling of the White House* (New York, 1946), 49; Ishbel Ross, *Power with Grace: The Life Story of Mrs. Woodrow Wilson* (New York, 1975), 13.

3. Edith Wilson, *My Memoir*, 10–12.

4. Edith Wilson, *My Memoir*, 1–10, 18.

5. Edith Wilson, *My Memoir*, 10–12; Phyllis Lee Levin, *Edith and Woodrow: The Wilson White House* (New York, 2001), 58–65; Edith Galt to Woodrow Wilson, Aug. 11, 1915, *PWW*, 34:172; Ray Stannard Baker, *Woodrow Wilson: Facing War, 1915–1917* (New York, 1937), 42.

6. Edith Wilson, *My Memoir*, 16–32; Levin, *Edith and Woodrow*, 69.

7. Edith Wilson, *My Memoir*, 16–32; Levin, *Edith and Woodrow*, 66–73.

8. Edith Wilson, *My Memoir*, 33–41; Betty Boyd Caroli, *First Ladies: From Martha Washington to Michelle Obama* (New York, 2010), 145–47.

9. Edith Wilson, *My Memoir*, 51–55; Cary Grayson to Edith Galt, Aug. 25, 1914, *PWW*, 31:563–64.

10. Edith Wilson, *My Memoir*, 57–67; Edith Galt to Woodrow Wilson, May 5, 7, 27, 1915, *PWW*, 33:109, 127, 274; Edwin Tribble, ed., *A President in Love: The Courtship Letters of Woodrow Wilson and Edith Bolling Galt* (Boston, 1981), 1–42.

11. Edith Galt to Woodrow Wilson, June 3, 10, 1915, *PWW*, 33:335, 382; Woodrow Wilson to Edith Galt, June 5, 1915, *PWW*, 33:345; Edith Galt to Woodrow Wilson, June 18, 1915, *PWW*, 33:421; Woodrow Wilson to Edith Galt, Aug. 13, 1915, *PWW*, 34:192; Levin, *Edith and Woodrow*, 74–98.

12. Edith Wilson, *My Memoir*, 60–73.

13. Levin, *Edith and Woodrow*, 99–108; Edith Galt to Woodrow Wilson, Aug. 11, 13, 1915, *PWW*, 34:172, 195; Woodrow Wilson to Edith Galt, Aug. 13, 1915, *PWW*, 34:190.

14. Edith Galt to Woodrow Wilson, Aug. 25, 26, 1915, *PWW*, 34:326–29, 336–39; Woodrow Wilson to Edith Galt, Aug. 28, 1915, *PWW*, 34:350–55.

15. Levin, *Edith and Woodrow*, 109–21, 139–49; Woodrow Wilson to Edith Galt, Sept. 18, 19, 1915, *PWW*, 34:489, 491; Edith Galt to Woodrow Wilson, Sept. 19, 1915, *PWW*, 34:490; Woodrow Wilson to Edith Galt, Oct. 7, 1915, *PWW*, 35:40; Starling, *Starling of the White House*, 56.

16. Miller, *Ellen and Edith*, 126, 133–36; Edith B. Wilson to Altrude G. Grayson, Feb. 11, 1916, Woodrow Wilson Presidential Library, Staunton, VA; Levin, *Edith and Woodrow*, 154–56; Ross, *Power with Grace*, 61–68.

17. Edith Wilson, *My Memoir*, 102–19; Miller, *Ellen and Edith*, 142–43.

18. House Diary, Jan. 3, 12, Mar. 3, 1917, Edward M. House Papers, Yale University Library.

19. Edith Wilson, *My Memoir*, 127–33; Levin, *Edith and Woodrow*, 176–79.

20. Edith Wilson, *My Memoir*, 134–43; Miller, *Ellen and Edith*, 149–57; Levin, *Edith and Woodrow*, 179–85.

21. Edith Wilson, *My Memoir*, 144–57; House Diary, Aug. 19, 1918, *PWW*, 49:294.

22. Edith Wilson, *My Memoir*, 170–71.

23. Edith Wilson, *My Memoir*, 172–75; Levin, *Edith and Woodrow*, 227–32; Edith Benham Diary, Dec. 10, 1918, *PWW*, 53:357.

24. Edith Wilson, *My Memoir*, 177–221; Edith Wilson to her family, Dec. 15, 1918, *PWW*, 53:396–99; Levin, *Edith and Woodrow*, 235.

25. Edith Benham Helm, *The Captains and Kings* (New York, 1954), 91–92; Edith Wilson, *My Memoir*, 222–35; Levin, *Edith and Woodrow*, 246.

26. Edith Wilson, *My Memoir*, 239.

27. Levin, *Edith and Woodrow*, 254–61; Edith Wilson, *My Memoir*, 241.

28. Edith Wilson, *My Memoir*, 245–46.

29. Grayson Diary, Apr. 3, 4, 1919, *PWW*, 56:554–57; Edith Wilson, *My Memoir*, 252.

30. Grayson Diary, Apr. 9, 1919, *PWW*, 57:145; Grayson Diary, May 3, 1919, *PWW*, 58:368.

31. Edith Wilson, *My Memoir*, 255.

32. Edith Wilson to Henry White, Aug. 4, 1919, *PWW*, 62:156; Edith Wilson, *My Memoir*, 273–74; Levin, *Edith and Woodrow*, 315–16.

33. Edith Wilson, *My Memoir*, 275–81; Starling, *Starling of the White House*, 150; Mary Allen Hulbert, *The Story of Mrs. Peck* (New York, 1933), 272.

34. Edith Wilson, *My Memoir*, 284–90; Miller, *Ellen and Edith*, 186–92; Edwin A. Weinstein, *Woodrow Wilson: A Medical and Psychological Biography* (Princeton, NJ, 1981), 360; John Milton Cooper Jr., *Woodrow Wilson: A* Biography (New York, 2009), 536.

35. Alden Hatch, *Edith Bolling Wilson: First Lady Extraordinary* (New York, 1961), 226; Miller, *Ellen and Edith*, 190–96; Edith Wilson, *My Memoir*, 289–90; A. Scott Berg, *Wilson* (New York, 2013), 643–45.

36. Baker Diary, Nov. 5, 1919, *PWW*, 63:619–22.

37. Miller, *Ellen and Edith*, 193–207; Edith Wilson, *My Memoir*, 296–303; Levin, *Edith and Woodrow*, 375–414.

38. Miller, *Ellen and Edith*, 209–22; Baker Diary, Jan. 23, 1920, *PWW*, 64:320–21; Edith Wilson to Kate Trask, May 27, 1920, *PWW*, 65:333; Edith Wilson to Woodrow Wilson, June 5, 1920, *PWW*, 65:377.

39. Levin, *Edith and Woodrow*, 451–83; Baker Diary, Jan. 22, 1921, *PWW*, 67:82; Cary Grayson to Altrude Grayson, July 15, 1922, Grayson Papers, in Miller, *Ellen and Edith*, 237; Cecil Diary, Apr. 21, 1923, *PWW*, 68:345; Swem Diary, Jan. 30, 1921, *PWW*, 67:103–4.

40. Woodrow Wilson to Edith Wilson, Aug. 29, 1923, *PWW*, 68:412; Miller, *Ellen and Edith*, 236–41; Edith Wilson, *My Memoir*, 351–60.

41. Miller, *Ellen and Edith*, 242–57; Levin, *Edith and Woodrow*, 494–511.

42. Levin, *Edith and Woodrow*, 496–97.

43. Levin, *Edith and Woodrow*, 512; Miller, *Ellen and Edith*, 255; Jonathan Daniels, *The Time between the Wars* (New York, 1966), 346.

44. Miller, *Ellen and Edith*, 258; Levin, *Edith and Woodrow*, 514–18.

Chapter 10 · Bernard Baruch

Chapter subtitle: Baruch to Wilson, Nov. 26, 1918, in Arthur S. Link, ed., *The Papers of Woodrow Wilson* [*PWW*], 69 vols. (Princeton, NJ, 1966–93), 53:209. In its larger context, the quotation reads: "In happier days to come, when the world has steadied and composed itself, countless millions will always be thankful to God for having given us Woodrow Wilson, in, perhaps, the greatest crisis of all times."

1. Bernard M. Baruch, *Baruch: The Public Years* (New York, 1960), 8–9; House Diary, Oct. 12, 1912, Edward M. House Papers, Yale University Library. Wilson, who was uncertain that he should meet with Baruch, a Wall Street broker, insisted that House stay for the entire conversation. Jordan A. Schwarz, *The Speculator: Bernard M. Baruch in Washington, 1917–1965* (Chapel Hill, NC, 1981), 36–37.

2. Bernard M. Baruch, *Baruch: My Own Story* (New York, 1957), 1–39; Margaret L. Coit, *Mr. Baruch* (Boston, 1957), 1–32.

3. Baruch, *My Own Story*, 1–39; Coit, *Mr. Baruch*, 1–32.

4. Baruch, *My Own Story*, 41–52; Coit, *Mr. Baruch*, 37–61; Schwarz, *The Speculator*, 8–10.

5. Baruch, *My Own Story*, 53–85; Coit, *Mr. Baruch*, 33–69; Schwarz, *The Speculator*, 13–15.

6. Baruch, *My Own Story*, 85–134; Coit, *Mr. Baruch*, 68–107; Schwarz, *The Speculator*, 31–35.

7. Baruch, *My Own Story*, 177–80; Coit, *Mr. Baruch*, 109–12.

8. Baruch, *My Own Story*, 185–232; Coit, *Mr. Baruch*, 113–30; Schwarz, *The* Speculator, 27–31.

9. Baruch, *My Own Story*, 267–304; Coit, *Mr. Baruch*, 313–38; Helen Lawrenson, *Stranger at the Party: A Memoir* (New York, 1972), 148–49.

10. Baruch, *The Public Years*, 2–20; Schwarz, *The Speculator*, 37–45.

11. Baruch, *The Public Years*, 21–30; Baruch to Wilson, Apr. 5, 1917, Wilson Papers, in Schwarz, *The Speculator*, 45–51; Meirion Harries and Susie Harries, *The Last Days of Innocence: America at War, 1917–18* (New York, 1917), 193–203.

12. Robert H. Zieger, *America's Great War: World War I and the American Experience* (Lanham, MD, 2000), 64–71; Tumulty to Wilson, Feb. 7, 1918, McAdoo to Wilson, Jan. 17, 27, 1918, Daniels to Wilson, Feb. 2, 1918, *PWW*, 46:269, 17, 111–12, 217; Baruch, *The Public Years*, 45.

13. Douglas B. Craig, *Progressives at War: William G. McAdoo and Newton D. Baker, 1863–1941* (Baltimore, MD, 2013), 182; Stephen Skowronek, *Building a New American State* (New York, 1982), 238; House Diary, May 27, 1917, House Papers; Wilson to Baruch, Mar. 4, 1918, *PWW*, 44:522.

14. Schwarz, *The Speculator*, 57–58; Coit, *Mr. Baruch*, 145–47; Baruch, *The Public Years*, 77–84.

15. Schwarz, *The Speculator*, 51–55; Coit, *Mr. Baruch*, 172–222.

16. Coit, *Mr. Baruch*, 195–222; John Milton Cooper Jr., *Woodrow Wilson: A Biography* (New York, 2009), 427; Robert D. Cuff, *The War Industries Board: Business-Government Relations during World War I* (Baltimore, MD, 1973), 269–71.

17. Schwarz, *The Speculator*, 66–69, 104–9; Baruch to House, July 24, 1918, House Papers.

18. E. David Cronon, ed., *The Cabinet Diaries of Josephus Daniels, 1913–1921* (Lincoln, NE, 1963), 350; James Grant, *Bernard M. Baruch: The Adventures of a Wall Street Legend* (New York, 1997), 166, 189–90.

19. Wilson to Baruch, Nov. 27, 1918, Dec. 7, 1918, *PWW*, 53:213–14, 334; Schwarz, *The Speculator*, 107–11; *Woodrow Wilson's Own Story*, ed. Donald Day (Boston, 1952) 303; Baruch, *The Public Years*, 102.

20. Schwarz, *The Speculator*, 112, 119; Diary of Lord Robert Cecil, British Museum, London; Arthur Krock, *Memoirs: Sixty Years on the Firing Line* (New York, 1968), 53; Coit, *Mr. Baruch*, 230.

21. Coit, *Mr. Baruch*, 228; Baruch, *The Public Years*, 84–102; Schwarz, *The Speculator*, 112–44.

22. Grayson Diary, March 30, 1919, *PWW*, 56:428; Charles E. Neu, *Colonel House: A Biography of Woodrow Wilson's Silent Partner* (New York, 2015), 414.

23. Baruch, *The Public Years*, 121–23; Baruch to Wilson, Apr. 24, 1919, *PWW*, 58:94; Thomas W. Lamont to Wilson, June 13, 1919, *PWW*, 60:538.

24. Baruch, *The Public Years*, 123–29.

25. Baruch, *The Public Years*, 123–29; Schwarz, *The Speculator*, 151–53.

26. Baruch, *The Public Years*, 139; Schwarz, *The Speculator* 161–67; Baruch to Wilson, Dec. 16, 1920, *PWW*, 66:525.

27. Baruch, *The Public Years*, 159–73; Schwarz, *The Speculator*, 175–82.

28. Baruch, *The Public Years*, 189–202; Schwarz, *The Speculator*, 182–92.

29. Schwarz, *The Speculator*, 167, 193–206; Lawrenson, *Stranger at the Party*, 149; Baruch, *The Public Years*, 135; Phyllis Lee Levin, *Edith and Woodrow: The Wilson White House* (New York, 2001), 62, 496, 504–8.

30. Baruch, *The Public Years*, 139–59, 203–5; Schwarz, *The Speculator*, 213–51; Baruch to Kenyon, Apr. 9, 1923, Bernard M. Baruch Papers, Princeton University Library.

31. Baruch, *The Public Years*, 207–17; Schwarz, *The Speculator*, 252; Michael Hiltzik, *The New Deal: A Modern History* (New York, 2011), 117–18.

32. Baruch, *The Public Years*, 221–32; Schwarz, *The Speculator*, 266–68; Coit, *Mr. Baruch*, 417–34.

33. Baruch, *The Public Years*, 234–45; Grant, *Bernard M. Baruch*, 240–62; Schwarz, *The Speculator*, 270–323; Joseph P. Lash, *Eleanor and Franklin* (New York, 1973), 538.

34. Baruch, *The Public Years*, 245–64; Schwarz, *The Speculator*, 331–447.

35. Baruch, *The Public Years*, 274–301; Schwarz, *The Speculator*, 415–16; Lawrenson, *Stranger at the Party*, 130–39.

36. Baruch, *The Public Years*, 315–36; Schwarz, *The Speculator*, 417–19.

37. Schwarz, *The Speculator*, 466–75; Baruch, *The Public Years*, 336–61.

38. Baruch, *The Public Years*, 367–85; Grant, *Bernard M. Baruch*, 304; Schwarz, *The Speculator*, 508–9, 539; Helen M. Lilienthal, ed., *The Journals of David E. Lilienthal: The Atomic Energy Years, 1945–1950* (New York, 1964), 163; Baruch to Doris Fleeson, May 25, 1953, Bernard M. Baruch Papers.

39. Coit, *Mr. Baruch*, 670–71; Schwarz, *The Speculator*, 542–46; Baruch to Eleanor Roosevelt, Sept. 19, 1952, Bernard M. Baruch Papers.

40. Tony Smith, *Why Wilson Matters: The Origin of American Liberal Internationalism and Its Crisis Today* (Princeton, NJ, 2017), 282–89; Baruch, "Woodrow Wilson's Claim to Greatness," *Vital Speeches of the Day*, Dec. 15, 1947; Baruch, "The Wilsonian Legacy for Us," address at the Washington Cathedral, Nov. 11, 1956, *New York Times Magazine*, Dec. 23, 1956; Schwarz, *The Speculator*, 547–80; Grant, *Bernard M. Baruch*, 215–17.

Chapter 11. Ray Stannard Baker

Chapter subtitle: "A Draft of an Article by Ray Stannard Baker, Nov. 29, 1920," in Arthur S. Link, ed., *The Papers of Woodrow Wilson* [*PWW*], 69 vols. (Princeton, NJ, 1966–93), 66:441. In its larger context, the quotation reads: "For this is certain: there will be no one judgment of history regarding Woodrow Wilson. He is the kind of man who has provoked controversy in his life, divided men into bitter opponents, or worshipful admirers, and so it will be to the end of time. The court of last resort, which history is supposed to be, will send down at last a divided opinion."

1. Ray Stannard Baker, *American Chronicle: The Autobiography of Ray Stannard Baker* (New York, 1945), 271–75.

2. Ray Stannard Baker, *Native American: The Book of My Youth* (New York, 1941), 1–129; John E. Semonche, *Ray Stannard Baker: A Quest for Democracy in Modern America* (Chapel Hill, NC, 1929), 7–12.

3. Baker, *Native American*, 157–91; Robert C. Bannister Jr., *Ray Stannard Baker: The Mind and Thought of a Progressive* (New Haven, CT, 1966), 24–36.

4. Baker, *Native American*, 217–58.

5. Baker, *Native American*, 259–336; Baker, *American Chronicle*, 1–68; Bannister, *Ray Stannard Baker*, 43.

6. Baker, *American Chronicle*, 69–82; Bannister, *Ray Stannard Baker*, 67.

7. Ida M. Tarbell, *All in the Day's Work: An Autobiography* (New York, 1939), 196–97; Baker, *American Chronicle*, 83–101; Doris Kearns Goodwin, *The Bully Pulpit: Theodore Roosevelt, William Howard Taft, and the Golden Age of American Journalism* (New York, 2013), 182, 187–202.

8. Baker, *American Chronicle*, 102–55.

9. Baker, *American Chronicle*, 158–89; Bannister, *Ray Stannard Baker*, 86–98; Goodwin, *The Bully Pulpit*, 354–65.

10. Bannister, *Ray Stannard Baker*, 126–32, 154–57, 275–76; Semonche, *Ray Stannard Baker*, 198–210.

11. Baker, *American Chronicle*, 186–212; Goodwin, *The Bully Pulpit*, 401–87; Bannister, *Ray Stannard Baker*, 96–103.

12. Baker, *American Chronicle*, 215–48; Goodwin, *The Bully Pulpit*, 492–93; Bannister, *Ray Stannard Baker*, 110–25.

13. Baker, *American Chronicle*, 249–60, 271–80; Goodwin, *The Bully Pulpit*, 588–728.

14. Bannister, *Ray Stannard Baker*, 152–65; Baker, *American Chronicle*, 276–87; "A Memorandum by Ray Stannard Baker of a Conversation at the White House," May 12, 1916, *PWW*, 37:31–38; John A. Thompson, *Reformers and War: American Progressive Publicists and the First World War* (Cambridge, UK, 1987), 88–89.

15. Baker, *American Chronicle*, 298–304; Daniel T. Rogers, *Atlantic Crossings: Social Politics in a Progressive Age* (Cambridge, MA, 1998), 73; Bannister, *Ray Stannard Baker*, 168–74; Ray Stannard Baker, *Woodrow Wilson: Life and Letters*, vol. 6, *Facing War, 1915–1917* (London, 1938), 429; Merrill D. Peterson, *The President and His Biographer: Woodrow Wilson and Ray Stannard Baker* (Charlottesville, VA, 2007), 81.

16. Thompson, *Reformers and War*; Baker, *American Chronicle*, 305–67; Bannister, *Ray Stannard Baker*, 177–83; John Maxwell Hamilton and Robert Mann, eds., *A Journalist's Diplomatic Mission: Ray Stannard Baker's World War I Diary* (Baton Rouge, LA, 2012), entries for July 12, Oct. 7, Oct. 14, and Dec. 6, 1918, 200–201, 207–9, 267–68.

17. Baker, *American Chronicle*, 368–89; Hamilton and Mann, *A Journalist's Diplomatic Mission*, Mar. 8, 1919, 294–99.

18. Baker, *American Chronicle*, 390–408; Hamilton and Mann, *A Journalist's Diplomatic Mission*, Apr. 3, 1919, 321.

19. Hamilton and Mann, *A Journalist's Diplomatic Mission*, Mar. 27, 1919, 310–12; Baker, *American Chronicle*, 400.

20. Baker, *American Chronicle*, 419–24; Hamilton and Mann, *A Journalist's Diplomatic Mission*, May 3, 9, 17, 19, 1919, 356–57, 364–84.

21. Baker, *American Chronicle*, 436–38; Hamilton and Mann, *A Journalist's Diplomatic Mission*, May 30, 1919, 400–402.

22. Baker, *American Chronicle*, 456, 459; Hamilton and Mann, *A Journalist's Diplomatic Mission*, July 1, 4, 8, 9, 1919, 445–57.

23. Baker, *American Chronicle*, 460–65; Bannister, *Ray Stannard Baker*, 197–98.

24. Baker, *American Chronicle*, 464–65; Baker Diary, Nov. 5, 1919, *PWW*, 63:619–22; Baker Diary, Nov. 18, 1919, *PWW*, 64:62.

25. Baker Diary, Jan. 23, 1919, *PWW*, 64:320–22; Baker, *American Chronicle*, 471–74; Baker to Edith Wilson, Jan. 25, 1920, *PWW*, 64:326–27.

26. Baker Diary, Feb. 3, 1920, *PWW*, 64:159–60.

27. Baker to Wilson, Dec. 16, 1920, Baker Diary, Dec. 16, 1920, *PWW*, 66:521–23; Baker Diary, Jan. 19, 22, 27, 1921, Mar. 22, 1921, *PWW*, 67:67–82, 71, 93, 238; Baker, *American Chronicle*, 487–98.

28. Baker Diary, Feb. 12, 1921, *PWW*, 67:129–30.

29. Baker Diary, May 25, 1921, *PWW*, 67:288–94.

30. Baker, *American Chronicle*, 497–98; Bannister, *Ray Stannard Baker*, 200–230; Baker, *Woodrow Wilson and the World Settlement*, 3 vols. (New York, 1922), 1:xxxv.

31. Bannister, *Ray Stannard Baker*, 241–44; Baker to Wilson, Jan. 7, 1924, Wilson to Baker, Jan. 8, 25, 1924, *PWW*, 68:523–24; Ishbel Ross, *Power with Grace: The Life Story of Mrs. Woodrow Wilson* (New York, 1975), 269–73; Kristie Miller, *Ellen and Edith: Woodrow Wilson's First Ladies* (Lawrence, KS, 2010), 246–48.

32. Ross, *Power with Grace*, 271; Baker, *Woodrow Wilson: Life and Letters*, vol. 1, *Youth, 1856–1890* (New York, 1927), xxxiii; Bannister, *Ray Stannard Baker*, 294–303.

33. Baker, *American Chronicle*, 499–502; Bannister, *Ray Stannard Baker*, 285–93; Otis L. Graham Jr., *An Encore for Reform: The Old Progressives and the New Deal* (New York, 1967), 70.

34. Baker, *American Chronicle*, 516.

Epilogue

1. Robert C. Bannister Jr., *Ray Stannard Baker: The Mind and Thought of a Progressive* (New Haven, CT, 1966), 307.

The literature on Woodrow Wilson is massive and constantly growing. The following essay will, I hope, give readers some suggestions for continuing their study of this remarkable man and those who advised him.

Woodrow Wilson

For those readers who wish to explore some of the primary sources of the Wilson era, Arthur S. Link, ed. *The Papers of Woodrow Wilson*, 69 volumes (Princeton, NJ, 1966–93), is the place to start. Wilson's daughter Eleanor collected many of the love letters of Ellen and Woodrow in *The Priceless Gift: The Love Letters of Woodrow Wilson and Ellen Axson Wilson* (New York, 1962).

Three recent biographies, all sympathetic, explore Wilson's life in considerable detail: John Milton Cooper Jr., *Woodrow Wilson: A Biography* (New York, 2009); A. Scott Berg, *Wilson* (New York, 2013); and Patricia O'Toole, *The Moralist: Woodrow Wilson and the World He Made* (New York, 2018). Of the short biographies, John A. Thompson's *Woodrow Wilson* (London, 2002) is the best. Edwin A. Weinstein's *Woodrow Wilson: A Medical and Psychological Biography* (Princeton, NJ, 1981) is a pioneering study, while W. Barksdale Maynard, *Woodrow Wilson: Princeton to the Presidency* (New Haven, CT, 2008), covers Wilson's pre-presidential years. Robert Alexander Kraig, *Woodrow Wilson and the Lost World of the Oratorical Statesman* (College Station, TX, 2004), and Malcolm D. Magee, *What the World Should Be: Woodrow Wilson and the Crafting of a Faith-Based Foreign Policy* (Waco, TX, 2008), focus on important themes in Wilson's life.

Two recent books reassess America's entry into World War I: Justus D. Doenecke, *Nothing Less Than War: A New History of America's Entry into World War I* (Lexington, KY, 2011), is a wide-ranging reassessment, while Robert E. Hannigan, *The Great War and American Foreign Policy, 1914–24* (Philadelphia, PA, 2017), is critical of Wilson's diplomacy. Michael Kazin, *War against War: The American Fight for Peace, 1914–1918* (New York, 2017), explores the antiwar movement and argues that the United States should have stayed out of World War I. John Milton Cooper Jr., *Breaking the Heart of the World: Woodrow Wilson and the Fight for the League of Nations* (New York, 2001), is an absorbing account of Wilson's doomed effort, and Erez Manela, *The Wilsonian Moment: Self-Determination and the International Origins of Anticolonial Nationalism* (New York, 2007), traces the worldwide influence of Wilson's ideas.

Many authors have sought to understand the long-term impact of Wilson's efforts to reshape American foreign policy. John B. Judis, *The Folly of Empire: What George W. Bush Could Learn from Theodore Roosevelt and Woodrow Wilson* (New York, 2004), contends that President Bush betrayed Wilson's vision; John A. Thompson, *A Sense of Power: The Roots of America's Global*

Role (Ithaca, NY, 2015), ponders the reasons for America's assumption of global responsibilities; Tony Smith, *Why Wilson Matters: The Origin of American Liberal Internationalism and Its Crisis Today* (Princeton, NJ, 2017), warns of the dangers of a betrayal of Wilson's vision. Several volumes include valuable essays on aspects of Wilson's presidency: John Milton Cooper Jr. and Charles E. Neu, eds., *The Wilson Era: Essays in Honor of Arthur S. Link* (Arlington Heights, IL, 1991), contains essays exploring Link's achievements; John Milton Cooper Jr., ed., *Reconsidering Woodrow Wilson: Progressivism, Internationalism, War, and Peace* (Washington, DC, 2008), contains eleven essays on a broad range of topics; John Milton Cooper Jr. and Thomas J. Knock, eds., *Jefferson, Lincoln, and Wilson: The American Dilemma of Race and Democracy* (Charlottesville, VA, 2010), puts Wilson's racism in historical perspective; Jeffrey A. Engel and Thomas J. Knock, eds., *When Life Strikes the President: Scandal, Death, and Illness in the White House* (New York, 2017), compares the breakdown of Wilson's health with the medical crises of other presidents. Two recent books assess the whole of Wilson's presidency: William E. Leuchtenburg, *The American President: From Teddy Roosevelt to Bill Clinton* (New York, 2015), includes a perceptive essay on Wilson; David Milne, *Worldmaking: The Art and Science of American Diplomacy* (New York, 2015), includes chapters on key figures in the shaping of American foreign policy. Finally, Michael Beschloss, *Presidents of War* (New York, 2018), examines each president's decision to lead the nation into war.

Ellen Axson Wilson

Two excellent biographies cover the whole of Ellen's life: Frances Wright Sanders, *First Lady between Two Worlds: Ellen Axson Wilson* (Chapel Hill, NC, 1985); and Kristie Miller, *Ellen and Edith: Woodrow Wilson's First Ladies* (Lawrence, KS, 2010). Frank J. Aucella and Patricia A. Piorkowski Hobbs, *Ellen Axson Wilson: First Lady and Artist* (Washington, DC, 1993), describes Ellen's considerable artistic talent, while three memoirs offer insight into her personality and her marriage to Woodrow: Stockton Axson, *Brother Woodrow: A Memoir of Woodrow Wilson*, ed. Arthur S. Link (Princeton, NJ, 1993); Margaret Axson Elliott, *My Aunt Louisa and Woodrow Wilson* (Chapel Hill, NC, 1944); and Eleanor Wilson McAdoo, *The Woodrow Wilsons* (New York, 1937). Ellen's role as First Lady is examined in Lewis L. Gould, ed., *American First Ladies: Their Lives and Their Legacy*, 2nd ed. (New York, 2001), and Betty Boyd Caroli, ed., *First Ladies: From Martha Washington to Michelle Obama* (New York, 2010).

Josephus Daniels

Daniels covered his long career in five volumes of detailed memoirs: *Tar Heel Editor* (Chapel Hill, NC, 1939); *Editor in Politics* (Chapel Hill, NC, 1941); *The Wilson Era: Years of Peace, 1910–1917* (Chapel Hill, NC, 1944); *The Wilson Era: Years of War and After* (Chapel Hill, NC, 1946); and *Shirt-Sleeve Diplomat* (Chapel Hill, NC, 1947). Daniels son Jonathan wrote an affectionate memoir, *The End of Innocence* (New York, 1954), while E. David Cronon edited *The Cabinet Diaries of Josephus Daniels, 1913–1921* (Lincoln, NE, 1963). Lee A. Craig, *Josephus Daniels: His Life and Times* (Chapel Hill, NC, 2013) is a full, up-to-date biography. Adriane Lentz-Smith, *Freedom Struggles: African Americans and World War I* (Cambridge, MA, 2009), explains Daniels's role in racial politics in North Carolina.

William Gibbs McAdoo

McAdoo's ghostwritten memoir, *Crowded Years: The Reminiscences of William G. McAdoo* (Boston, 1931), appeared ten years before his death. John J. Broesamle, *William Gibbs McAdoo: A Passion for Change, 1863–1917* (Port Washington, NY, 1973), carries the story of his life down to America's entry into World War I, while Douglas B. Craig, *Progressives at War: William G. McAdoo and Newton D. Baker, 1863–1941* (Baltimore, MD, 2013), is a dual biography based on thorough research in relevant manuscript collections. The history of McAdoo's greatest achievement, the creation of the Federal Reserve System, is told in Roger Lowenstein, *America's Bank: The Epic Struggle to Create the Federal Reserve* (New York, 2015). Two monographs assess his role in segregation during the Wilson administration: Adriane Lentz-Smith, *Freedom Struggles: African Americans and World War I* (Cambridge, MA, 2009); and Eric S. Yellin, *Racism in the Nation's Service: Government Workers and the Color Line in Woodrow Wilson's America* (Chapel Hill, NC, 2013). Douglas B. Craig, *After Wilson: The Struggle for the Democratic Party, 1920–1934* (Chapel Hill, NC, 1992), analyzes Democratic Party politics in the 1920s and early 1930s, and Jordan A. Schwarz, *The New Dealers: Power Politics in the Age of Roosevelt* (New York, 1993), covers McAdoo's relationship to FDR and the New Deal.

Joseph Patrick Tumulty

Tumulty's *Woodrow Wilson as I Know Him* (Garden City, NY, 1921), was the first memoir written by one of the president's close advisers. John M. Blum's *Joe Tumulty and the Wilson Era* (Boston, 1951), is perceptive on Tumulty's role, although it is thin on his life after 1921. Tumulty awaits his biographer. David Greenberg, *Republic of Spin: An Inside History of the American Presidency* (New York, 2016), has sections on Tumulty's relationship to the press. Virtually all of the memoirs written by those close to Wilson include descriptions of his personal secretary.

Colonel Edward M. House

House wrote two memoirs, *Reminiscences*, in 1916, and *Memories*, in 1929. Both are in the Edward M. House Papers at Yale University Library. His novel of the future, *Philip Dru: Administrator*, appeared in 1912. On September 25, 1912—when he was convinced that Wilson would win the presidency—he began keeping a diary, one that would eventually total nearly three thousand typed pages. Since House recorded all of his conversations with the president, his diary is one of the most important documents of the Wilson era. It is not, however, always reliable and should be used with caution. House was worried about his place in history, and in the early 1920s he commissioned Charles Seymour, a Yale University historian, to edit his diary. The result, *The Intimate Papers of Colonel House*, 4 vols. (Boston, 1926–28), was controversial. Rupert Norval Richardson, *Colonel Edward M. House: The Texas Years, 1858–1912* (Abilene, TX, 1964), has valuable information on House's early years, while Alexander L. George and Juliette L. George, *Woodrow Wilson and Colonel House: A Personality Study* (New York, 1956), is a pioneering psychological look at the relationship between the two men. In recent years, two biographies have appeared: Godfrey Hodgson, *Woodrow Wilson's Right Hand: The Life of Colonel Edward M. House* (New Haven, CT, 2006), is a brief, favorable biography, while Charles E. Neu, *Colonel House: A Biography of Woodrow Wilson's Silent Partner* (New York, 2015), is longer and more critical.

Cary T. Grayson

In 1924, Grayson recorded some impressions of Wilson, which were published posthumously as *Woodrow Wilson: An Intimate Memoir* (New York, 1960). Grayson kept a diary during and after the Paris Peace Conference; most of his diary entries can be found in various volumes of *The Papers of Woodrow Wilson*. Ludwig M. Deppisch, *The White House Physician: A History from Washington to George W. Bush* (Jefferson, NC, 2007), puts Grayson's role in historical perspective, while the essays on Wilson's health in three volumes assess Grayson's contribution: Bert Edward Park, *The Impact of Illness on World Leaders* (Philadelphia, PA, 1986); Park, *Ailing, Aging, Addicted: Studies of Compromised Leadership* (Lexington, KY, 1993), and Jeffrey A. Engel and Thomas J. Knock, eds., *When Life Strikes the President: Scandal, Death, and Illness in the White House* (New York, 2017).

Newton D. Baker

Baker never wrote a memoir and was contemptuous of those who did so or who kept diaries. Douglas B. Craig, *Progressives at War: William G. McAdoo and Newton D. Baker, 1863–1941* (Baltimore, MD, 2013), is the most recent biography. Two books analyze Baker's direction of the American army: Edward M. Coffman, *The Regulars: The American Army, 1898–1941* (Cambridge, MA, 2004); and David R. Woodward, *The American Army and the First World War* (Cambridge, UK, 2014). David R. Woodward, *Trial by Friendship: Anglo-American Relations, 1917–1918* (Lexington, KY, 1993), covers Baker's role in this difficult relationship. Baker's attitude toward Afro-Americans is explored in Adriane Lentz-Smith, *Freedom Struggles: African Americans and World War I* (Cambridge, MA, 2009). For the American experience in World War I, consult Robert H. Zieger, *America's Great War: World War I and the American Experience* (Lanham, MD, 2000); and Meirion Harries and Susie Harries, *The Last Days of Innocence: America at War, 1917–1918* (New York, 1997). Finally, two recent books look at important aspects of America's wartime experiment: Christopher Capozzola, *Uncle Sam Wants You: World War I and the Making of the Modern American Citizen* (New York, 2008); and Andrew Carroll, *My Fellow Soldiers: General John Pershing and the Americans Who Helped Win the Great War* (New York, 2017).

Edith Bolling Galt

Edith's *My Memoir* (Indianapolis, IN, 1938), is a spirited, if sometimes inaccurate, story of her life and defense of her role after the collapse of Woodrow's health. Edith and Woodrow's love letters can be found in various volumes of *The Papers of Woodrow Wilson*, but Edwin Tribble, ed., *A President in Love: The Courtship Letters of Woodrow Wilson and Edith Bolling Galt* (Boston, 1981), is an edited, more readable version of these 250 letters. Phyllis Lee Levin, *Edith and Woodrow: The Wilson White House* (New York, 2001), is a thorough reassessment of their relationship based on primary sources. It is marred, however, by the author's animus toward Edith. Kristie Miller, *Ellen and Edith: Woodrow Wilson's First Ladies* (Lawrence, KS, 2010), is a shorter, more balanced account. Two edited volumes place Edith's role as First Lady in historical perspective: Betty Boyd Caroli, ed., *First Ladies: From Martha Washington to Michelle Obama* (New York, 2010); and Lewis Gould, ed., *American First Ladies: Their Lives and Their Legacy*, 2nd ed. (New York, 2001).

Bernard M. Baruch

Baruch wrote two volumes of memoirs, *Baruch: My Own Story* (New York, 1957), and *Baruch: The Public Years* (New York, 1960). Jordan A. Schwarz, *The Speculator: Bernard M. Baruch in Washington* (Chapel Hill, NC, 1981), emphasizes his public career but neglects his personal life. James Grant, *Bernard M. Baruch: The Adventures of a Wall Street Legend* (New York, 1997), is a briefer, more recent biography. Baruch's leadership of the War Industries Board is covered in Robert D. Cuff, *The War Industries Board: Business-Government Relations during World War I* (Baltimore, MD, 1973), while the story of his chief journalistic promoter is told in E. J. Kahn Jr., *The World of Swope* (New York, 1965). Helen Lawrenson, *Stranger at the Party: A Memoir* (New York, 1972), paints an unflattering portrait of the speculator; and Michael Hiltzik, *The New Deal: A Modern History* (New York, 2011), explores Baruch's tense relationship with FDR and the New Deal.

Ray Stannard Baker

Baker wrote two thoughtful memoirs, *Native American: The Book of My Youth* (New York, 1941), and *American Chronicle: The Autobiography of Ray Stannard Baker* (New York, 1945). Portions of his diary are reprinted in various volumes of *The Papers of Woodrow Wilson*, and all of his diary entries written while he was a special diplomatic agent in 1918 and press secretary of the American Peace Commission are included in John Maxwell Hamilton and Robert Mann, eds., *A Journalist's Diplomatic Mission: Ray Stannard Baker's World War I Diary* (Baton Rouge, LA, 2012). Two studies explore many aspects of Baker's life: John E. Semonche, *Ray Stannard Baker: A Quest for Democracy in Modern America, 1870–1918* (Chapel Hill, NC, 1969); and Robert C. Bannister Jr., *Ray Stannard Baker: The Mind and Thought of a Progressive* (New Haven, CT, 1966). John A. Thompson, *Reformers and War: American Progressive Publicists and the First World War* (Cambridge, UK, 1987), explores the thinking of Baker and of other progressive journalists. Doris Kearns Goodwin, *The Bully Pulpit: Theodore Roosevelt, William Howard Taft, and the Golden Age of Journalism* (New York, 2013), covers the careers of Baker and other muckrakers, while Merrill D. Peterson, *The President and His Biographer* (Charlottesville, VA, 2007), focuses on Baker's relationship with Woodrow Wilson.

Baruch, Bernard M., 76, 77, 149, 193; as adviser to
Franklin Roosevelt, 213, 214–15; as adviser to
Wilson, xi, 22, 26, 131, 199, 204, 205–6, 208, 210;
African Americans as viewed by, 203; as an
agnostic Jew, 201; and Newton Baker, 205;
Baruch: My Own Story, 236; *Baruch: The Public
Years*, 236; on the civil rights movement, 216;
and Josephus Daniels, 205; death of, 217; early
years of, 199; on economic regulation, 212;
education of, 201; and the Great Depression,
213; and Cary Grayson, 155–56, 195, 208, 212; on
Hitler, 214; at Hobcaw Barony, 203; and Edward
House, 205, 212; and impressions of Wilson, 199;
as head of the War Industries Board, 73, 169,
205–6; as investor in raw materials, 202–3; and
William McAdoo, 205, 206–7, 211, 212; in New
York City, 200–201; at the Paris peace conference, 207–8; photographs of, 198, 209; and
Eleanor Roosevelt, 213; and Harry Truman,
215–16; and Joseph Tumulty, 205; as supporter
of Wilson, 204; as Wall Street speculator, 201–2;
as wartime statesman, 206–7; and Edith Wilson,
208, 210, 212; on Wilson's legacy, 211, 216–17;
during World War I, 125, 199, 204
Baruch, Simon, 199; as physician, 200, 202
Baum, Mannes, 199–200
Beal, William J., 220
Birth of a Nation, The, 55
Bolling, Anne, 180, 181
Bolling, John Randolph, 30, 99
Bolling, Randolph, 196
Bolling, Sallie White, 180
Bolling, William Holcombe, 180
Bones, Helen, 20, 114, 142, 179, 182
Brandeis, Louis D., 20, 69
Bryan, William Jennings, ix, 53, 56, 67, 70, 84, 87,
109, 160, 162, 183, 203, 221; Josephus Daniels's
friendship with, 49, 51
Bryn Mawr College: Wilson as teacher at, 6
Burleson, Albert, ix, x, 41, 52, 54, 57, 69, 223, 225
Butt, Archie, 138

Cárdenas, Lázaro, 60
Cecil, Lord Robert, 194–95, 208
Chamberlain, George E., 168
Churchill, Winston, 203
Clayton Antitrust Act, 16

Clemenceau, Georges, 129, 149, 189, 208, 226
Cleveland Electric Railway Company, 161
Cleveland, Grover, 48, 67, 160
Cleveland, Ohio: Newton Baker as mayor of,
161–62
Colby, Bainbridge, 59
College of New Jersey. *See* Princeton University
Columbia Theological Seminary: Wilson as pro-
fessor at, 4
Coolidge, Calvin, 233
Cooper, John Milton, Jr., ix, 11
Council for National Defense, 165, 204
Council of Four, 25, 148, 149, 190
Council of Ten, 127–28, 147
Cox, James M., 59, 75, 98, 99, 131, 154, 233
Coxey, "General" Jacob, 221
Craig, Douglas B., 73
Cram, Ralph Adams, 8
Creel, George, 22; on McAdoo, 80
Cross, Doris, 78
Culberson, Charles Allen, 106–7, 108

Daniels, Adelaide Bagley "Addie," 45, 47, 52, 58
Daniels, Jonathan, 53
Daniels, Josephus, x, 15, 68, 69, 97, 196, 225; as
adviser to Wilson, 45, 51–52, 61; as ambassador
to Mexico, 60–61, 236; and Newton Baker, 166,
168; and Bernard Baruch, 205; and William
Jennings Bryan, 49, 51; and concerns about
Wilson's condition, 58–59; death of, 61; early
years of, 45–47; as editor of the *Advance*, 46–47;
as editor of the Raleigh *News and Observer*, 45,
48–50, 59; as editor of the *State Chronicle*, 47–48;
and Cary Grayson, 136–38, 144, 153; and Edward
House, 52–53, 92, 110; in the Interior Department, 48; marriage of, 47; and William McAdoo,
52; and peace treaty negotiations, 58; photograph
of, 44; political views of, 48–50; reforms recommended by, 53–54; and Franklin Roosevelt, 54,
60, 236; as secretary of the navy, 45, 51, 53–58,
137–38; as supporter of Woodrow Wilson, 45,
50–51; and Joseph Tumulty, 52, 53, 58; and Ellen
Wilson, 52; white supremacist views of, 49, 50,
51; and Ellen Wilson, 40; *The Wilson Era: Years
of Peace*, 61, 236; *The Wilson Era: Years of War
and After*, 61, 236; during World War I, 56–57,
168